Introduction to the Library and Information Professions

Introduction to the Library and Information Professions

ROGER C. GREER
ROBERT J. GROVER
SUSAN G. FOWLER

LIBRARIES
U N L I M I T E D
A Member of the Greenwood Publishing Group
Westport, Connecticut • London

Library of Congress Cataloging-in-Publication Data

Greer, Roger C., 1928–
    Introduction to the library and information professions / Roger C. Greer, Robert J.
Grover, and Susan G. Fowler.
        p. cm.
    Includes bibliographical references and index.
    ISBN-13: 978–1–59158–486–5 (alk. paper)
    1. Information science – Philosophy.   2. Library science – Philosophy.
3. Information services.   4. Information policy.   5. Information society.
6. Knowledge, theory of.   7. Learning and scholarship.   I. Grover, Robert J., 1942–
II. Fowler, Susan G., 1958–   III. Title.
    Z665.G87   2007
    020 – dc   2007013540

British Library Cataloguing in Publication Data is available.

Library of Congress Catalog Card Number: 2007013540
ISBN-13: 978–1–59158–486–5

First published in 2007

Libraries Unlimited, 88 Post Road West, Westport, CT 06881
A Member of the Greenwood Publishing Group, Inc.
www.lu.com

Printed in the United States of America

The paper used in this book complies with the
Permanent Paper Standard issued by the National
Information Standards Organization (Z39.48–1984).

10 9 8 7 6 5 4 3 2 1

This book is a collection of ideas, theories, and models—the result of a professional lifetime of discussions, teaching, thought, and work in the library and information professions. Influential in this thinking was the critical input for almost 50 years of Natalia Greer, wife of Roger. She was a librarian responsible for influencing Roger to enter that profession, and she was always there, critiquing his thinking and offering constructive and sometimes acerbic suggestions as we did our work.

Nat left us in September 2003, but our memories of her and her contributions to our thinking are indelible. To her we dedicate this book.

Roger C. Greer
Bob Grover
Susan G. Fowler

Contents

Acknowledgments

A special "thank you" is extended to Dr. Martha Hale. She participated in the development of the theories, models, and perspectives in this book through her work with the Community Analysis Research Institute at the University of Denver and the development of the new curricula launched at the University of Southern California and Emporia State University. Her tireless enthusiasm and creative insights were fundamental to the evolution of this publication.

We would like to thank the professional colleagues who shared their ideas with us: Sue Blechl, Director, Emporia Public Library; Sharon Coatney, Acquisitions Editor, Libraries Unlimited; Joyce Davis, Dean of Libraries and Archives, Emporia State University; Dalene Hawthorne, Head of Systems and Technical Services, Emporia State University; and Heather Wade, Archivist, Emporia State University.

We are also grateful to Waseem Afzal, doctoral student, who assisted with a review of literature and helped with various aspects of the book preparation.

Following is a special acknowledgment from coauthor Susan Fowler:

Years ago, I was a graduate assistant at Emporia State University's School of Library and Information Management (SLIM). During an orientation session for new library school students, Dean Marty Hale asked each of us to introduce ourselves by sharing a life-changing moment. Herbert Achleitner summed it up for many of us that day: "I met Roger Greer."

Fifteen years later, I still feel that way. I was fortunate to be Roger's graduate assistant and later, research assistant. In those days he had a huge chalkboard in his office on which he diagrammed emerging models. I was there the day he discovered the catalyst that moves a library (in its community's mind) from a monument to a utility. I likened the moment to what Albert Einstein's graduate assistant must have experienced, a compliment Roger has never accepted.

He can refute it all he wants, but the fact remains that many of us—either alumnae of Syracuse, Denver, University of Southern California, Rutgers, or ESU—owe our careers to Roger's genius. His ideas were the fuel for SLIM's revolutionary curriculum change in the early 1980s, and they are the core of this book. He is generous with his ideas and happiest when others implement them. His pleasure comes not from accolades but from seeing his ideas in action and the resulting contributions to our profession's body of knowledge.

Writing this book with Roger and my husband, Bob Grover, was possible through Bob's superb organization skills (Roger and I are much more the creative types). It is with a profound sense of gratitude that I thank my coauthors for letting me in on the fun.

1

Introduction: Purpose and Objectives of This Book

Chapter Overview

This chapter is an introduction to the book, its intended audience, and its scope. The information professions are defined within the context of our knowledge society. Key terms are explained, including "theory," "data," "information," "knowledge," and "wisdom." Characteristics of a profession are described, and the roles of such information professionals as information managers, records managers, librarians, archivists, and information entrepreneurs are compared. The differences between a professional and technician are examined.

Why Read This Book?

Why should you read this book? What is its importance? These are important questions for those who have an interest in learning more about the information professions and want to expand their knowledge to be a more effective professional.

In this book we define the role of library and information professionals and present a conceptual framework—a way of thinking about professional work in the library and information field. We present you with an idea "tool box" which you will be able to use as you enter the profession and as you continue through it. You are entering a society of information professionals (whenever we use the term "information professional" we include librarians) which has the very important role of helping others to use information effectively.

This book will provide you with the background to prepare you for the problems that we in the information professions encounter. Consequently, graduate students in professional programs will find this book useful as an introduction, and practicing professionals will find it helpful as a guide to the current issues with a theoretical framework (a way to think about) the various issues associated with information services today.

The Intended Audience

This book is an introduction to the information professions for individuals who need a broad perspective of professional service—professionals who are familiar with the field of information work but want to know the "why" behind their professional practice. This book can be used for continuing education of professionals who have been "kicked upstairs" to a new leadership role and need to make decisions for an organization—they want to understand the "big picture" of information service. This work is also intended as an introductory text for students beginning a course of study in the information professions. The goal is to ground these studies in a theoretical and social perspective—how information work fits into our society and our economy. Practicing professionals and technicians who want to understand their work beyond the level of every day practicalities will find this book of value.

The theoretical perspective considers the information professions and their roles and functions in the dynamics of a social system, i.e., in our contemporary knowledge society. In addition, the scope and importance of the various fields or service areas in the information professions are explored.

The social perspective serves two functions: first, the sociology of information is examined from its creation to issues of preservation or discarding. Second, we examine the characteristics of the information infrastructure at the global, national, and local levels. We relate both of these elements to the role of the information professions.

Scope of the Book

The design of this work moves from the general to the specific. The earlier chapters (1–5) explore the role of information in society, change as reflected in paradigm shifts, the theory and processes of information transfer, the characteristics of professions, the national information infrastructure, and the cycle of professional service. We explore the theory base from which the information professions draw direction in the delivery of services. This discussion focuses on four fields of study, which provide a framework for research efforts necessary for the development of theory to employ in professional practice—the sociology of information, information psychology, information organization management, and information engineering.

The second half of the book (Chapters 6–10) concentrates on professional practice. It focuses on the processes involved in the design and management of information systems. It includes the following topics: information reproduction, identification, evaluation, selection, acquisition, organization, storage and retrieval, preservation, and disposal.

Chapter 9 addresses the characteristics of a professional infrastructure necessary for societal recognition of professional status. These characteristics are identified by the sociology of professions and generally fall into nine categories. Each category will be considered in terms of its strengths and weaknesses with respect to the different information professions. In addition to a science or theory base, these characteristics include the existence of professional organizations, a formal education system, communication mechanism (journal literature), code of ethics, licensing, history of service, standards of performance, and general recognition of the public.

Because of the broad sweep of the scope of this work, many topics will be treated at the definition and identification level while others will be examined in greater depth. It is the intention of the authors to present guides to further study in each area discussed. Topics lacking consensus on core issues will be presented from two or more perspectives as found in the professional literature.

We begin with an introductory look at professionals and what we mean by the term "professional."

The Role of Professionals

Information professionals must understand their special role in society and *why* they do things as well as *how* they do things. First, let's look back in time to the history of the information professions, which began with the storage of the written word on clay tablets. Cultures have realized that in order to evolve, they had to have access to their past. For nearly 5,000 years, librarians (although they weren't always called that) were responsible for those collections by acquiring, storing, retrieving, organizing, and preserving the documents of their society. The idea that these responsibilities included the needs of specific users did not come to prominence in the library/information field until Melvil Dewey in the 1870s urged librarians to include direct service to their clients as a relevant duty:

> It is not enough that the books are cared for properly, are well arranged, and are never lost. It is not enough that he [the librarian] can, when asked, give advice as to the best books in his collection on any given subject. All these things are indispensable, but not all these are enough for our ideal. He must see that his library contains, as far as possible, the best books on the best subjects, regarding carefully the wants of his special community. Then, having the best books, he must create among his people, his pupils, and a desire to read these books.... The time *was* when a library was very like a museum, and a librarian was a mouser in musty books, and visitors looked with curious eyes at ancient tomes and manuscripts. The time *is* when a library is a school, and the librarian is in the highest sense a teacher, and the visitor is a reader among the books as a workman among his tools. Will any man deny to the high calling of such a librarianship the title of profession? (Dewey 1976, 21–23)

A contemporary of Dewey's, Samuel S. Green, shared Dewey's concept of service in libraries and promoted "personal intercourse" between the librarian and the client. Green noted, "When scholars and persons of high social position come to a library, they have confidence enough, in regard to the cordiality of their reception, to make known their wishes without timidity or reserve" (Green 1976, 319). However, that confidence is not evidenced in all library clientele, and Green noted that "Persons who use a popular library for purposes of investigation generally need a great deal of assistance" (Ibid.). Green also suggested that sometimes "... it is practicable to refer applicants for information which you cannot supply, to libraries in larger cities in the neighborhood of your own library, or to other institutions in your own town" (p. 324).

Green recommended that librarians engage in "personal intercourse" with clientele in order to improve service to individuals. He saw the following benefits of this intercourse:

- Gain the respect and confidence of clientele to afford opportunities to direct users to the best sources of information.
- Learn what books (and other resources) the users of the library need, helping the librarian to make better selection decisions.
- "Mingle freely" with users to be available to provide help when needed, which will make the library indispensable within the community.
- The collection will reflect the varying interests, abilities, and needs of the community. (p. 326)

Service should be a fundamental concern in libraries, Green argued, "A librarian should be as unwilling to allow an inquirer to leave the library with his question unanswered as a shopkeeper is to have a customer go out of his store without making a purchase" (p. 327). Attention to the needs and interests of the user was first articulated by Green, and it is the focus for our philosophy in this book. It is interesting to see that this focus began with Dewey and Green, yet we must be reminded of this philosophy today, when so many agencies of all types disregard it.

The Value of Theory

During the second half of the nineteenth century, most of the social science disciplines were developing. These new disciplines were oriented to the behaviors and characteristics of individuals, groups, organizations, and cultures. Methodologies for conducting research and extrapolating theory evolved too. Other professions and other professional services, recognizing their roles of providing services to specific clients, took advantage of social science research. Because librarians continued their preoccupation with housekeeping collections, the profession was immune to these developments in the social sciences, prompting Pierce Butler (1933) to decry the pragmatism in the library profession:

Unlike his colleagues in other fields of social activity the librarian is strangely uninterested in the theoretical aspects of his profession. He seems to possess a unique immunity to that curiosity which elsewhere drives modern man to attempt, somehow, an orientation of his particular labors with the main stream of human life. The librarian apparently stands alone in the simplicity of his pragmatism: a rationalization of each immediate technical process by itself seems to satisfy his intellectual interest. Indeed any endeavor to generalize these rationalizations into a professional philosophy appears to him, not merely futile, but positively dangerous. (pp. xi–xii)

Butler noted that early library schools contributed to this pragmatism by continuing to provide the vocational training that had been done in libraries. Butler noted that library schools "... were founded in an age when librarians thought too exclusively in terms of library technology. Library education was, therefore, conceived as primarily training in the niceties of cataloging and classification" (Butler 1976, 28).

Scholarship has advanced considerably with the application of social science theory to the information needs and use patterns of information consumers. However, scholarship in librarianship was unaffected by the advances in the social sciences because librarians continued to concentrate on the traditional processes of storing and retrieving books. Scholarship in the field of library science moved forward when propelled by new advances in technology—beginning with the typewriter.

Theory in the Information Professions Today

Recalling Pierce Butler's statement in the 1950s that "... the librarian is strangely uninterested in the theoretical aspects of his profession," it is noteworthy that the information profession today still misses the point about theory. The information professions have not contributed a great deal to the theoretical base, especially in management. Until the 1950s, management theory and pedagogy were dominated by Gulick's model (Gulick 1937) until management began to adopt sociology theories, e.g., Karl Weick and Garreth Morgan. Management has become one of the best fields to adopt social science methodology. Industrial psychology, sociology, and anthropology are looking at their functions as they influence society. During the last two decades, numerous scholars in the information profession began incorporating social science theory into their research. Among the earliest to do so were Elfreda Chatman, Carol Kuhlthau, Michael Harris, and T.D. Wilson. More will be discussed regarding this trend in Chapter 10.

Although progress has been made with the production of research which centers on the clientele of information organizations, practice is often focused on the information package, the software, or the hardware. While bibliography is still an important function of information professionals and has expanded to other media (including such formats as journals, videos, CDs, and Web sites), scholarship has advanced considerably to the application of social science theory to the information needs and use patterns of information consumers. However, scholarship in librarianship moved forward only with advances in technology, beginning with the typewriter. The library profession saw an expansion of bibliography after World War II. With the development of bibliography as a discipline and the process of identification of acquisition, description, organization, retrieval began to take hold after World War II.

With the evolution of scholarship and bibliography and with the introduction of theories from the social sciences it became apparent that the passive librarian had a more proactive role in society. During the 1970s, Roger Greer pursued this study of the librarian's role through his study of information needs of public library clientele. The study of more than fifty communities resulted in the development of theory base for study of the information professions (Greer and Hale 1982; Greer 1987). Regardless of the role of an information professional, Greer asserts that there are four features in common across the information professions:

- The information professional works with individuals, who have unique information requirements and a unique style for finding and using information. We refer to this study as "information psychology."

- The information professional works with groups of individuals, and these groups have definable and unique information needs and patterns for use. We have given this study the designation "sociology of information."

- The information professional manages an organization comprising staff, budget, and facilities. We call this "information organization management."

- The information professional organizes and maintains an information storage and retrieval system to meet the needs of the organization's clientele. For this function, we use the term "information engineering."

These four fields of study lead to the following questions for society to address:

- How do individuals know they need information?

- How does a dynamic society create information? What do they do about it?

- How does one manage an organization whose product is information? What's different about this kind of management?

- How does one build a database within an organization? Is an archival database different than others?

This book addresses these questions and builds on the tradition of scholarship in the social sciences because the role of information professionals is to focus on the information needs of individuals and groups. These four fields are central to all of the information professions. In this book we address the differences of technology types and the role of this profession in society and its impact on society.

Still today, there are information professionals more devoted to acquisition, storage, retrieval, and preservation than they are devoted to people and to service. This book addresses the need for the application of theory to practice:

- We urge a shift from a focus on collections to a focus on people.

- We urge a shift to an understanding of theory as a basis for guiding practice.

- We provide the reader with a toolbox of theories and models which will serve as a framework for practice in the information professions.

- We provide an agenda—a "road map"—for research needed to benefit practice.

Theory and Its Uses in Professional Service

Theory can most easily be defined as "a generalization" (Grover and Glazier 1986; Glazier and Grover 2002). We suggest that a theory is a statement that explains, describes, or predicts a possible outcome of an event or circumstance. Applied to the study of information use, theory is in the realm of the social sciences because information is created, disseminated, and used by people. Since people's behavior is often unpredictable, social science theory cannot be predicted as accurately as theory in the sciences. A theory must be practical (i.e., capable of being applied to a part of reality) or verified or refuted through research. Abstractions, constructs, and conjectures are not theories because they lack one or more of the properties stated above. In this book we introduce numerous theories that may be collected in a conceptual "toolbox" of professional theories to be employed in delivering services.

In our daily lives we have formed generalizations, or general ideas, that we believe to be true, and we act upon them. For example, we may have accepted a theory that brushing our teeth prevents tooth decay, and that theory prompts us to brush our teeth once or more each day. That theory has been presented to us over our lifetime through our learning in school, reading of studies in newspapers and magazines, taught by our parents, and reinforced through toothpaste commercials and advertisements. Consequently, the relationship between brushing teeth and fighting tooth decay is an accepted generalization in our personal paradigm. Indeed, a theory is a generalized statement about a relationship between or among two or more factors, e.g., between brushing and tooth decay.

Theory is an essential part of professional work. The primary function of any professional is diagnosis. A professional diagnoses need, i.e., a physician diagnoses a patient's ailment, an accountant diagnoses accounting issues of a company, or an information professional diagnoses the information need of a client or group of clients. It is necessary to apply theory in this process to have an accurate diagnosis. Diagnostic theory primarily comes from psychology, the study of human behavior. The psychological theories that apply to information professions are defined as "information psychology," a developing field which is outlined later in this chapter. Unless theory is applied to diagnosis, an information professional is functioning as a technician.

Here's an example of a professional using theory. If you want to build a deck on your house and you decide where you want it, you find a carpenter and say you want a deck. Can you build it? The carpenter says, "Sure! Do you want stairs? How large do you want it? What kind of wood do you want to use?" If you go to an architect, s/he will ask what you want to do on that deck. When will you use it—what time of day? How will you incorporate the deck into your lifestyle? Meanwhile, the architect has not done any design work. S/he first determines needs. Based on the client's needs, the architect then starts planning the patio. The product is customized to the client.

Unless a product is customized, it is not the product of a professional. The carpenter is more concerned about the deck itself and does not diagnose customer needs. It's a very pragmatic approach which may not address the actual needs of the customer. In our society we tend to label all kinds of abstract statements as theoretical, thereby demeaning the significance of theory. However, theory is not just abstract, it is applicable. It must be susceptible to being tested. If one takes the abstract concept of "love" it's hard to define; it cannot be validated with a measuring instrument. "Liberty" is a construct too. We can measure the lack of liberty, but such constructs we use to embellish descriptions of reality and not necessarily embellish the truth of our reality. Theories are verifiable statements that must be capable of being tested in a systematic way.

Theories are necessary for a manager because they (1) tell the individual both what is important and what can be safely ignored, and (2) group a great deal of different and disparate pieces of information into patterns or concepts (Bolman and Deal 2003). Theories help us to determine what's important and what's not important. Theories help us to see trends. Management which uses theory goes beyond "seat of the pants" decisions; a manager cannot respond effectively to trends by intuition and by "what feels good." Effective managers must know what they're doing and why they're doing it. Theory helps the manager in those thought processes.

In summary, theory enables professionals to see relationships and to make reasonable decisions based on these relationships. Just as we use our theory about tooth decay to influence our behavior daily, theories can influence our professional behavior as well. The distinction between professional service and that provided by a technician is in the product or service, as demonstrated by the architect/carpenter example. Professionals provide customized products (e.g., databases, mediagraphies, and Web sites) or services (e.g., reference assistance, answers to questions, and organization of information resources) for individual clients, while technicians apply generalized rules to fit a problem. (More discussion of the role of professionals and technicians follows later in this chapter.)

In order to provide this service, professionals must draw upon a body of theory to diagnose the particular needs of individuals or groups and to provide the needed service or product. For example, Carol Kuhlthau has conducted research and generated a theory on information-seeking behavior. This theory enables information professionals to identify the stages an information seeker experiences in a quest for information (Kuhlthau 1993, 2004). Through an understanding of these stages, the librarian can better assess which stage a particular client is in this quest. This enables the information professional to formulate an appropriate response to the query and suggest information sources or strategies to satisfy the information need.

Using the information-seeking example, the model developed by Kuhlthau (2004, 81–84) enables professionals to anticipate the six steps in the information-seeking process:

Stage 1. Initiation: A person first becomes aware of a need for information to complete a task or assignment. This step is usually accompanied by feelings of apprehension or uncertainty.

Stage 2. Selection: The information seeker identifies a subject or topic to investigate. After a topic is identified, the feelings of uncertainty usually give way to feelings of optimism.

Stage 3. Exploration: The searcher begins to locate information in an effort to better understand and narrow the topic. This stage of the search is accompanied by feelings of uncertainty, confusion, and doubt.

Stage 4. Formulation: The information seeker uses information found to form a focus for the task or assignment. At this point in the search, uncertainty diminishes and is replaced by confidence.

Stage 5. Collection: The individual gathers information on the selected topic, using a library or other information system. Feelings of confidence increase and feelings of uncertainty subside.

Stage 6. Presentation: The search is completed, and the information is prepared for use. This stage is usually accompanied by feelings of relief. If the search has been successful, there is a feeling of satisfaction; if unsuccessful, the searcher may have feelings of disappointment.

Kuhlthau's analysis of the information-seeking process provides both an explanation of the client's behavior and feelings, and a prediction of subsequent behaviors which enables information professionals to anticipate client behavior and needs as the search continues. Generally, theory is formulated from research data and/or from observation over a long period of time. As such, theory is likely to be tested formally or informally and can be considered a desirable guideline for professional behavior. Theory enables us to explain relationships in a professional environment and can also help us predict the future.

The information professions have generated numerous theories to aid in the delivery of professional service. In addition, relevant theories from other professions and disciplines are employed when relevant. For example, theory has been generated in management, sociology, anthropology, psychology, education, and other fields that can be used to inform the practice of information professionals. This book introduces numerous theories that will provide a framework for understanding the information professions and the nature of professional work.

Defining Terms

In a lay person's conversation, and even among information professionals, the terms "information" and "knowledge" often are used interchangeably. It is important to distinguish the differences between these terms, but to do so we must also look at the terms "data" and "wisdom." Harland Cleveland defined these terms effectively in his book *The Knowledge Executive* (1985).

Data

Data are the rough materials from which information and knowledge are formed, i.e., undigested observations, or unvarnished facts, as Cleveland calls them (p. 22). For example, researchers collect data from interviews, observations, surveys, and other means in order to analyze it for research purposes. We are bombarded with data all the time. To make sense of it, data must be synthesized. Data may take the form of words, numbers, and visual images. By themselves, data make no sense. For example, these data alone have no meaning unless placed in a context, as noted below: 76, 6, 2, August.

Information

Using Cleveland's definition, information is organized data (p. 22). Given connections or context, data can form information. In this case, we may be listening to the radio on an August morning; the radio voice wishes us a good morning and announces that it is August the second, the time is 6:00 A.M., and the current temperature in our town is 76 degrees. Now we have information because we have put the numbers together in a meaningful way.

Knowledge

Knowledge, according to Cleveland, " . . . is organized information, internalized by me, integrated with everything else I know from experience or study or intuition, and therefore useful in guiding my life and work" (p. 22). The noise of a distant train's whistle, a passing car, conversation in the next room, the sound of a furnace or air conditioner, or the television in the background as we read all give us data or information that we may reject or do not retain or remember. When we watch the television news or read the newspaper; we remember only a small percentage of what we read, view, or listen to. That which we remember or incorporate in our memory bank becomes knowledge. In other words, information that is processed, selected, and synthesized by a human becomes knowledge.

Knowledge is also processed by groups of people, and we will refer to social knowledge when we discuss information transfer and knowledge diffusion. As with personal knowledge, social knowledge requires analysis, selection, and synthesis of information in order to be accepted as knowledge. We discuss this process in much more detail in Chapters 2 and 5.

Wisdom

When knowledge is integrated into the thinking of human beings and incorporated into their decision-making processes, it becomes wisdom. Cleveland defines wisdom as:

> [Wisdom] is integrated knowledge, information made super-useful by theory, which relates bits and field of knowledge to each other, which in turn enables me to use the knowledge to do something. (p. 23)

Using the example of the above weather report which indicated that the temperature at six o'clock in the morning is 76 degrees, will tell an individual that the day is probably going to be a hot one. That information (time and temperature) alone, combined with an individual's experience of many August days (in the Northern hemisphere) over a lifetime suggests guidelines for dress: lightweight, light colors, loose fitting if spending time outdoors. In other words, new information is taken in, evaluated, and acted upon based upon the existing store of accumulated knowledge or wisdom. Wisdom, then, is the accumulation of a lifetime's experience and testing of knowledge.

Information and Communication Professions: Convergence and Divergences

The information professions are those professions ("profession" is defined later in this chapter) which focus on some aspect of information creation, collection, organization, storage, dissemination, diffusion, or utilization. Mason, Mason, and Culnan (1995) have offered a satisfactory definition of information professionals:

> Information professionals possess specialized knowledge about information, knowledge, and information technology. That is, they are skilled at processing symbols. They deal primarily with codified or objectified information rather than information in a subjective form. (p. 155)

As noted by Greer (1987) and described above, all information professionals have four characteristics in common:

1. Responsibility for accommodating the information needs and behavioral characteristics of a specific client population by working with individuals;

2. Responsibility for enhancing the processes of information transfer among a clientele group;

3. Responsibility for the design and management of an organization consisting of staff, equipment, space, and financial resources to provide the interface between the information system and the potential user;

4. Responsibility for the design and management of an information system encompassing a database.

Each of these factors is described briefly below and in more detail in Chapter 4.

Work with Individuals

All information professionals spend a portion of their time working with individual clients. For example, a librarian in a public library will answer questions of a businessman who is asking for a description of a certain company in which he wishes to invest, or school library media specialists who work with a fifth grade teacher to plan a science unit that will study bears and include development of student skills in gathering and organizing information. In both examples the information professional identifies the need of the client and attempts to address that need by identifying and providing appropriate information sources.

Work with Groups

In the example above the school library media specialist, might also work with the entire fifth grade class, teaming with the teacher in the science unit. Likewise, a public librarian might organize and present a program on financial planning to groups of people planning for retirement. Or a university librarian might prepare an instructional unit for an advanced education teaching methods class about to embark on a library research project. In each case the group has identifiable characteristics (fifth grade, retirees, and upper division education students) and fulfills a role which has certain predictable elements. Identifying the role of a retiree, for example, gives librarians an instant understanding of the group's social characteristics and helps them to focus their efforts to locate appropriate information and to instruct the members of the group.

Greer has noted that groups have unique and predictable patterns for the creation, recording, mass production, dissemination, organization, diffusion, utilization, and preservation/destruction of information. He has labeled this an "information transfer" process. Considerable research is necessary to understand the information transfer patterns of various social groups. It is possible to investigate the information transfer patterns of those with which we are unfamiliar by interviewing members of those groups to identify these patterns. Among the differences that exist between the information professions is the types of groups with whom information professionals work. Other differences are described below.

Manage an Organization

Information professionals must design and manage the organization of services and resources for the delivery of information to individuals and groups who are the agency's clientele. The professional must manage a budget, the collection, staff, and facilities. Effective management requires an understanding of theory associated with the management of organizations. Management is a fundamental part of all information professions, and all information professionals borrow from this body of knowledge.

Maintain a Collection of Recorded Information

Every information professional is charged with the responsibility for a collection—books, journals, reports, audio and video recordings, microforms, CD-ROMs, databases, Web sites, and electronic books are examples of the wide variety of formats now available. A professional is responsible for identifying appropriate items for an agency's clientele, selecting resources, and organizing them, storing them, retrieving them, and preserving them. Knowing the characteristics of the individuals and groups using these resources is important in order to select and organize the resources in a manner that will be most convenient for the clientele. Knowledge of organization theory, organizational schemes, and information transfer patterns is essential for organizing and retrieving information in a collection or database.

While all the information professions share these characteristics, differences exist in the way that the four fields are practiced. Those differences are discussed in the section which follows.

Similarities and Differences among the Information Professions

We have used the term "information professions" frequently. Who is included in this category of professional? Our definition is, "those professions which are engaged in the creation, organization, diffusion, and preservation of information and knowledge." The information professions are in concurrence with the definition of "librarian," but there is no consensus on other terms used. Therefore, we define these professions and discuss the differences in categories below to provide a consistent vocabulary for the remainder of this book.

Librarians

The librarian traditionally has concentrated on the organization and storage of books, journals, and other published information sources. However, advances in technology have changed the nature of the library and the library profession as noted in this description of "librarians" published in the U.S. Government's *Occupational Outlook Handbook 2006–2007*:

> The traditional concept of a library is being redefined from a place to access paper records or books to one that also houses the most advanced media, including CD-ROM, the Internet, virtual libraries, and remote access to a wide range of resources. Consequently, librarians, or information professionals, increasingly are

combining traditional duties with tasks involving quickly changing technology. Librarians assist people in finding information and using it effectively for personal and professional purposes. Librarians must have knowledge of a wide variety of scholarly and public information sources and must follow trends related to publishing, computers, and the media in order to oversee the selection and organization of library materials. Librarians manage staff and develop and direct information programs and systems for the public, to ensure that information is organized in a manner that meets users' needs.

In other words, the librarian is a professional who assesses the information needs of a clientele and selects the appropriate packaged resources to meet those needs. Maintaining this collection requires a large facility, furnishings, and staff to select and acquire the resources, organize them, and make them available for use by the library's public. Consequently, management of this organization is a big job and takes a considerable amount of a librarian's time and energy. The traditional librarian rarely repackages information by writing reports, reformatting, or in other ways customizing the information package for individuals or groups. Librarians are found in a variety of organizations, public libraries, schools, colleges and universities, and in many kinds of "special" libraries, including law firms, medical and health facilities, archives, and government agencies at all levels.

Archives Managers or Archivists

Archives management is primarily concerned with the organization and storage of items important to the operation of an enterprise. Preservation for future use is a major concern for the archivist. Recent advances in technology have changed the role of the archivist as well. Below is a description of the work of archivists:

Archivists collect, organize, and maintain control over a wide range of information deemed important enough for permanent safekeeping. This information takes many forms: photographs, films, video and sound recordings, computer tapes, and video and optical disks, as well as more traditional paper records, letters, and documents. Archivists work for a variety of organizations, including government agencies, museums, historical societies, corporations, and educational institutions that use or generate records of great potential value to researchers, exhibitors, genealogists, and others who would benefit from having access to original source material. Archivists maintain records in accordance with accepted standards and practices that ensure the long-term preservation and easy retrieval of the documents. Records may be saved on any medium, including paper, film, videotape, audiotape, electronic disk, or computer. (*Handbook, 2006–2007 Edition*, Archivists, Curators, and Museum Technicians, available at http://www.bls.gov/oco/ocos065.htm)

Information Managers/Information Resources Managers

ARMA International, the professional association for records managers, combines records and information management, defining records management on its Web site as "The systematic control of records throughout their life cycle...."

An information manager usually works for a private agency, although s/he may also work for a public agency. The clientele of an information or records manager is more clearly defined than the clientele of a library, i.e., the number of clientele is usually a relatively small group of people whose needs are clearly identified by the information manager. While there may be a small collection of frequently used resources, the information manager typically relies more on access to information resources rather than a collection. The information manager rarely gives clientele an information package without repackaging it for the client; for example, a client may request detailed and recent information that might be found in a journal article or book, but the information manager will write a digest of the article or book chapters pertinent to the needs of the client. Handing a busy client a book is not a service that will help busy clients.

Levitan's (1982, 237) review of literature notes that information resource management (IRM) and information management have similar objectives, whether applied to public or private agencies. Among the objectives of information management are:

- To establish a system that applies only relevant information to corporate decisions.

- To change attitudes, polices, and practices so that information is viewed as a major asset of the enterprise.

- To legitimize the role of the information professional.

- To establish information skills training programs for all managers and employers.

- To identify research and development activities that improve information systems as they influence decision-making.

- To determine responsibilities for information acquisition and utilization throughout the organization.

- To integrate consideration of corporate information needs into the management routines of the organization.

Clearly, the terms for various aspects of the profession are still blurred as technology merges some specialties and assists in the creation of others.

Information Scientists/Theorists

Information scientists and theorists are concerned with the theories, philosophy, and study of the creation, use, and dissemination of information and knowledge. An information scientist or theorist is most likely an academic who teaches and conducts research in professional schools.

A leading professional organization for theorists is the Association for Library and Information Science Education (ALISE), which is composed primarily of faculty in professional schools accredited by the American Library Association. However, information theorists may be found in schools of business, archives programs in history departments, museum management programs, and school library programs in schools of education.

Information Systems Specialists

Sometimes called management information systems (MIS) specialists, these professionals typically work within a corporate environment. Their role is to develop internal systems for the management of information within the company. The largest volume of this information is from internally generated data, including personnel information, budget, product information, and measures of productivity of the organization.

Knowledge Managers

The knowledge manager works primarily with information that has been distilled and processed by groups. To become knowledge, information has been refined and accepted by an organization, a profession, or a group of some type. Part of the knowledge manager's role is to collect that knowledge which is acceptable and appropriate for the clientele. This is done by conducting a needs analysis, selecting appropriate information, and recommending it to the information consumer.

Information Entrepreneurs

With the expansion of the information field and with the transformation of the economy to include more information and knowledge-based jobs, people with training in information work can apply this knowledge in unique ways. Following is an account from *Occupational Outlook Handbook 2006–2007* regarding the potential future for librarians as information entrepreneurs:

> More and more, librarians are applying their information management and research skills to arenas outside of libraries, for example, database development, reference tool development, information systems, publishing, Internet coordination, marketing, Web content management and design, and training of database users. Entrepreneurial librarians sometimes start their own consulting practices, acting as freelance librarians or information brokers and providing services to other libraries, businesses, or government agencies.

The Association of Independent Information Professionals describes on its Web site the work of information entrepreneurs: "Our members provide a wide variety of services including specialized research; information, knowledge, and records management; writing; editing; indexing; training; translations; database design; and web page development."

Records Managers

Records managers may work for a public or private agency, and they are primarily concerned with the recorded documents generated within the agency. Internal correspondence and correspondence sent to individuals outside the agency are part of the information base to be managed. Records may be on paper or, increasingly, digital in format. A major concern of records managers is the organization, storage, and preservation of records for future retrieval and use. The terms "records manager" and "information manager" are sometimes used interchangeably. See "Information Manager" above.

Characteristics of a Profession

An important concept to consider is the difference between a professional and a technician or paraprofessional. As we advance through the Knowledge Society, the role of knowledge workers increases—the number of people engaged in the use of knowledge as their work increases. Professionals are knowledge workers, and so are paraprofessionals and technicians. But what is the difference in their work?

In summary, a professional is a person who masters and applies a body of knowledge in a specific area of inquiry. For example, an attorney has mastered the body of knowledge associated with the practice of law; a psychologist has learned and practiced the general or specific knowledge related to human behavior. However, the definition of a profession is more complex. According to Flexner (1915), a profession is characterized by the following: A body of knowledge, a body of literature, professional associations, an accreditation or licensure process, a system of education, a system of ethics. In other words, a profession has a unique culture, and a professional school is a purveyor of that culture.

Body of Knowledge

A body of knowledge is central to a profession. The professional is expert in an area of knowledge that can be applied in a professional practice. A teacher has studied learning theory and techniques for applying pedagogy to learners—usually specializing in pedagogy for an age group. In addition, a teacher has mastered the subject matter to be taught, including the rudimentary knowledge taught in elementary schools. The information professional has mastered a body of knowledge related to the creation, dissemination, diffusion, organization, preservation, and recording of knowledge. We submit that the body of knowledge is the four fields which are described above— information psychology, sociology of information, information organization management, and information engineering.

Body of Literature

The knowledge that a professional masters is recorded and available through a body of literature, which is organized, stored, indexed, and retrievable using the terms specific to the field of specialization. The information profession has many journals that record the research and current thinking, new techniques, and issues related to the practice of the information professions. Included are such journals as *American Libraries*. Of course, many books are published as textbooks and professional reading by such publishers as the American Library Association, Sage, H. W. Wilson, Scarecrow Press, Libraries Unlimited, and Marcel Dekker. Increasingly, journals and books are being published online, especially more specialized titles which cannot be justified financially by publishing in paper.

Professional Associations

Professional associations provide forums for the exchange of knowledge in the field and for dissemination of new knowledge related to practice. They contribute professional newsletters and journals which publish news of the organization and record accomplishments, trends, research, and innovative practices in the profession. Associations encourage networking among professionals through listservs; local, state, regional, national, and perhaps international conferences and provide opportunities to present new practices, research, and issues at conferences. Through committee work, new policies and procedures for practice are developed, implemented, and evaluated.

System of Education

The body of knowledge, the literature, the ethics and values, the system of literature—the culture of a profession—must be conveyed to prospective members of a profession in a systematic way. Professional schools have evolved to diffuse the knowledge and culture of professions.

Accreditation System

Professions have some form of authentication, i.e., some way of identifying individuals who have gained the professional knowledge of the field through an accepted system of licensure or certification. For example, the medical, law, and accounting fields have exams and/or review boards at the local or state levels to monitor the administration of exams to test standards set at the national level. Accreditation of library and information programs is granted by the American Library Association.

Ethics

Professions have a system of ethics by which their members practice the profession. The ethics of the information profession, as presented by the various professional associations, articulate a common thread of high standards for the profession. Examples of these statements are found in the Appendix. Ethics are an essential part of a profession, and the other elements have been described above. These characteristics of a profession are discussed in more detail in Chapter 9; however, the differences between professionals and technicians is an important distinction which is further described below.

Library Technicians

"Technicians" do not have the status as professionals, nor do they have the education of professionals. In short, technicians have more defined duties than professionals and do not have the overall responsibility for decision-making that is required by professionals. Technicians may have the title "aide" or "assistant," and their role is to assist the information professional to accomplish her/his work. Technicians may work with the clientele, helping them to use the information services, and they may have specialized duties, as described below:

Library technicians both help librarians acquire, prepare, and organize material and assist users in finding information. Library technicians usually work under the supervision of a librarian, although they work independently in certain situations. Technicians in small libraries handle a range of duties; those in large libraries usually specialize. As libraries increasingly use new technologies—such as CD-ROM, the Internet, virtual libraries, and automated databases—the duties of library technicians will expand and evolve accordingly. Library technicians are assuming greater responsibilities, in some cases taking on tasks previously performed by librarians .... In addition, technicians instruct patrons in how to use computer systems to access data. The increased automation of recordkeeping has reduced the amount of clerical work performed by library technicians. Many libraries now offer self-service registration and circulation areas with computers, decreasing the time library technicians spend manually recording and inputting records. (*Handbook 2006–2007*, "Library Technician")

Similarly, technicians or paraprofessionals in any aspect of the information professions or any other professions do not have the depth of knowledge or other aspects of a profession as defined earlier. While they have skills which can contribute to the profession, technicians do not have the breadth of knowledge, the understanding of ethics, the values, the mastery of the literature, and membership in the culture of the profession.

Conclusion

In this chapter we have introduced this book and the information professions. We have described the elements of a profession, with a brief discussion of the difference between a professional and a technician. The knowledge base of the information professions has been introduced, and those ideas will be explored in more depth in succeeding chapters.

References

ARMA International. What is 'records management'? Why should I care? http://www.arma.org/pdf/WhatIsRIM.pdf (accessed July 21, 2005).

Bolman, Lee. G, and Terrence E. Deal. 2003. *Reframing organizations: Artistry, choice, and leadership*. 3rd ed. San Francisco, CA: Jossey-Bass.

Bureau of Labor Statistics, U.S. Department of Labor. *Occupational Outlook Handbook, 2006–2007 Edition*, Archivists, Curators, and Museum Technicians. on the Internet at http://www.bls.gov/oco/ocos065.htm (accessed June 30, 2007).

———. *Occupational Outlook Handbook, 2006–07 Edition*, Librarians. http://www.bls.gov/oco/ocos068.htm (accessed June 30, 2007).

Butler, Pierce. 1933. *An introduction to library science*. Chicago: The University of Chicago Press.

———. 1976. "Librarianship as a profession." In *Landmarks of library literature 1876–1975*, ed. Dianne J. Ellsworth and Norman D. Stevens, 24–43. Metuchen, NJ: The Scarecrow Press.

Cleveland, Harlan. 1985. *The knowledge executive; leadership in an information society*. New York: Truman Talley Books/E.P. Dutton.

Debons, Anthony, Esther Horne, and Scott Croneweth. 1985. *Information science: An integrated view*. Boston: G.H. Hall. Cited in Rubin, *Foundations of library and information science*, 479–480.

Dewey, Melvil. 1976. "The profession." In *Landmarks of library literature 1876–1975*, ed. Dianne J. Ellsworth and Norman D. Stevens, 21–23. Metuchen, NJ: The Scarecrow Press.

Flexner, Abraham. 1915. Is social work a profession? Paper presented at the National Conference on Charities and Correction.

Glazier, Jack and Robert Grover. 2002. A multidisciplinary framework for theory building. *Library Trends* 50: 317–332.

Green, Samuel S. 1976. "Personal relations between librarians and readers." In *Landmarks of library literature 1876–1976*, ed. Dianne J. Ellsworth and Norman D. Stevens, 319–330. Metuchen, NJ: The Scarecrow Press.

Greer, Roger C. 1987. "A model for the discipline of information science." In *Intellectual foundations for information professionals*, ed. Herbert K. Achleitner, 3–25. Boulder, CO: Social Science Monographs; New York: Distributed by Columbia University Press.

Greer, Roger C. and Martha L. Hale. 1982. "The community analysis process." In *Public librarianship, a reader*, ed. Jane Robbins-Carter, 358–366. Littleton, CO: Libraries Unlimited.

Grover, Robert and Jack D.Glazier.1986. A conceptual framework for theory building in library and information science. *Library and Information Science Research* 8: 227–242.

Gulick, Luther. 1937. "Notes on the theory of organization." In *Papers on the science of administration*, ed. Luther Gulick and Lyndall Urwick, 191–195. New York: Institute of Public Administration, Columbia University.

Kuhlthau, Carol Collier. 1993. *Seeking meaning: A process approach to library and information services*. Norwood, NJ: Ablex.

———. 2004. *Seeking meaning: A process approach to library and information services*. 2nd ed. Westport, CT: Libraries Unlimited.

Levitan, Karen B. Information resource(s) management—IRM. *Annual Review of Information Science and Technology (ARIST)* 17 (1982):227–266.

Mason, Richard O., Florence M. Mason, and Mary J. Culnan. 1995. *Ethics of information management*. Thousand Oaks, CA: Sage Publications (Sage Series in Business Ethics).

2

Creation, Diffusion, and Utilization of Knowledge

Chapter Overview

The creation, diffusion, and utilization of information is explained and illustrated with a graphic model. The roles of universities, professions, and public policy are explored. Implications for information professionals are suggested with examples.

Introduction

To understand the functions and objectives of the information professions in society, it is necessary to place them in the context of the social structure of society. The overall goal of the information professions is to enhance the flow of information in and around the elements of society. An understanding of information flow begins with an awareness of the fundamental actions that encompass information in its service to society.

Information in a society can be compared with the function of blood in a human body. In order to sustain life, blood must be created and renewed constantly; similarly, information must be created continuously to maintain a dynamic momentum in a society. As blood nourishes part of the body as it circulates in the body, so does information nourish a society through the processes of information transfer.

This chapter examines that process by focusing on the creation, diffusion, and utilization of information and knowledge. We examine and define "data," "information," and "knowledge" and explore how new knowledge is created, diffused in society, and put to use. Below we define key terms before discussing them in more detail later in this chapter.

Information and Data

In Chapter 1 we used Cleveland's definition for "information," i.e., information is organized data (Cleveland 1985, 22). "Data" are the rough materials from which information and knowledge are formed, i.e., undigested observations, or unvarnished facts. Given connections or context, data can form information. Furthermore, information can be generated by all kinds of natural and unnatural phenomena, e.g., weather, weather reports, news events, or the work of professionals of various types.

Knowledge

That information which we remember or incorporate into our memory becomes knowledge. In other words, information that is processed, selected, and synthesized by a human becomes knowledge. Knowledge is also processed by groups of people, and we will refer to social knowledge when we discuss information transfer and knowledge diffusion. If information is read into a computer, it can be synthesized, but our definition of knowledge is consistent with that of Patrick Wilson, who contends that knowledge requires a knower (Wilson 1977).

Creation of Knowledge

Creation of knowledge refers to the creation of new social knowledge—new knowledge for groups in our society. Research produces new social knowledge, and research is conducted in universities, government agencies, and private sector think tanks. Creation of new knowledge for an individual is not considered knowledge creation in this discussion.

Dissemination

Webster's Collegiate Dictionary defines "dissemination": "to spread abroad as though sowing seed." Applied to information, we use this term similarly—to spread information widely. For example, broadcast news is dissemination, as is newspaper publishing and Web sites. The audience is often of a general nature, and the acceptance of the information is uncertain.

Diffusion

"Diffusion" is the transmission of knowledge from one individual or group to another individual or group in such a way that the recipients absorb or transfer the knowledge into personal action. Learning must occur for diffusion to be successful. Schools and colleges are social institutions, which are part of the knowledge infrastructure designed by society to diffuse knowledge from one generation to another.

Utilization

After individuals or groups have adopted new knowledge and, after it has been diffused to them, the knowledge may be put to use, or utilized. Knowledge that has been learned has been employed for some benefit to the user or to the group. Information professionals exist for the purpose of converting knowledge into practical advantage.

Change and the Evolution of Professions

In today's dynamic society, new knowledge increases exponentially. De Solla Price (1975) was one of the earlier scientists to write about the information explosion. He noted that the number of scientific journals increased exponentially, not linearly. "The constant involved is actually about fifteen years for a doubling, corresponding to a power of ten in fifty years and a factor of one thousand in a century and a half" (p. 169).

A recent study conducted by researchers at the School of Information Management and Systems, University of California-Berkeley, estimated ". . . the amount of new information stored on paper, film, magnetic, and optical media has about doubled in the last three years" (Lyman and Varian 2003). Furthermore, the same study estimated that the amount of new stored information grew approximately 30 percent each year between 1999 and 2002. The study also reported that the amount of information printed on paper continues to grow, but 92 percent of new information is stored on magnetic media—mostly hard disks. Ninety-two percent of new information is stored on magnetic media, primarily hard disks. Paper accounts for only .01 percent of new information.

New knowledge often brings new technologies to simplify or satisfy emerging needs. New technology has brought us such conveniences as garage door openers, microwave ovens, and cable or satellite television. Similarly, some of these same technologies often bring more complexities to daily living and may even change how we view reality. An example of this change in attitudes is the simultaneous coverage of news events as the events occur. We hear reporters speculate as they observe an attack on a platoon of U.S. soldiers in Baghdad, and when the speculation is negated by events in the next few hours, our confidence in news coverage is influenced. Likewise, we observe events transmitted instantaneously, and we compare what we see with later statements by government officials which seem to contradict our observations. Our personal views are shaped by the coverage of news events made possible by communications technologies.

While satellite transmission brings us instant coverage of news stories, we have access to several hundred channels of entertainment and news programming, more than we can possibly attend to or comprehend. Similarly, the palmtop computer enables us to carry address books, to-do lists, documents, pictures, and movies in our purses or pockets; however, we must be disciplined to learn to use this technology and to use it to our advantage. If we are not careful, this technology can be a distraction instead of a useful tool.

As social organizations develop and social interaction becomes more diverse and complex, new technologies appear to assist in dealing with emerging issues and problems, as do new occupations. These occupations provide an expertise in the exploitation of new technologies as well as dynamic components of society. While computers enable the production, storage, and retrieval of vast amounts of information, the resulting information explosion poses gigantic problems for people to access, organize, and use information effectively. As a result, the information professions have proliferated and transformed to address these needs.

Occupations evolve from the mere application of simple rules and techniques to resolve problems at a more sophisticated level of service. To do this, a process of analysis of circumstances and customization of service is required. When the occupation matures to the point of providing a customized solution to address a client's unique need, the occupation must have developed a base of specialized knowledge, a theory base. With the accumulation of a sufficiently broad knowledge base, an in-depth collection of relevant theories, and an ethical commitment to serving the public, an occupation evolves from the level of a technician applying memorized rules and formulas to that of a profession, drawing upon theory for a diagnosis that will lead to a customized service.

The information profession is an example of such an evolution based on societal need. Until the formation of the American Library Association in 1876, librarians learned their occupation on the job—learning to obtain, organize, and retrieve books from senior staff. Early preparation for librarians occurred as internships at libraries. Melvil Dewey formed the first school for the preparation of librarians at Columbia College (now Columbia University) in 1887. As the field became more complex, the education of library professionals expanded to the graduate level at the University of Chicago in 1928 and expanded beyond libraries during the 1960s and 1970s. Now the field assumes the moniker "library and information science" to recognize the breadth of the field.

Stated in general terms, the function of professions in society is to provide customized services employing specialized knowledge in an ethical manner. Therefore, professionals are partners of academicians in colleges and universities because professions convert new and existing knowledge for societal advantage. Academics are defined here as individuals engaged in the processes of creating new knowledge through research and diffusing this knowledge to members of society through a formal educational system. Researchers pursue the quest for new knowledge because of a curiosity about the nature of reality. The objective of developing something of use in solving social or intellectual problems is often the motivation to do research. In summary, professions are a significant component of the creation, diffusion, utilization of knowledge. That role is described in the model which follows.

A Model for Explaining the Creation, Diffusion, and Utilization of Knowledge

The way that new knowledge is created, diffused, and used in a society is complex. To assist in presenting these ideas, we will refer to the model below to explain the processes of knowledge creation, diffusion, and utilization. This model (Figure 2.1) is a simplified, idealized graphic description of a complex knowledge infrastructure. A model is like a formula which helps to identify the core concepts associated with a complex system. Since it is a generalization, it is considered a type of theory (Grover and Glazier, 1986; Glazier and Grover, 2002).

Although a model is a simplification of a complex idea or system, the diffusion model in Figure 2.1 attempts to cluster a number of concepts, organizations, and activities associated with the role of information in society, a segment of the societal infrastructure or fabric associated with information and knowledge. In reading the model, begin at the center and move toward the perimeter.

In the knowledge infrastructure portrayed in this model, the Ph.D. degree (center of the model) is a societal construct that exists and is designed specifically to provoke the process of creating new knowledge. Unlike other places and ways that new knowledge is created, the objective of the Ph.D.

Figure 2.1. Creation, Diffusion, Utilization of Information

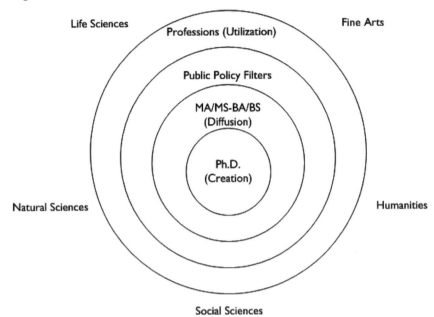

process is to produce acceptable new knowledge for society. Think tanks and other private enterprise research organizations produce new knowledge, but that knowledge often tends to be a synthesis or new application of old or existing knowledge.

Divisions identified in the model represent the traditional academic environment—fine arts, humanities, social sciences, natural sciences, and life sciences. The diffusion "ring" or circle of the model represents the teaching/learning process that is the core social responsibility of the academic infrastructure, i.e., the transfer of knowledge from one generation to the next. Additional rings of public policy and the professions should also be interpreted to receive knowledge from the creation circle.

The public policy filters ring of this model is intended to show the role that public policy plays in the diffusion and utilization of information. Public policy is a conglomeration of laws, regulations, and rules that we need in order to maintain stability and structure in society. Public policy represents those actions of a corporate body or public agency like a public library where policies are articulated to affect use of information. Public policy can enhance or inhibit the flow of information. For example, information creation is enhanced when an agency like the National Science Foundation funds a research effort like hydrogen fuel, research on information systems, or stem cell research. On the other hand, government policy can withhold funds for certain projects like stem cell research, because the policy reflects values of the prevailing government, while public policy also can be harmful to a society or to a prevailing belief system because it makes available contrary information.

The professions/utilization "ring" of the model shows that as public policy is a filter, professions are a screening process whereby public policy is converted knowledge for utilization by society. Professions, as defined in Chapter 1, include professional education schools to teach new theories and methods, researchers to create new theories and models for practicing the profession, journals and professional organizations to communicate new ideas and best practices.

As noted above, this model is a simplified perspective on the formal research and education infrastructure for the creation and diffusion of new knowledge in society through colleges and universities. In recent years, educational programs in private enterprise and online universities have changed the structure of higher education and secondary/elementary education. Despite the application of new technologies, this model reflects the concepts that are operative in the research and teaching functions of our educational institutions.

Creating New Knowledge

Research in Colleges and Universities

Traditionally, society has invested the responsibility for creating new knowledge in the course of study leading to a doctor of philosophy degree (Ph.D.). The typical curriculum associated with this course of study focuses on the accepted research methodologies, accepted theories, and values associated with particular disciplines. The doctorate is not given until new knowledge is endorsed by a doctoral committee of seasoned experts in a field of study. The new knowledge produced by doctorates is often embodied in theory, generalizations which can be applied to problems in a discipline or profession. Doctoral research must conform to the accepted research methods and theories of a field; in other words, new knowledge must conform to the prevailing paradigm of the field. Paradigms are discussed in depth in Chapter 3.

Conventionally, colleges are organized around a broad arrangement of academic divisions: Humanities, Life Sciences, Fine Arts, Social Science, and Physical Sciences. Depending on the size of the institutions, these divisions are further subdivided by disciplines: social sciences include history, sociology, political science, and geography. Among the Life Sciences are biology and zoology. Physics, geology, earth science, and chemistry are among the Physical Sciences. Languages and literature are included in the Humanities, along with the Fine Arts, which include music, the performing arts, and graphic arts.

During the latter part of the twentieth century, disciplines expanded into hyphenated areas cutting across the boundaries of other fields, generating labels such as biochemistry, economic geography, social psychology, etc. Consequently, the current organization of colleges varies from the historical, depending upon size, mission, physical plant, and an assortment of practical considerations rather than an intellectual ideal. When professional schools and graduate programs are added to the campus, the college becomes a university.

While academic disciplines comprise the elements of the typical college of arts and sciences on a campus, the professions add a cluster of graduate schools to the organization that comprises the university. Traditionally, graduate programs designed to educate practitioners in diverse professions range from 1 to 3 years. In addition, some professions require additional time spent in an internship status working as a practitioner under the supervision of a mentor. These professional programs build upon undergraduate academic degrees. For example, a student will learn relevant theories in an undergraduate program in biology for advanced applications in the professional fields of medicine. Professions, like disciplines, adopt value systems which include research methods, best practices, service attitudes, ethics, and other values which comprise a paradigmatic perspective on their profession. As undergraduates pursue a major field of study, they learn the attributes of the paradigm in that major, and students become members of that discipline when they have accepted the values of that paradigm.

Other Sponsors of Research

Although conducting research is a fundamental responsibility of academics, in reality, this source of new knowledge is probably a minor portion of the total production of new knowledge in a dynamic and sophisticated society. Most major industries have large budgetary and personnel commitments to conduct research. So-called "think tanks" or institutes and foundations, a phenomenon of the latter half of the twentieth century, are also engaged in the production of knowledge. It is common and desirable for a company to invest a percentage of its annual budget in research and development.

Government laboratories such as the Livermore Laboratory at the University of California-Berkley and agencies such as the National Aeronautics and Space Administration (NASA) produce knowledge to address specific goals or questions. Professional organizations and academic societies are also engaged in the production of useful new knowledge. In essence, new knowledge is produced in almost all segments of society. Much of it is new and involves an application on behalf of society.

In summary, academic components of higher education in society have responsibility for research to create new knowledge. In addition, these disciplines are responsible for the diffusion of knowledge through a formal system of advanced education. This diffusion process encompasses each succeeding generation.

Diffusion of Knowledge

As noted above, colleges, universities, and schools, all educational institutions, are designed to serve societal goals of diffusion of knowledge. Academic members of faculty in colleges and universities have a dual role—creating new knowledge through research and diffusing it through their classes and through institutes, workshops, and various forms of presentation of their findings. It should be noted that publication of research is considered "dissemination" because the mass publication and distribution of ideas through journals or electronic publications is not diffusion as workshops or classes. The entire education system is concerned with diffusion of knowledge. The key to knowledge diffusion is *learning*, and learning is enhanced through the application of theories derived in educational psychology. In other words, learning theory suggests ways for teachers to enhance the teaching/learning process. Research on individual learning styles is applied to instruction for the benefit of learners.

New knowledge may be published in books, journals, and other formats, and the knowledge may then be the subject of teaching in higher education and/or secondary level schools. Specialized knowledge may also be diffused through specialty education programs in public or private agencies; for that matter, teachers of all types are engaged in diffusion. It is their professional calling, and learning theory and cognitive style are part of their theory base.

However, teachers are not the only professionals engaged in the diffusion of new knowledge. Some information professionals also have diffusion as their goal. The challenge of information professionals is to help information users, their clients, to derive meaning from the information or knowledge sources they are using. Information professionals have the responsibility of not only disseminating information to the right person at the right time, they have the responsibility of helping the information users to understand the information presented and to use the information effectively. To accomplish this, the information professional must analyze the client's learning style, matching the user's needs and preferences for learning to the information or knowledge available. The information professional must enable users to use information in their own contexts. With children, information professionals can determine the grade level that a child is in to gain a partial understanding of their audience. When information professionals work with young adults and adults, the diagnostic process is more complex and is discussed in Chapter 6, "The Cycle of Professional Service."

Public Policy

Every society attempts to protect itself from harmful knowledge and its use, as well as, benefit as early and diversely as possible from beneficial knowledge. The mechanism most useful in this process is the development and application of public policy. Public policy is a consequence of governmental action that affects certain aspects of a society. Public policy related to the development and utilization of information and knowledge comes in many forms.

Most directly related is the Copyright Law, which guarantees an author or creator of an intellectual property the right of ownership. Thus, this public policy is designed to enhance the value of an individual's creativity both for the sake of the individual by receiving income from its dissemination and for society by making knowledge available to everyone. Another example of the application of public policy in the development, dissemination, and utilization of new knowledge is the creation of a new drug for the treatment of some known disease. Once the knowledge of the composition of a new drug is converted to a manufacturing process, the Pure Food and Drug Agency, conducts appropriate tests to determine if it is indeed of value to society.

Another example of public policy involvement in the development and implementation of new knowledge is in the roles of the National Science Foundation or the National Institutes of Health. These agencies enhance the development of new knowledge through grants and contracts, on the one hand, and promote the dissemination by providing funds for the process.

Thus, it is evident that public policy at the national level is profoundly relevant to the creation, diffusion, and utilization of knowledge by society. At the regional and local level, governments and public agencies, such as universities and public libraries, have a corresponding impact on these societal processes. For example, a public library's lending policies have an impact in a limited way on the ability of citizens to access information.

Role of Professions in the Utilization of Knowledge

Diffusion and utilization could be concurrent for those who learn by doing. We artificially separate these processes, but the three processes are so interlinked it is impossible to separate them. We separate them for the purpose of this discussion, but they can occur simultaneously.

Above we called the education profession a "diffusion" profession. The information professions are "utilization" professions, joining physicians, attorneys, architects, financial planners, managers, accountants, and other professionals as those who take knowledge and make it practical.

Professions have the responsibility of adding new knowledge to the existing mass of what is known and converting it for practical use by the public. On this continuum from the production and diffusion of new knowledge to its practical employment is the role of public policy. Every society attempts to protect itself from harmful knowledge and its use and benefit as early and diversely as possible from beneficial knowledge. The mechanism most useful in this process is the development and application of public policy.

Implications for Information Professionals

Information professionals, including archivists, librarians of all types, information specialists, researchers, information entrepreneurs, database managers, Web masters, and others in information intensive professions have a vital role to plan in the creation, diffusion, and utilization of knowledge.

Facilitating Knowledge Creation

The creation of new knowledge takes many forms, as noted in the discussion above. More specific discussions will be found in other chapters; however, examples of information professionals assisting clients with knowledge creating include the following:

- A university librarian discusses a research project with a university professor and conducts an online search to provide interdisciplinary research which contributes to an understanding of the problem the professor is investigating.

- A public librarian, at the request of the city manager, prepares a report on current trends in e-commerce.

- An information entrepreneur contracts with a public health agency to review research on "second hand smoke" in order to prepare a public information campaign citing the impact of second hand smoke on children.

Diffusing Knowledge

Following are examples of information professionals engaged in the diffusion of knowledge:

- A school library media specialist teams with a fifth grade teacher to collaborate on a unit which will require students to conduct searches online and using the school library media center. The library media specialist will review appropriate resources and search strategies with the students and teach note-taking. The final product will be a science fair in the classroom.

- A law librarian conducts a workshop for attorneys during lunch hour in a community law library. The librarian instructs attorneys in the types of information available in the data bases and teaches search strategies.

- A college librarian lectures an introductory history class on the ethics of using online sources for reports.

- A public librarian teaches retired citizens the resources available for planning a healthy lifestyle. A physical education instructor from a local community college lectures on the topic at the same meeting.

Knowledge Utilization

Utilization requires the information professional to help the information user derive meaning from information. Here are a few examples:

- All the diffusion examples above are the first step in facilitating knowledge utilization. Additional diagnosis of the individual's particular interests and needs will enable the information professional to prescribe unique strategies for the user.

- A school library media specialist joins a middle school class writing a history report. The librarian teaches a unit on synthesizing information—assembling notes in a logical manner, without plagiarizing.

- A public librarian helps a father planning a trip for his family. The librarian selects a number of printed travel guides, shows the uses of each, and demonstrates an online navigation system.

Summary

Information professionals in any work setting can and should engage in the promotion of knowledge creation, diffusion, and utilization. This role is a departure from the traditional role of many librarians who see their role as maintaining collections of books, periodicals, and databases. The role can, and should be, much more collaborative and complex. In essence, the information professional must collaborate with information users to understand their information needs, and prescribe appropriate information resources and strategies for using them. The information professional works with people and information or knowledge. More specific models and strategies for accomplishing this important professional work are explained in chapters that follow.

References

Cleveland, Harlan. 1985. *The knowledge executive; leadership in an information society.* New York: Truman Talley Books/E.P. Dutton.

de Solla Price, Derek. 1975. *Science since Babylon.* Enlarged Edition. New Haven, CT: Yale University Press.

Glazier, Jack D. and Robert Grover. 2002. A multidisciplinary framework for theory building. *Library Trends* 50: 317–332.

Grover, Robert and Jack Glazier. 1986. A conceptual framework for theory building in library and information science. *Library and Information Science Research* 8: 227–242.

Lyman, Peter and Hal R. Varian. 2003. How much information. http://www.sims.berkeley.edu/how-much-info-2003 (accessed on January 18, 2007).

U.S. Department of Labor, Bureau of Labor Statistics. *Occupational outlook handbook 2006–2007.* http://www.bls.gov/oco/ (accessed March 21, 2006).

Webster's Collegiate Dictionary. http://www.merriam-webster.com/dictionary/disseminate (accessed January 17, 2007).

Wilson, Patrick. 1977. *Public knowledge and private ignorance.* Westport, CT: Greenwood Press.

3

The Role of Professionals as Change Agents

Chapter Overview

As professionals, we must be aware of the "big picture." We must understand our current society and the role of our profession in that society. In this chapter, we examine change in our world—the different kinds of change, and the implications of that change for the library and information professions. We then explore the shift that has occurred in the information professions and how that shift influences the way we think about library and information service. We provide an outline of levels of service and types of services that can be provided to our changing society.

The Impact of Change on Society

Professions are socially anchored. As noted in Chapter 2, the function of professions in society is to provide customized services employing specialized knowledge in an ethical manner. To be effective they must reflect in some measure the currents of thought, activity, and social dynamic of the parent society. While there are many adjectives one may choose to describe the social environment at the beginning of the third millennium, perhaps the most compelling and all encompassing is the concept of change.

Change is a byproduct of many distinct and separate variables evolving and simultaneously interacting with each other. A list of some of the ubiquitous variables can lead us to a broader understanding of the concept of change. Perhaps the dominant variable among the developed societies of the world is the current cornucopia of new technologies which appear at an unprecedented rate.

Each new technology seeks to improve our ability to manage our daily occupational and domestic chores and routines. Moreover, the addition of a new technology is not necessarily a replacement for an existing tool, but often is merely an additional device or methodology. A person wishing to attend to a task or engage in an activity has more options in choice of tools or techniques to employ. With the addition of more options comes increased complexity.

New technologies lead to greater complexity because of things that can be accomplished now which were impossible in the past. The astonishing developments in space exploration are compelling examples of this change. Advances in medical technologies and techniques have advanced longevity. New drugs designed to pinpoint and ameliorate the effects of illness from deadly cancer to simple headaches are contributing to the general expansion of the human races. Increased population combined with enhanced communication and transportation technologies has profoundly contributed to the reality of the concept of a global economy.

More people, and more social complexity through enhanced communication and transportation, necessarily provoke a deluge of information to provide the glue necessary for the maintenance of a dynamic society. All these developments contribute to an accelerated rate of change impacting every individual, organization, community, society, and culture in the world. Understanding the existence of this run-away explosion of change is essential for professions and professionals seeking means of satisfying individual needs.

Categories of Change

The three types of change include incremental, cataclysmic, and paradigmatic. Each will be discussed below and related to implications for information professionals.

Incremental Change

Incremental change is that which happens every day. It is continuous and imperceptible unless closely scrutinized. It is the process of transforming in micro increments the condition of anything that is subject to time and the environment. Thus the process of human aging is evidence of incremental change. The status of aging is only recognized when we are presented with a picture of ourselves from an earlier time. The changing seasons of weather are another example of incremental change. As the earth rotates on its axis and traverses its orbit around the sun, there is a continuous transformation that is barely perceptible at any one moment. The daily routine of light and darkness are processes of incremental change. Similarly the evolution of the four seasons demonstrates another process of incremental change.

In all these examples the rate of change differs but often remains imperceptible. It is the process that is inexorable in most living things, and inanimate things also change incrementally, e.g., a car gradually deteriorates. Incremental change is normal, and we go on with our lives.

At certain points we may observe a fundamental change, e.g., a child moves from childhood to adolescence, then from adolescence to young adult, and from young adult to mature adult. We adjust to these changes. With these changes comes a shift in perspective and values, a shift in understanding, a shift in awareness of ourselves as part of the universe. This happens three or four times during our lifetimes.

An accumulation of incremental change eventually becomes a fundamental shift in perspective. As an example, the United States population has grown to 280 million; the perspective of rural living is largely gone because we have been urbanized by the mass media, television, radio, film, and the Internet. Societies move and have transitions as they grow and evolve.

Incremental change is ubiquitous and continuous, resulting in periodic shifts in values.

Cataclysmic Change

Cataclysmic change is a consequence of uncontrollable natural or social phenomena. Examples of natural phenomena are earthquakes, tornados, tidal waves, hurricanes, floods, or wildfires. The impact of these natural phenomena is immediate and sometimes inexorable. Frequently the change is brought about by the process of reconstruction. In every instance the change is more or less permanent.

Other forms of cataclysmic change occur as a consequence of dramatic social activities. These include wars, riots, revolutions, and man-made conflagrations. Government policy resulting in huge undertakings such as dams, reservoirs, housing developments, or urban renewal projects can also induce cataclysmic change in an environment. Cataclysmic change is like the impact of the terrorist attacks on September 11, 2001—dynamic, unforeseen, and horrendous. Cataclysmic change may take decades for the country and world to accept it. It is unbelievable change. Lifestyle changes have occurred as a result, and often dominate our conversation and media.

Paradigmatic Change

A third type of change is considerably more inclusive in its impact than the other two. This example of change is identified as a paradigm shift. According to current researchers and popular authors (e.g., Toffler 1980, Kuhn 1962), societal and global paradigm shifts occur over one or more centuries (Burke 1985) or even millennia. The reason for this seemingly long time frame is associated with changes in paradigms which frame reality in mental constructs.

Before we can understand the concept of a paradigm shift, we must explore the role of paradigms in providing societies with coherent and common views of reality. The term paradigm is being used rather casually in popular dialog these days; consequently, its meaning and significance tend to be distorted. A paradigm is neither a new technology nor new technique in doing a task or activity. It is a new way of perceiving what was known before. This new perception is so profound that it alters how we define a previously known "truth."

A well articulated definition by Schwartz and Ogilvy follows: "A paradigm is, broadly construed, the set of those beliefs, axioms, assumptions, givens, or fundamentals that order and provide coherence to our picture of what it is and how it works" (Schwartz and Ogilvy 1979, 179).

Paradigm is described by the metaphor of a lens—the lens we use to view the world. It brings into focus what we deem important and excludes what is deemed irrelevant at the moment. As a lens, it may be focused on the most distant of objects as a telescope or minute entities as a microscope. In every instance, it provides meaning to what is being perceived. This meaning is achieved by ordering the assumptions, beliefs, axioms, givens, and fundamentals that we have organized around the object being viewed. In other words, a paradigm encompasses the values that we have devised to assist in making sense of the world. Values are designed by humankind and dominate societies for centuries, even millennia.

The Paradigm Shift in Western Society

Schwartz and Ogilvy (1979) applied the paradigm concept of Thomas Kuhn to the changes in Western society. They noted a shift as follows:

From	To
Simple	Complex
Hierarchy	Heterarchy
Mechanical	Holographic
Determinate	Indeterminate
Linearly causal	Mutually causal
Assembly	Morphogenesis
Objective	Perspective
Analog	Digital

Simple to Complex

The emergent paradigm recognizes the complexity of contemporary society. As a result, simple solutions have given away to complexity. Even the marketplace is much more complex. For example, the "big three" auto makers (General Motors, Ford, and Chrysler) have given way to a multitude of international manufacturers which often rival or surpass American auto makers in quality. In addition to the expanded market of autos from France, Great Britain, Germany, Japan, Korea, and China, among others, each auto maker has a plethora of models, colors, and options to choose from. To complicate further the auto market, it is increasingly difficult to identify the nationality of the manufacturer. Until the 1990s, American cars were made with parts made in the United States, and foreign cars were made in their home country. Now American cars are built with parts made in the United States and several other countries. Japanese, German, and other foreign auto makers now manufacture or assemble many of their models in the United States.

Similarly, life has become more complex. New technologies provide many options for entertainment and for information sources. News is available to us in printed newspapers and magazines, television, radio, via the telephone, Internet, and through informal networks. Furthermore, the complexity is exasperated by the rate of change. New inventions are invading the marketplace and being adopted at a rapid pace. This pace causes frustration, and some people throw up their hands, exclaiming that they have given up on keeping up.

Hierarchy to Heterarchy

The structure of organizations has changed from a traditional hierarchical structure like that of the military with generals, colonels, majors, captains, lieutenants, and noncommissioned officers to a flattened heterarchy. A hierarchy has specified levels of authority, with communication from top down, or from bottom up, in a specified linear pattern. The communication is expected to follow the levels of authority one by one.

A heterarchy, by contrast, is more fluid and more casual in organization and communication. A marriage relationship is a heterarchy when the couple negotiates who is in charge, and that may vary according to the situation.

Currently, an Anglo-American marriage is likely to be a partnership, not a dominating relationship. In families, parents do not rely on their status as parents for authority, they must reason with their children.

In organizations, a heterarchical or flattened structure enables people at any point in the organization to have access to decision makers at any level. Heterarchy is the new paradigm organization plan in organizations; the top management is likely to be more interested in the content of employees' heads than the use of their hands. One of the characteristics of e-mail and instant messaging is that any member of the organization can be reached at any time by any other member of the organization via electronic mail. As a result, the hierarchy is deflated and replaced by a heterarchy. The inflexibility of communication by level in the hierarchical organization is replaced by flexibility in the communication system, making the organization more fluid and responsive to the need for change.

Similarly, library and information systems like indexing can be made more flexible and responsive to the needs of clientele by using natural language searching or by creating multiple access points using many indexing terms. The former limitations of paper information sources and their consequent necessity to limit indexing terms has been replaced by the use of large numbers of terms and natural language searching.

Mechanical to Holographic

This evolution recognizes the advancement from physical or mechanical objects to a virtual reality. For example, we are accustomed to visiting an actual library where we can sit down and examine a catalog, either by sitting before a computer screen, book catalog, or card catalog (now nearly extinct!). We then can note the books or other items that we want and physically locate them. A virtual library would enable us to browse the stacks on our computer screen, select the time, and check it out online.

A holograph is a lifelike, three dimensional representation of reality. However, it is not real; it is virtual reality. The concept of a holograph is that a portion or part lets us see the whole, a piece contains all the elements of a whole. For example, a case study helps us to understand issues of a larger population, e.g., studying a cohort to understand distance education issues.

We are seeing many examples of virtual reality in video games in which the player may be driving a race car or hunting wild animals in a jungle. With increased sophistication and diminishing cost of computer technology, the possibilities for additional simulation of reality may become an integral part of our lives as an instructional or informational tool. For example, we might sit down at a computer screen to take a virtual tour of Disney World or the city of Seattle before we make a decision to take a family vacation. Tour books and brochures may give way to virtual reality introductions to places we may want to visit.

Determinate to Indeterminate

Determinate solutions are not possible in a complex society. Nothing has a definite answer. Facts that were once certain are no longer certain. The complexity in contemporary society leads to insoluble problems. There are few absolutes in today's world. For example, we ask questions about our society and seek answers which are not forthcoming. We see criminal behavior and want to know ways that such behavior can be curbed.

We receive news reports of indisputable signs that our world is experiencing global warming. What are the causes? The United States engages in military conflicts in Iraq; how can the conflict be resolved so that troops can be returned home and the Iraqis can administer their own government? How can inflation be controlled? How can the size of government be controlled?

The solutions of social problems may have been contemplated, addressed, and resolved more simply in past generations. For example, cures could be found for polio, small pox, and other diseases. Public health issues were addressed through public policy which stopped the spread of disease. The American economy was more independent from the economies of other countries. Families were fairly stable, but now we have blended families whereby father and mother bring together children from previous relationships. Even the home life has become more complex. As a result of the complexity in our society, the resolution of problems is much more complex. Few simple solutions are appropriate; solutions which were once determinate are now indeterminate. Solutions to social issues are likely to be short- rather than long-term.

Linearly Causal to Mutually Causal

The causes of phenomena have also become more complex. Mutually causal suggests that there is not a straight line cause/effect relationship. Influence goes both ways and a researcher can influence effects. Whereas A caused B and C caused D, we now find that D is caused by A plus B plus C.

To say that criminal behavior is caused by the home environment is inadequate. Criminal behavior may be caused by a congenital psychological defect exacerbated by home environment and social interactions with peers. Similarly, when an information professional is asked, "What is the population of Chicago?" we have an apparently simple question. However, does the client want the current population? How current? Does s/he want the city as defined by the city limits? Or the metropolitan area? Even the simplest question is more complex than it appears.

While we may yearn for simplistic solutions to problems like poverty, crime, and the rising cost of living, such issues have multiple causes. However, politicians running for office still attempt to apply linearly causal solutions to mutually caused social problems. As information professionals, we must resist the urge to provide simplistic answers to complex questions and problems. We have a professional obligation to help our clients understand the complexity of issues by providing them with examples of various viewpoints.

Objective to Perspective

The term "objective" refers to things outside our thoughts and feelings. This term suggests the presentation of facts without bias. Although it is commonly suggested that we should be "objective" about an issue or a person,. However, individuals are influenced by their experiences over time, and we form opinions about issues. Since we cannot be totally objective, let us recognize that we have a perspective, and it is an important perspective. As information professionals, we must be aware of our perspective on issues and be willing to announce our biases when dealing with sensitive issues.

Figure 3.1. Thomas Kuhn's Conception
of a Paradigm Shift

The Paradigm Shift in Disciplines
and Professions

Thomas Kuhn (1962) described the paradigm shift in disciplines as shown in   Figure 3.1. An existing paradigm used to provide sense to an area of consideration, e.g., a discipline, is discovered to have anomalies, which eventually develop into a crisis state, which results in a revolution and a new paradigm.

In disciplines, the existing theories have been demonstrated as effective, and the methodologies used in the field explain the value system—what is accepted, what is valid, and what is not. Then some anomalies are noted. When a sufficient number of anomalies are recognized, there is a crisis, and the luminaries in a field are at odds. When a crisis is reached, there follows a revolution, and a new perspective is developed to accommodate the anomalies. A new paradigm has becomes dominant, and the cycle commences again. Paradigms help us to understand what acceptable knowledge is and why people think and believe the way they do.

The paradigm which we use to give meaning to reality includes the assumptions we have accepted about the nature of things and how they work. These assumptions include an image of the universe, the position of the planet earth, the sun and other elements in the natural world including humans and other living beings.

Over the last 5,000 years (a relatively recent period in the known history of humankind) assumptions about the position and relationships of each of these components have changed drastically and with relative infrequency. Recent changes have been motivated by discoveries of empirical evidence which refuted previously held views of reality. Perhaps the most profound and sweeping examples are the works of Copernicus in the sixteenth century and, approximately 100 years later, the contribution of Galileo. Previous views, based more or less on Aristotle's "Mechanics," provided coherence for the Western world's views of reality. This scenario also reflected in the Old Testament and early religions placed the earth at the center of the universe with the sun and other celestial bodies revolving around the earth.

These changed views of the universe affected existing assumptions, beliefs, givens, and fundamentals about the organization of the universe. This challenge to existing values associated with the proper order of things was indeed a paradigm shift. The new paradigm placed the sun at the center of the universe and recognized that the planets, including earth, revolved around the sun while simultaneously rotating on their axis. Other changes that occurred during these centuries of paradigm shifting, included the Reformation (Luther's dictum that everyman was his own priest changed the view of the role of the church), the rise of nationalism with the dissolution of the concept of the divine right of kings, and inexorable tendency toward individual liberty and the age of exploration.

Paradigms are the boxes we use to contain our values about the way things should work. Paradigms are socially constructed. They describe the right way and the wrong way, the just and the unjust, the logical and the illogical for any one group of people or any one culture.

When someone is "thinking outside the box," it is likely that they have transcended the boundaries of the dominant paradigm. Similarly, "straying outside the lines" is another way of suggesting a violation of the limits of the paradigm governing the situation.

The concept of a paradigm is difficult to grasp because it can refer to very broad concepts and cultural entities, while relating to a narrow environment such as an academic discipline or an organization. Essentially, paradigms associated with narrower and smaller aspects of social life are in some manner derivative of the broadest values of a culture.

A complex society such as the United States in the beginning of the third millennia has an almost boundless collection of paradigms which govern the behavior of the citizenry. While these paradigms may be in conflict with each other, they are all subordinate to the dominant national paradigm articulated by the U. S. Constitution and the Bill of Rights. As mentioned earlier, disciplines, organizations, professions, and other social entities are more or less governed by dominant paradigms that are taught to new initiates through practice, education, indoctrination, or tradition. The groups generally share in the ennui that ensues when a larger societal paradigm is undergoing a transformation.

Much has been written about the transformation taking place in this period of our history. From the industrial revolution and mechanistic, positivistic view of reality to something profoundly different fueled by the new knowledge derived from computer and telecommunication technologies. This transformation has affected almost every segment of society in some measure, from the relationships of the sexes, families, churches, communities, and governments, to views of functions and management of agencies and organizations providing services and products to the inhabitants of the planet.

In each of the paradigm transformations, the process involves a discarding of accepted values and adopting new ones. It is likely the process will take several decades or more to affect a complete change.

Paradigm Shift in the Information Professions

As paradigms have shifted in society and academic disciplines, so have paradigm shifts occurred in the professions serving society, especially the library and information professions. That shift is from a "bibliographic" to a "client-centered" paradigm. That shift is from a preoccupation with the housekeeping the information packages to a concern for the users of information. Without users there would be no need to manage information, and yet some in the library and information discipline have only transitioned from a focus on the format (book) to a focus on the content (information). While their new paradigm may sound more up-to-date, it lacks substance if it doesn't put people first.

The Bibliographic Paradigm

The information professions, along with most other professions of society, are experiencing a paradigm shift in how they serve society. The traditional paradigm valued the acquisition, collection, organization, storage, and making accessible the records of society. Kuhlthau (1993) describes the "bibliographic paradigm" as follows:

> Traditionally, library and information services have centered on sources and technology. Libraries have developed sophisticated systems for collecting, organizing, and retrieving texts and have applied advanced technology to provide access to vast sources of information. This bibliographic paradigm of collecting and classifying texts and devising search strategies for their retrieval has promoted a view of information use from the system's perspective. For the most part, library and information science has concentrated on the system's representation of texts rather than on users' tasks, problems, and processes in information gathering. (p. 1)

The objective of the bibliographic paradigm is to acquire as many of the current, important, or prized publications as possible. The goal is to provide well-rounded collections of materials representing the dominant fields and views of our society. The dominant value in this paradigm is size. The largest library building, the largest staff, the largest collection of materials, and the largest budget are automatically considered the best within this paradigm.

The bibliographic paradigm is not restricted to books, journals, and "traditional" formats of information. Databases and digital information can be planned, developed, and offered to clientele in ways that do not meet the needs of the using clientele. Herein rests the key principle underlying the bibliographic paradigm—the focus is on the information, not the people.

The People Paradigm

In 1887, Melvil Dewey committed some of his resources to a staff person to be a reference librarian. This is the first example of the new paradigm in LIS, when service replaced the collection as evidence of quality. His essay "The Profession" in the first issue of *Library Journal* provided a harbinger of this paradigm:

> The time **was** when a library was very like a museum, and a librarian was a mouser in musty books, and visitors looked with curious eyes at ancient tomes and manuscripts. The time **is** when a library is a school, and the librarian is in the highest sense a teacher, and the visitor is a reader among the books as a workman among his tools. Will any man deny to the high calling of such a librarianship the title of a profession? (p. 23)

Helping to establish meaning (diffusion of knowledge) requires a professional to translate information or knowledge into the paradigmatic structure of a culture. An example is that in our societal paradigm, we do not believe in the existence of UFOs. We have anecdotal evidence, first-hand accounts, but our society does not accept such evidence. It is outside the current paradigm which requires scientific evidence before something is accepted. Logical positivism is the philosophy supporting scientific thought.

The "people paradigm" replaces the focus on collection of information with a focus on people. This is a relatively simple concept, but one that is often overlooked in professional practice. To illustrate the impact of user-centered professional library and information service, we present below a model for planning levels of service.

Levels of User-Centered Services

A model for outlining levels of service was first introduced by Greer and Hale (1982) and uses the following terms:

- Passive level of service, which provides the resources (books, journals, computer software, etc.) for use with no help from the professional staff.

- Reactive level of service, which provides professional assistance when the information user requests help

- Assertive level of service, which anticipates the needs of clientele based upon the results of a systematic community analysis

These levels of service can be applied to the various information services provided in a library or information center. Types of services are discussed in Chapter 8, The Processes and Functions of Information Professionals: educational, informational, research, cultural, recreational, and bibliographic or archival.

Conclusion

Perhaps the only constant in contemporary Western society is change. In this chapter we identified three categories of change—incremental, cataclysmic, and paradigmatic. We discussed the paradigm shift in the information professions, noting the shift from a focus on the acquisition, organization, and preservation of materials to the identification of users' needs and provision of services to address those needs. We identified three levels of service (passive, reactive, and assertive), and suggest that assertive level of service is based on a knowledge of user needs. If we are to provide information service in the "client-centered" paradigm, we must continuously assess client needs so that assertive level of services can be offered.

References

Burke, James. 1985. *The day the universe changed*. Boston: Little, Brown.

Dewey, Melvil. 1976. The profession, in *Landmarks of library literature 1876–1976*, ed. Dianne J. Ellsworth and Norman D. Stevens, 21–23. Metuchen, NJ: The Scarecrow Press.

Greer, Roger C. and Martha L. Hale. 1982. "The community analysis process." In *Public librarianship, a reader*, ed. Jane Robbins-Carter, 358–366. Littleton, CO: Libraries Unlimited.

Kuhlthau, Carol Collier. 2004. *Seeking meaning: A process approach to library and information services*. Westport, CT: Libraries Unlimited.

Kuhn, Thomas S. 1962. *The structure of scientific revolutions*. Chicago: University of Chicago Press.

Schwartz, Peter and James Ogilvy. 1979. *The emergent paradigm: Changing patterns of thought and belief*. Report issued by the Values and Lifestyles Program, April 1979. In Yvonne S. Lincoln and Egon G. Guba. 1985. *Naturalistic inquiry*. Newbury Park, CA: Sage Publications.

Toffler, Alvin. 1980. *The third wave*. New York: Morrow.

4

The Science Supporting the Information Professions

Chapter Overview

This chapter identifies, justifies, and describes the scope of the science necessary to develop customized services beyond the level of "cookie cutter" nonprofessional output—making professional decisions that do not consider the needs of clientele. Types or levels of theory are defined, and the common features of the library and information professions are described, and these features are extrapolated into a theory base for the library and information professions. This theory base is proposed as the theoretical core of library and information science.

Introduction

As mentioned in earlier chapters, professions have three distinct elements that distinguish them from technician level occupations. These are: (1) a science; (2) a technology; and (3) an art or infrastructure.

Each of these elements fulfills a distinct role in the development and delivery of a service to the public. The science provides the theoretical underpinning for the design of these customized products for a clientele. The technology provides the methods and modes for organizing and delivering service, while the art or infrastructure provides the paradigmatic framework for the entire cycle of service. That means it provides the values, customs, and context for the analysis, design, and delivery of the service.

The Importance of Theory to Professionals

As indicated in Chapter 1, theory is the bedrock of professional practice. We feel that we cannot emphasize enough that the object of professional service is to create and deliver customized products to a specified clientele, whether an individual, group, community, organization, or society. Customization is an ad hoc process wherein each product is fashioned to satisfy the identified or diagnosed needs of a client. To distinguish the customized product of a professional from the efforts of a talented and well meaning lay person or technician requires the application of theory.

Theory represents the body of knowledge a profession acquires over time. This acquisition may be from a variety of means, from vigorous scientific study to accumulated layers of anecdotal experiences. Its function is to provide guidance in deriving meaning from information acquired during the diagnostic process. Once the meaning associated with data is understood, theory may also provide direction and parameters for the development of the service to satisfy the needs of the client.

Another objective of theory is to predict an outcome when certain characteristics are present. In the case of human behavior, the goal of prediction is less attainable than areas of the physical and biological sciences. Nevertheless, identification of trends is a meaningful function of theory and serves in the diagnostic process.

Levels of Theory

"Theory" has been described as "generalizations that seek to explain relationships among phenomena" (Glazier and Grover 2002, 319). Theory helps us to understand "why" things happen and help us to anticipate what will happen when similar circumstances are present at a different time. For example, Newton's theory of gravity says that any object which leaves the surface of the earth is drawn back down.

Several types and levels of generalization have been observed; however, even in academic discourse, levels of theory may not be specified. Grover and Glazier (1986, 2002) reviewed the literature of the social sciences and outlined a taxonomy of theory which designated three main levels of theory: Substantive theory, formal theory, and grand theory. Each is defined below.

Substantive Theory

The first level of theory is defined as "A set of propositions which furnish an explanation for an applied area of inquiry" (Grover and Glazier 1986, 233). In other words, substantive theory is a level of generalization applied to a profession and provides guidelines for practice.

An example of substantive level theory is Kuhlthau's theory of information-seeking behavior (See Chapter 1), which enables information professionals to identify the stages an information seeker experiences in a quest for information. Through an understanding of these stages, the librarian or other information professional can better assess which stage of search a client is in and can more effectively assist with the information search.

Formal Theory

Formal theory is defined as "A set of propositions which furnish an explanation for a formal or conceptual area of inquiry, that is, a discipline . . . ." (Grover and Glazier 1986, 234). Formal theory, discipline level theory, can be generalized more broadly than substantive theory. For example, theories of psychology may apply to any profession which is concerned with serving people as individuals. However, theory which applies to the information professions may not apply effectively to another profession like the practice of law.

Maslow's (1954) original theory of human motivation is an example of a formal theory within the discipline of psychology. According to this theory, human needs can be classified into five categories: physiological needs, safety needs, belonging and love needs, esteem needs, and the need for self-actualization. This broad theory, based on Maslow's research, has broad application within behavioral science for explaining human motivation.

Grand Theory

Grand theory is defined as "a set of theories or generalizations that transcend the borders of disciplines to explain relationships among phenomena" (Glazier and Grover 2002, 321). An example of a grand theory is Ludwig von Bertalanfy's (1969) general systems theory, which applies across disciplines and professions. This theory explains the interrelationship among phenomena, and takes a holistic view of complex phenomena.

The practice of the library and information professions applies all these theory levels. Researchers may borrow from any or all these levels of theory as they attempt to find solutions to professional problems. As a result of applying a theory, gathering and analyzing data, and restating theory to "fit" the results of research, researchers can add to the body of theory which supports the practice of the library and information professions. This body of theory comprises the "science" of the field and is the subject matter taught in professional programs. The discussion which follows explores the theory base which supports the practice of library and information science.

Characteristics Common to the Information Professions

The library and other information professions are far-reaching in the range of service provided. In some positions, information professionals have wide-ranging responsibilities, i.e., school library media specialists, public librarians in smaller libraries, and one-person libraries. Other information professionals are specialized, e.g., map librarians, some archivists, law librarians, corporate librarians, acquisition librarians, reference librarians, research specialists, catalogers, and music librarians. Because of their responsibilities, information professionals may be called librarians, information specialists, researchers, archivists, information brokers, information entrepreneurs, or other terms.

All these information professionals share the following characteristics which were first described by Greer (1987, 7) and are adapted and updated here.

1. Responsibility for the commodity "information" and the objective of enhancing the processes of information transfer.

2. Responsibility for accommodating the information needs and behavioral characteristics of a specific client population.

3. Responsibility for the design and management of an organization consisting of staff, equipment, space, and financial resources to provide the interface between the information system and the potential user.

4. Responsibility for the design and management of an information system encompassing a database—a collection of information in any format.

The knowledge required to practice these shared characteristics is the knowledge base for the library and information professions—the science of the information professions. This theory base is amplified in the discussion that follows.

The Science of the Information Professions

The science for the information professions may be properly called "information science." However, that term, information science, is frequently used to designate the application of technology to the acquisition, storage, retrieval, and dissemination of information.

While some aspects of this science are consistent with the so-called hard sciences, for the most part, its domain is related to the social sciences, specifically psychological and sociological perspectives. Consequently, information science quite rightly belongs within the family disciplines commonly associated with the social sciences.

Information science seeks to address the four common areas of focus of information professionals listed above by posing the following questions and identifying the field of study in parentheses:

1. How is knowledge converted to information, reproduced, and disseminated to society (sociology of information)?

2. How do individuals seek and acquire information (information psychology)?

3. How are organizations for the management of information organized and managed (management of information organizations)?

4. How are databases developed and maintained for a particular purpose (information engineering)?

The objective of this chapter is to explore each of these fields which we maintain belong within the discipline of information science, following the model first articulated by Greer (1987). Each exploration will include a description of the scope of the field. In addition, suggestions will be indicated for areas of research and theory development needed to serve the needs of practicing information professionals. To begin this exploration, we will consider the role of information in a society.

Sociology of Information

Since information is, metaphorically speaking, the life blood of any society and culture, it is fundamentally at the core of whatever dynamics exist in that society. The study of the role of information in society and the systems, processes, and patterns of information transfer must draw its perspectives from the discipline of sociology. This field, which we choose to label the "sociology of information," must address issues associated with the creation of knowledge, its recording, and reproduction, and the various social systems involved in its dissemination and utilization. This field seeks to understand and predict the steps involved in the creation, recording, mass production, dissemination, collection, organization, storage, retrieval, preservation, discarding, and destruction of information in society.

The activities associated with the sociology of information relate to the role of information in society, from creation to ultimate preservation or discarding. As indicated earlier, information is defined as knowledge recorded. That is, it exists independently of any human intelligence and does not convert to knowledge until it is diffused into the intellect of another person. Once information is incorporated in a human intelligence, it acquires meaning and may become a building block toward wisdom.

The social processes of this field are reflected in the following questions:

1. What are the patterns of knowledge creation? How is new knowledge created? What are the accepted research methods?

2. What are the systems for recording knowledge? As research is conducted and new knowledge is created, how are the data recorded? What technologies are used in the recording process?

3. What are the mechanisms for the mass production of information? After research is completed, how is this research packaged for distribution to a large audience? What are the accepted presses for publishing? Which electronic media are used?

4. What varieties of systems are employed in the dissemination of information? When the new knowledge has been packaged for mass distribution, what are the professional associations, professional conferences, publishers, conferences, mass media, and Web sites used to distribute the new knowledge?

5. What systems for bibliographic control of the records are being produced in society? What are the bibliographies, Webographies, indexes, and other organizing tools which organize knowledge in this area and make it available to audiences?

6. What is the paradigmatic structure for the organization of information by subject fields? Within this specialty area, how does this knowledge fit into the discipline or profession? What special terms are used to organize and retrieve this knowledge?

7. What are the patterns of diffusion of knowledge? How and through what social organizations is this new knowledge likely to be taught to others? What are the leading universities or other social agencies which specialize in passing on new knowledge in the field?

8. How is information used in society? What are likely user groups who would put this new knowledge to use?

9. What systems exist for the preservation of information? Which agencies are likely to preserve this knowledge? What means would be used to maintain the knowledge?

Among the fields of study which contribute to an understanding of sociology of information are the following:

1. Sociology, including sociology of knowledge and symbolic interactionism

2. Economics

3. Intellectual history

4. Political science

5. Cultural anthropology

6. Cybernetics

7. Bibliometrics

8. Socio-linguistics

9. Information psychology

10. Information engineering

11. Information organization management

The sociology of information is explored in more detail in Chapter 5, "Information Transfer in the Information Professions."

Information Psychology

The goal of information professionals is to create and operate information systems and services which accommodate the information needs and behavioral characteristics of a specific client population. This goal of customizing information service requires knowledge of human behavior associated with the acquisition and use of information. Information psychology is the field of information science concerned with the development of this theory of human behavior. Information psychology applies behavioral theory to the library and information professions in the same way that educational psychology is an application of psychology to the education profession.

Knowledge of an individual's processing of information is vital to the identification of information sources to meet the needs of that individual. Likewise, knowledge of information psychology is required for a library and information professional to design and implement an information service which addresses the information needs and preferences of individuals.

The field of information psychology addresses the following questions:

1. How does a person decide that there is need for information? What are the conditions or motives that provoke this awareness?

2. What processes are involved in decisions to satisfy or ignore the need?

3. What are strategies employed in searching for information and how does this differ among individuals?

4. What are the variations in behaviors associated with the search for information? How does the configuration of the use of a particular information system affect these behaviors?

5. How does the medium of the information (book, electronic publication, video, etc.) influence the individual's selection and use of the information?

6. What methods and criteria are employed in evaluating the relevance of information acquired?

7. What are the behaviors associated with the processes of assimilating information? How does information become knowledge? How does format and system design affect this aspect of behavior?

8. What cognitive styles are employed in information processing? How does learning style influence information searching, information retrieval, and information use?

9. How do individuals organize, store, and retrieve information from memory?

10. What are the varieties of forms and patterns of information utilization?

Contributing to an understanding of these questions are the research and theory from the following fields:

1. Behavioral psychology, including personality theory, perception theory, motivation theory, attitude theory, cognitive science, theories of intelligence, role theory, learning theory

2. Psycholinguistics

3. Physiology

4. Religion

5. Educational psychology

6. Social psychology

7. Sociology of information

8. Information engineering

9. Information organization management

As noted above, role theory contributes to an understanding of the information user's needs. Role theory is a subdiscipline of psychology that studies the activity of people as they spend much of their time in groups. In the groups, these individuals engage in expected behaviors and take certain positions. Each of these positions is called a "role." Each role that an individual fulfills suggests information needs. For example, the role of parent suggests a need for information about children—their health, diet, psychology, recreation, education, and other aspects of child rearing. Similarly, occupational or professional role implies other needs which drive the individual's need for information.

Both information psychology and sociology of information provide the background knowledge which enables a library and information professional to conduct an effective information needs assessment. Information psychology provides the knowledge of how individuals use information. Sociology of information provides insight from the perspective of an individual's membership in a group.

The information organization management and information engineering fields (described below) relate to the information processes—what information professionals DO with information. These two areas of applied theory are unique to the practice of library and information professionals.

Information Organization Management

An information agency includes a collection of information resources, facilities, budget, and staff. We define "Information Organization Management" as the field responsible for managing human, financial, and physical resources to create information collections and to deliver information services to a client population.

The professional processes associated with information organization management are listed as follows:

1. Define the mission of the organization
2. Assess the information needs of clients
3. Define objectives for the organization
4. Develop policies, strategies, and procedures
5. Implement plans
6. Operate and supervise the organization
7. Develop feedback mechanisms and evaluate effectiveness of the organization
8. Modification of the system

Related fields of study which contribute to an understanding of information organization management include the following:

1. Organization theory
2. Management theory
3. Systems theory
4. Change theory
5. Sociology of the professions
6. Sociology of information
7. Information psychology
8. Information engineering

Management is usually studied in one or more courses in a master's degree program; since this book is an introduction to the field, we will make no attempt to provide more detail of this field of study.

Information Engineering

Information professionals are responsible for the design and management of an information system encompassing a database which may comprise information in a variety of formats. We list the processes essential to the design and management of data bases as follows:

1. Needs assessment: the analysis of the information needs and behaviors of the client population(s) being served by the database.

2. System design: planning and designing the architecture of a database oriented to the needs and behaviors of the client population(s).

3. Identification of relevant data/information for potential inclusion in the database.

4. Data evaluation and selection—analysis of quality and relevance of specific data/information for inclusion in the database.

5. Data/information acquisition—the process of acquiring materials from a vendor or publisher or inputting data to a computer.

6. Organization of data/information for storage—cataloging/programming.

7. Retrieval of data/information.

8. Repackaging or reorganizing data/information.

9. Dissemination or delivery of information to clients.

10. Discarding/withdrawing of data/information from the database.

Following are disciplines and fields of inquiry which contribute an understanding to the field of information engineering:

1. Operations research

2. Networking theory

3. Communication theory

4. Information processing theory, including artificial intelligence

5. Classification theory

6. Sociology of information

7. Information psychology

8. Information organization management

Since the creation of a resource collection is a major activity of an information professional, the functions and processes related to this area will be discussed in subsequent chapters—especially Chapter 8, The Functions and Processes of Information Professionals.

Policy and Environmental Context

The professional processes associated with the four fields of study (sociology of information, information psychology, information organization management, and information engineering) are influenced by variables external to the practice of the library and information professions. We call these variables "the environmental and social context." These variables apply to all four fields and are listed below.

1. Culture—language, philosophical and moral values, educational system, concept of time, historical background, and all features which comprise a community's culture.

2. Physical geography—aspects such as climate and topographical characteristics.

3. Political structure of society—the system for governance and underlying values regarding the role of government in a dynamic society.

4. Legislation and regulations issued by legislative and regulatory agencies of government.

5. The economic system under which the culture functions.

6. Technology—the level of sophistication in terms of computer and telecommunication technology.

7. Information policy—copyright laws, policies regarding secrecy, censorship, privacy, ownership, the public's right to know, and government responsibility to inform.

These variables apply to all four fields of study; however, the application of the processes in each field is influenced by the policy and environmental variables in the community as the culture varies. Examples of each environmental context variable follows.

Culture

We often think of culture very broadly—the culture of an ethnic group or country. For example, the language, history, music, and dress of Mexico vary considerably from those attributes of France or parts of the United States. We can also think of culture variance as we think of communities within the United States. The local idioms, food, entertainment, history, and dress of rural Kansas vary considerably from the culture of New Orleans or New York City. The meanings associated with language vary, and attitudes will also vary. These factors influence how people perceive information—how they think.

Physical Geography

The climate of a community influences lifestyle, use of leisure time, and the culture of a community. California and the American south boast a climate that encourages outdoor activities most of the year. While residents of southern California, the Southwest, the Gulf Coast, and Florida are playing tennis on weekends, those of us in the rest of the country are indoors watching movies on DVD, bowling, attending basketball games, or otherwise staying indoors during the winter. The weather influences recreational activities provided by libraries, and lifestyle differences influence attitudes.

Geographic features likewise inhibit or encourage travel and lifestyle. The congestion of cities is a stark contrast to the wide expanses of mid-America, where residents may drive 30 to 100 miles to the nearest city. Although technology shaves distances, attaining broad band Internet service and the latest network technologies is still difficult for residents of remote areas in the United States and other countries in the world. Such difficulties have a significant impact of the currency of information available to these residents.

Political Structure

The system for governance in an agency influences the flow of information. A hierarchy generally requires that information flows up the organization and down according to the rank of the individual. An organization that is more informal usually encourages information flow in a casual manner without regard to status of the sender or receiver. In such organizations, information flow can be fast and unencumbered by status. Political structure can also influence the content of information; for example, the values of a dominant political party may suppress information which is opposed to the prevailing views, and this suppressed information may find outlet through "underground" or illicit channels. This political structure may be dictated by the culture of the organization and by the leadership style of those in leadership positions. Similarly, the format of the information may be dictated by the political structure, e.g., print is preferred to electronic sources; narrative is preferred to charts or diagrams.

Some leaders subscribe to an organizational philosophy that information must be controlled and that power or authority is derived from the control of information. Other leaders may believe that information should be shared among leaders and among all workers. These leaders will treat new information in a manner much different than those who wish to control. In these examples, the philosophy of management focuses on the locus of control, and that control is determined to a large extent by access to information. How information is controlled and distributed, is dependent on leadership style or philosophy.

Legislation and Regulations

Legislation and regulations are issued by legislative and regulatory agencies of government. Where the political paradigm is controlled by the scope and limits of a constitution (e.g., the United States Constitution), freedom of access to information is at the core of this paradigm and is the bedrock of any information system designed for public use. The United States Constitution guarantees through the first amendment the right of free expression of ideas, and other laws, e.g., copyright law, also protects individuals or groups who create new packages of information so that others will not steal those ideas and call them their own. Copyright protects various forms of expression, including songs and music, as well as prose and poetry. Similarly, patents protect the rights of inventors who create new products of various kinds, including hardware and software which may access, organize, store, or retrieve information. Still other laws, like securities laws, provide a framework for the exchange of stock information, determining when this information can be exchanged fairly, and when it is considered "insider" illegal trading of information.

Economic System

The economic system supports a culture and social system financially. If capitalism is the basis for economic activity in a society, information is a commodity that appears in the market-place as well as in the halls of the academies. Privacy and proprietary perspectives are very evident in this society. Other economic systems, e.g., communism, employ different approaches to the creation, reproduction, and distribution of information.

In a capitalistic society, the marketplace determines the marketability of a product. Since information is a commodity, the format and content of information is influenced substantially by the economic feasibility of the information package. For example, the marketability of a new information system, like the Internet, must be accompanied by affordable accessibility. The Internet was created in the 1960s by the U.S. government to exchange defense information, using state-of-the-art computers, software, and networking technologies of the 1960s. This system was not available to the public until personal computers, telecommunications, and software became affordable to regional, state, regional, and local government agencies and individuals. The widespread availability of the Internet became a reality in the mid-1990s with the confluence of technology and affordability.

The diffusion of the Internet into municipal governments, schools, colleges and universities, and individual homes took approximately 30 years. Often the diffusion process occurs first through the diffusion of information for recreation, followed by use for educational purposes. The use of film, audio recordings, compact discs, and digital video all found their way into the marketplace first as entertainment packages. To anticipate changes in technology applications, information professionals are advised to watch trends in the use of new technologies for entertainment as possible precursors of information use for other purposes.

Technology

The level of sophistication in terms of computer and telecommunication technology becomes increasingly relevant to the processes of information transfer in a society. As noted above, the application of new technology to the transfer of information is dictated by economics. Affordability precedes adaptation on a wide scale in society.

Moore's Law is a theory which helps us understand the affordability of technology. Gordon Moore, cofounder of Intel, made this prediction in 1965:

> The number of transistors on a chip roughly doubles every two years. As a result the scale gets smaller and smaller. (http://www. intel.com/technology/mooreslaw/index.htm)

Technology innovation has transformed all aspects of information creation, recording, mass production, distribution, organization, storage, retrieval, and use. With the rapid change in technology, the transfer of information has been changed dramatically. The ability to transmit information using cell phone technologies, to store and retrieve information on palmtop computers, and the availability of instant messaging has had a major impact on daily life and on the practice of the information professions. This impact is discussed throughout this book, and the influence of technology is a major trend discussed in Chapter 10. Providing guidelines for the fair and equitable use of information in this age of technology is determined through laws and through information policies, as outlined below.

Information Policy

Copyright laws, policies regarding secrecy, censorship, privacy, ownership, the public's right to know, and government responsibility to inform. Legislation is a formal policy adopted by a governmental body at the local, state, national, or international level and is addressed in the "legislation and regulation" section above. Those laws and regulations which specifically address the creation, production, distribution, use, and storage of information may also be considered information policy. However, policy may be adopted within small and large agencies and groups of all types.

A policy is a generalization or general statement which provides guidelines for the transfer or use of information. For example, any social organization, school, library, college or university, business, or government agency at any level may articulate a policy for information use. A small business may elect to keep no papers or financial records after 7 years because tax records may be kept for 7 years. Another small business, conscious of its historic contribution to a community, may elect to preserve all correspondence and donate them after 5 years to a local historical museum. While the practices outlined are much different, they are both policies which govern the transfer of information for their respective agencies and are consistent with their culture.

All the above variables influence each other and, in turn, influence the professional processes of each of the four fields of information science.

Conclusion

Professions have three distinct elements that distinguish them from technician level occupations. These are: (1) a science; (2) a technology; and (3) an art or infrastructure. This chapter is intended to identify, justify, and describe the scope of the science necessary to construct customized information services. It focuses on the science which provides an intellectual foundation for the practice of the library and information professions, providing the theoretical underpinning for the design of customized services and products for a clientele. We have outlined levels of theory which can be used to explain how and why people use and transfer information and outlined four fields which comprise the study of information science: (1) Sociology of information, (2) information psychology, (3) information organization management, and (4) information engineering. These theories will be applied as we explore further the role of library and information professionals.

References

Bertalanffy, Ludwig von. 1969. *General system theory; foundations, development, applications*. New York: G. Braziller.

Glazier, Jack D. and Robert Grover. 2002. A multidisciplinary framework for theory building. *Library Trends* 50: 317–332

Greer, Roger C. 1987. "A model for the discipline of information science." In *Intellectual foundations for information professionals*, ed. Herbert K. Achleitner, 3–25. Boulder, CO: Social Science Monographs; New York: Distributed by Columbia University Press.

Grover, Robert and Jack Glazier. 1986. A conceptual framework for theory building in library and information science. *Library and Information Science Research* 8 (July-September 1986): 227–242.

Maslow, Abraham H. 1954. *Motivation and personality*. New York: Harper & Row.

Moore's Law. http://www.intel.com/technology/mooreslaw/index.htm.

5

Information Transfer in the
Information Professions

Chapter Overview

This chapter introduces the concept of information transfer as a way of conceptualizing the work of information professionals. The information transfer model is linked to the information professions and the roles that they play in the information transfer process. Finally, this chapter examines the application of the information transfer model to information agencies in order to create "information utilities" which serve the information needs of their communities.

Introduction to Information Transfer

"Information transfer" is a type of communication. It can be defined as the communication of a recorded message from one human or human mind to another. Unlike communication which assumes that the sender and receiver of a message are contemporaries, information transfer requires a recorded message transmitted on a medium that enables senders to transmit ideas to people who are not their contemporaries. In other words, information transfer is asynchronous.

The information transfer model is a variation of the communication model by Shannon and Weaver (1963). A graphic representation of the information transfer model appears in Figure 5.1 below.

The triangle represents the *sender* of a message—a person with an idea who expresses that idea in a *recorded message*, such as a journal article, a book, a video production, or a software package. Any format for recording the idea fits this model.

The recorded message can be stored in an *information system*, represented by a second larger square. This information system can be a library, a computer storage device, or any kind of system which collects, organizes, stores, and makes available for *information users* the information created by the sender and recorded as an information package.

The traditional system requires information users to go to the system—the library, computer, or other collection of information. The motivation to

Figure 5.1. Conventional Library Service Model

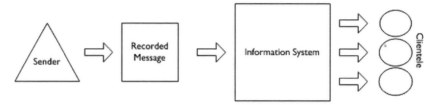

use the information system is on the user of the information, and the information system itself is designed more on behalf of preserving the information than it is on meeting the users' needs.

An example of this traditional form of information transfer might be the librarian in a library who is careful to maintain a well-organized collection but offers few services to address the needs of its users or potential users. No assessment is made of information needs. Instead, the library is open at hours that are convenient for the staff; the collection is organized by format so that the books are together in one place, the magazines in another, and software in another. Care is taken to keep the collection in order, but there is little or no effort to determine priorities for purchase based on a systematic needs assessment. Neither is there an effort to design services to meet client needs. The collection is simply "there."

The same principle of the traditional view of information transfer applies to databases which are designed without the users in mind. A database should be made as "transparent" as possible for potential users—using familiar terms and the specialized language of the user group(s). In addition, this information system should provide for user assistance to facilitate easy use of the database. A computer with a specialized database is like a collection of books without user aids. Both are passive collections of information which require initiative of the users.

The preoccupation with this conventional view is with the message (or the information package—book, journal, or software). By contrast, it is possible to design an information transfer system that better meets the needs of clientele. Such a system is presented in Figure 5.2 below.

Again the triangle above represents the *sender* of a message—a person with an idea who expresses that idea in a *recorded message*, as represented by the rectangle. Again, any format for recording the idea fits into this model, and the recorded message can be stored in an *information system*.

In this information transfer model, however, the recorded message is stored in a different type of information system, this time represented by a *circle*. As before, this information system can be a library or a computer storage device, or any kind of system which collects, organizes, stores, and makes available for information users the information created by the sender and recorded as an information package.

While the conventional system requires information users to go to the system, the information transfer model provides an information system *designed to meet the needs of information users*. As indicated by the two-way arrows, the information system is designed to meet the needs of current and potential users by reaching out to clientele, conducting a systematic needs assessment, and shaping the information system to address those needs.

This new paradigm in information service indicates that the information agency looks like the receiver. The value is centered on the receiver

Figure 5.2. Information Transfer Model

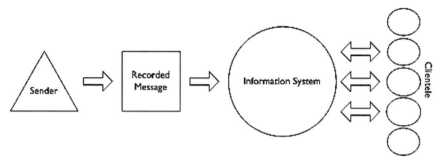

of the message, not the message itself, a profound difference. An example can be found in facilities design. Should a library be designed that fits the needs of people and looks like a supermarket, or should it be designed as a monument? Architects often want to build monuments to gain recognition, but form and function should be happily married in the design of a building.

An example of such a system is a library whose staff is continuously mindful of their clientele and their needs. By systematically conducting needs assessments through such means as casual conversations, systematic client surveys, use of advisory groups, and periodic community analyses, the librarian continuously monitors the community to select formats and information sources that meet the needs of that public. Using the user data, the staff continuously assesses their services and makes changes to keep pace with people's changing information needs.

Indeed, many libraries and information agencies reflect the service paradigm model which focuses on client needs. Some agencies are completely devoted to customer service; others provide client-centered service in some areas. As with any paradigm, the difference begins with the value system. Leaders in a client-centered organization must work to promote a focus on the client through example, training, policies, and administration of the agency. Maintaining client-centered service is an ongoing mission because the tendency of staff is to slip into focus on what is easy for them instead of what is best for the clients. The mission to become a client-centered agency is a journey which never ends.

A Closer Look at Information Transfer

The information transfer model shown and discussed earlier in this chapter is an overview of a much more complex concept. In this section, we will look at the *information transfer cycle*—the life cycle of information from "cradle to grave."

Information has a "life" as people do; those steps along the journey of information's life are listed below:

1. Creation

2. Recording

3. Reproduction

4. Dissemination

5. Bibliographic control

6. Organization by disciplines

7. Diffusion

8. Utilization

9. Preservation

10. Deletion

Each of these steps or stages of the information transfer cycle is described below.

Creation

Information is created in a variety of ways. Research is a formal process in the creation of information and will be used as an example throughout this discussion of the information transfer cycle. Research may be conducted in universities, think tanks, by reporters for new media, or others engaged in the creation of new information or knowledge. Information is created by the assembly of data in ways that provide new meanings or understandings that show new relationships. For example, researchers may conduct a formal study of the way that a group of people use information. These researchers define a social group (for example, corporate managers), identify exemplars of that group, and determine methods or strategies for gathering data about their information needs. Data may be collected using questionnaires, interviews, observations, analysis of records, or other means. After the data are collected, the data are analyzed to address the questions or hypotheses that were used to frame the research process. This is an example of the beginning of the formal research process.

Another example might be the coverage of a news event by a reporter for a local newspaper, television, or radio station. The editor assigns a reporter to cover a meeting of the local school board. The reporter attends the meeting, takes notes, and, at the conclusion of the meeting interviews the chair of the school board and the superintendent to get their reactions to the key agenda items discussed and action taken.

In both these examples, the creation of new information was accomplished. Data were assembled into new information. However, this is only the first step in the information transfer process, and the information has little meaning until it is synthesized and recorded.

Recording

After information is created, it must be recorded in some format so that eventually it can be disseminated and used by others. In the case of formal research, researchers collected data, and the data were analyzed to reveal trends. The analysis of data is synthesized into a report of the research process and the findings. This preparation of a report is the recording stage. In the example of a news event, the reporter has attended a meeting and must now assemble her notes into a report of the event, a school board meeting. The audio or video recording and/or written notes from the interviews are integrated into the report.

In both examples, data which were collected have been synthesized and recorded. The recording may be accomplished digitally, using a word processor in both cases. If the reporter were working for a television station, her report might be recorded on videotape after she had reported live during the local 10:00 p.m. televised news program. Regardless of format, the new information has been recorded as the second stage of the information transfer cycle.

Reproduction

Reproduction of information requires the copying of the information so that it can be distributed, although with electronic journalism, the mass production may be instantaneous with the dissemination. In the example of formal research, researchers send their finished report of the research project to a journal which is likely to publish a report on the topic. At this point an evaluation process occurs. A scholarly journal editor will scan the manuscript and select a group of peers to review the report, usually a "blind" review process in which the readers do not know the identity of the report author(s). If the reviewers concur that the researcher has used appropriate methods, and the topic and findings are a significant contribution to the discipline's or profession's body of knowledge, the reviewers provide a favorable evaluation, and the editor publishes the report. If one or more reviewers raise serious concerns about methodology and/or conclusions, the editor may ask the researcher to revise the manuscript to address the concerns of reviewers. If the reviewers have raised serious concerns, the editor will reject the manuscript.

When issues raised by reviewers and the editor have been satisfactorily addressed by the researcher, the manuscript may be accepted for publication. The journal may be mass produced in paper format, or a scholarly journal may be published electronically. In either case, the review by peers is a critical part of scholarly mass production of information and knowledge.

A newspaper or other mass media outlet has in place a similar review process before a story is published, aired, or placed on a Web page. An editor reviews the report by the reporter or staff writer, and with the concurrence of the managing editor assigns the story to a place in the newspaper so that it can be mass produced. A television news reporter, like a newspaper reporter, covers stories assigned by an editor. Similarly, stories that are aired are selected by a news director. Most newspapers, radio, and television news outlets now post stories and supplementary information on their Web sites.

Note that scholarly and popular news media have in place an editing or content screening process. However, technological advances have reduced the cost of mass production so that desk-top publishing and Internet publishing enable individuals to mass produce vast quantities of information without benefit of the screening which has been a common feature in the past. As a result, it is much easier for unauthenticated information to be mass produced.

Dissemination

After reproduction, information can be distributed to a vast audience. Technology has created new channels for the dissemination of information more quickly and more cheaply than ever before. Examples are discussed below.

To decrease the rising cost of publishing scholarly journals with small circulations, an increasing number of scholarly journals are published only in electronic format. As noted, the review process is retained, but an accepted research report can be posted on a journal Web site, accessible only to those who have subscribed. The authority of the review process of the scholarly journal preserves the integrity of the scholarly review process, and the new information is disseminated to a wide scholarly audience.

Newspapers usually distribute via both printed and electronic formats. The distribution is fast and to a large audience, including individuals and institutions. Television news also is usually disseminated both during live newscasts and on a station Web site, which may provide additional background information to a current story or additional information that was deemed of limited interest to a mass audience.

Libraries and other information agencies are the depositories of mass produced information of both a scholarly and popular nature. Libraries throughout history have collected recorded information that has been mass produced as books, serials, and audio and video recordings. Librarians collect such information packages, organize them, and make them available for use by their audiences. Indeed, libraries have been a major point of dissemination for new information and knowledge and continue to be so.

Bibliographic Control

The organization of information for accessing is referred to as "bibliographic control." Downs (1975) defined the term as follows:

> In its broadest sense, perfect bibliographical control would mean a complete record of the existence and location of every book and of all other materials of concern to libraries. It is doubtful that we shall ever reach such a utopia. (p. 124)

Throughout the history of the library profession, bibliography has been central to the profession. The result of this professional focus has been the creation of such societal mechanisms as national libraries, the copyright law, and national bibliographies.

According to Downs (1975), bibliographical control consists of the following four activities:

1. Complete recording of all types of printed and other formats of resources as they are produced.
2. Systematic acquisition of these resources in libraries and other information agencies.
3. Location of these resources through a union catalog and other devices.
4. Provision of subject bibliography in all areas. (p. 126)

It should be noted that bibliography is essential to the efficient retrieval and use of information; however, the library profession has taken a general approach to organizing information. Terms used for subject headings are standardized but are not necessarily the terms used by the library's clientele.

In the examples used previously, researchers in library and information science might publish their research in a library and information science professional or research journal. It might be purchased by a university library and integrated into the general collection of periodicals. Similarly, a newspaper could be displayed, stored, and perhaps microfilmed for storage in the university's newspaper collection. In both cases, a general scheme for organizing the periodicals would be employed.

Organization by Discipline

While bibliographic control is concerned with the generic organization of information and knowledge, groups of people may design unique systems for organizing information for their use. For example, a public health agency may design a system of subject headings and a code for classifying (cataloging) their printed resources. The scheme would use an organizational scheme which would facilitate browsing and use by the clientele. Terms assigned as subject headings for the agency's catalog would be those used by the agency.

Disciplines have produced their own indexes as examples of organization by discipline. *Psychological Abstracts* provides subject access to psychology research, and the Modern Language Association (MLA) *Bibliography* are two examples of the many specialized indexes and bibliographies available to provide access to the new knowledge in a discipline or profession.

Diffusion

After information is disseminated and organized, it is the mission of librarians and other information professionals to diffuse the information, i.e., to help information users to understand this information and to make sense of it. As noted above, it has long been the recognized task of librarians to acquire, organize, and disseminate information for their publics. With the infusion of technology into the information transfer process, and with the profusion of information and knowledge in contemporary society, it is increasingly important for librarians and other information professionals to assume an assertive role in the diffusion as well as the dissemination of information.

How do diffusion and dissemination differ? Dissemination is making information available, as a newspaper makes information available to the public. Diffusion is assisting in the understanding of information, as a teacher interprets a story in a newspaper to help a child understand a news event. History books disseminate information about world events; history teachers are engaged in diffusion of history.

In the research example, a university library might have the article on information transfer research published by the authors. The library has *disseminated* the research. When a library and information studies teacher discusses that article in a class, relates the research results to practice in the library and information professions, and helps a student to understand the article, the research results have been *diffused*.

Our educational institutions are engaged in the diffusion of knowledge. Public and private schools and colleges are dedicated to teaching (diffusing) basic cultural knowledge to new generations of young people. Parents, churches, libraries, and such organizations as 4-H, Girl Scouts, Cub Scouts, and Brownies also promote the diffusion of knowledge to youth. Undergraduate and graduate programs in colleges and universities prepare people for professions and disciplines through their educational programs. Doctoral programs prepare researchers to conduct research, creating new knowledge, and to diffuse this knowledge to students in undergraduate and graduate programs. The processes of diffusion and utilization are also described in Chapter 2.

Utilization

The role of professions in society is to facilitate the use of information. Professionals apply knowledge to use for the betterment of humankind. For example, medical doctors acquire knowledge of the human body, treatments, and medicine, and apply that knowledge to the treatment of human illnesses. Similarly, information professionals convert knowledge about the creation, dissemination, organization, and utilization of knowledge to using knowledge effectively.

Individuals must be able to take information that has been disseminated in libraries or through other channels of communication and use that information in their lives. It is the role of information professionals to help people understand information—to give it meaning—so that people can use information in the personal or professional lives (see diffusion, above).

As an example, an information professional who has become aware of new research in the field and understands the implications of this new knowledge can put that information to use in the practice of the profession. If the research is concerned with the information use patterns of a particular type of clientele, the information professional can use the research results to design information services for that user group.

Preservation

Preservation is concerned with the retention of recorded information for future audiences. Three aspects of preservation must be considered: (1) preservation of the artifact or physical information package, e.g., book, journal, etc.; (2) preservation of the content—the ideas; (3) the context of the work—it's meaning at the time of its writing or production.

A rare book, for example, may be valued as a physical object for historical or legal purposes, e.g., the published product of a particular printer or publisher. Also, it may be the first edition of a celebrated author, e.g., a first edition of Rudyard Kipling's first novel. First editions of the "Dick and Jane" readers from the 1940s and 1950s are valuable because of their popularity and sentimental value to millions of people educated during that time period. The physical object itself has value.

A second aspect of preservation is preservation of the content, the words used by the author. The author's thinking or ideas may be timeless—have value today although written many years ago and perhaps in a different culture. The ideas themselves are worthy of study today. Examples might include the writing of Aristotle, Francis Bacon, or Karl Marx; these are authors whose ideas are relevant today.

A third aspect of a work is best described in terms of context. Closely associated with content, context is concerned with the meaning of words and writings in the time and culture in which written. For example, literary scholars analyze literature in terms of the author's society so that current readers can better understand the author's meaning when a literary piece was written. Meanings of words change in time, and the meaning of a work in the time written must be considered. Consequently, a work must be evaluated in terms of its value for informing us about the time and society in which it was written.

When thinking about preserving records for future users, we must think in the terms noted above—the physical object, content, and context. From a societal view, information professionals would want to preserve records for all three purposes. However, it is usually not practical in all locales. The decision to preserve a given record depends on the mission of the library or information agency. For example, the Library of Congress would save for all three purposes. In a smaller library a record's content might be preserved in a digital format both to preserve the content and its meaning in context.

Records which address a library's mission and warrant preservation may be preserved in paper or digital formats. Preservation techniques are a specialized study in the library field. Those records assessed unworthy of preservation are discarded, as described below.

Deletion

Records may be removed from collections and destroyed if the content is irrelevant or obsolete, or if the physical object is damaged beyond repair. When discarding the information professional must consider the three aspects of a record as noted in "preservation" above. Items not preserved should be discarded—removed from a collection. Another way of thinking about this process is that resources must be evaluated regularly, just as information professionals evaluate services; in fact, most information professionals consider provision of a "collection"—books, videos, CDs, serials, etc.—a service. When resources are no longer contributing to the mission of the agency, they should be discarded.

Summary

The information transfer cycle represents the life cycle of information, regardless of format. Electronic resources, of course, also have this life cycle. It is helpful to consider this model when thinking about the role of information professionals because our profession is engaged in all aspects of this cycle. The role of information professionals is investigated in the next section.

Information Professions and Information Transfer

The information transfer cycle above provides a useful framework for thinking about the work of professionals. As noted in Chapter 1, members of professions have a major responsibility for converting new knowledge (research) into useful knowledge that can be used gainfully in society. For example, the medical profession applies new knowledge from medical research in the treatment of disease and physical problems. Also, all professions are engaged in research to create new knowledge which is mass produced, disseminated, organized, diffused, utilized, preserved, or discarded.

Where do the information professions fit in the information transfer process? Actually, they play a leading role in each of the stages of the information transfer cycle described above. It is appropriate to say that the information professions "pump the gas" for the "engine" of information diffusion and utilization. In other words, information professionals play a vital role is assisting other professions to teach or diffuse new knowledge so that it can be used effectively. Let's examine the stages of the information transfer cycle to examine the role of the information professional.

In the creation of information the information professional can be a guide to researchers identifying the "state of the art" of research in a given area of study. Information professionals are usually generalists who know the indexes, abstracts, catalogs, databases, and bibliographies which serve as finding tools for the existing knowledge in the field. Also, information professionals are able to identify the standard texts on which the field builds its research and investigates key issues. Information professionals can assist researchers in the identification of other researchers in related areas to interrelate research from related disciplines—to support interdisciplinary research and discovery.

Information professionals may also be engaged in the recording and reproduction of information, especially as new technologies are used in this process. Information professionals include individuals with highly developed skills in the development and organization of Web pages and Internet-based information resources. More traditionally, information professionals may work as editors, proof readers, and analysts in the publishing industry. Information professionals may develop and implement market surveys and needs analyses to determine the need for books and other information packages on topics in a field.

Dissemination is the historical work of librarians, who identify resources of any format for their publics. Librarians acquire, organize, and store information resources and make them available for general use, a dissemination service. Librarians produce bibliographies, indexes, pathfinders, and other aids to help clientele to locate information that they need. Librarians are heavily engaged in the bibliographic control function as part of dissemination. Specialized indexing or cataloging, using terms specific to a discipline or profession may also be accomplished by librarians.

With the proliferation of information now available, it is incumbent upon information professionals to go beyond dissemination to diffusion—helping information users to understand the new knowledge in a field, to help them make meaning of the research. As a result, librarians and other information professionals are engaging in information skills instruction, a.k.a., "bibliographic instruction." Professional literature documents the increasing importance of the information professional's role as a teacher—someone actively engaged in the diffusion of new knowledge.

In a similar vein, information professionals serve in roles as advisors and counselors to information users to help with the utilization of knowledge. Kuhlthau (2004, 114–120) identified five levels of mediation with a client: organizer, locator, identifier, advisor, and counselor. Each is identified below.

1. *The organizer* has no direct intervention with the client. However, the organizer organizes the facility and the collection of resources for effective and efficient client use. Although the organizer does not interact directly with clientele, all services and all other levels of intervention are dependent upon the organizer's work to be successful. Included in organization is cataloging and classifying resources, indexing, creating access tools, physical organization of resources, finding aids of various types, signage, and all aspects of organizing resources for easy retrieval.

2. *The locator* offers a level of intervention often referred to as "ready reference" service. A client has a request for a specific bit of information or a specific information source (e.g., book title) and has a clear, simple question. A simple search is conducted by the information professional and is located for the client. As Kuhlthau notes (p. 116), this type of mediation is source oriented, and the process

used by the client is not a consideration. This type of intervention may be useful in the later stages of a complex search, but this level of intervention is not helpful when the client's need is ambiguous, vague, or complex.

3. *The identifier* conducts an interview of the searcher's needs and locates titles of resources that address those needs. However, there is no effort to prioritize the sources in terms of relevance. The process is one of matching topics articulated by the searchers with resources in the library's collection. This interaction is one time only, and there is no attempt to clarify or to customize the resources to the specific needs of the searcher. Kuhlthau explains the identifier's role as follows: "Typically, when the user comes to the collection with a general topic, seeking information from a number of sources, one comprehensive search is conducted and a 'pile' of information is identified as relevant to the general topic without consideration for the users' particular point of view, level of knowledge, or stage in the process" (p. 117). There is no advising provided in this level of mediation.

4. *The Advisor* works with information users to help them use information resources that have been identified. However, the emphasis in helping users in on the information sources, which are assumed to be used in a particular sequence or in a particular way. As Kuhlthau points out, there is no attempt to approach the advising from the user's viewpoint, taking into consideration the unique learning and searching styles of individuals.

5. *The counselor* conducts a careful interview to determine the needs and learning preferences of the information user.

Kuhlthau notes,

The underlying assumption is that the user is learning from information in a constructive process as the information search proceeds. There is no one right answer and no fixed sequence for all. The person's problem determines the intervention. The holistic experience is understood, acknowledged, and articulated as an important aspect of mediation. The user and the mediator enter into a dialogue regarding the user's problem over time. (p. 119)

Consequently, the counselor's role is an attempt to customize the information to the user's needs and to help the user to use information effectively, a vital approach in the diffusion of information. As Kuhlthau points out, the information intermediary may be relatively uninvolved with the information seeker, or the information professional may be a partner in the information seeker's quest, as indicated in the role of the counselor.

Finally, the information professional may be involved in the decision to preserve or to discard information in the final stages of the information transfer cycle. Information professionals will assess the value of a given document (print or electronic) to determine its relevance to the agency mission and its potential for providing a valuable artifact, vital content, or informative context. To make an effective decision, the information professional must collaborate with information users and agency decision makers to develop policies and procedures for effective preservation or discarding of information packages.

A Model for Managing an Information Utility

The goal of information professionals is to diffuse information and knowledge, as noted in the discussion above, as professionals work with individual clients. A second challenge is for the information professional to design services which promote the diffusion of information and knowledge. How can information agencies in general, and libraries in particular, promote the diffusion process? A model for converting a traditional library from disseminating to diffusing information is discussed below, using a public library as an example.

Characteristics of an Information Utility

Public libraries are community agencies which exist to satisfy the information needs of their publics. Every member of a community needs information. The need for convenient, appropriate, and responsive information increases for everyone every day. The computer/telecommunication industry is spending millions of dollars to develop the technology, influence public policy, and position their organizations to capture the market for satisfying the information needs of potential customers—the same people served by libraries.

Initially, this communication/information industry will focus on information delivery systems utilizing phone and cable lines as well as the air waves. In other words, these industries are concentrating on the opportunity to provide access to any information desired and deliver it as conveniently as possible when and where it is wanted. This is a *dissemination* process.

The delivered information will be purchased and owned by the customer. It may be useful or inadequate depending upon the customer's ability to determine exactly what information is needed, and at what depth, breadth, currency, and accuracy. Additionally, this customer will need to be skilled in choosing and accessing the appropriate databases, software, CD-ROM, and Internet sources to serve these specific needs.

Eventually, these commercial services will add an interactive component which will provide personal assistance to the customer to assist in defining the need and providing direction in selecting the right resource.

Characteristics of Traditional Libraries

Traditionally, libraries and some other information agencies have functioned more or less as warehouses, providing *access* to as many resources as the community can afford to own; and as a conduit to the national information infrastructure to provide access to material which may be borrowed. In this mode, the primary focus is on our buildings, collections, and technologies for networking.

This shift of focus to become an information utility is to shift from a preoccupation with collections and systems to a preoccupation with users and their information needs. While the library as warehouse values books and the items warehoused, the alternative information utility places value on serving its customers. Since service is the valued commodity, the staff providing service is a more important commodity than the information packages which make up the library collection (the client-centered information transfer model depicted in Figure 5.2 above).

As other agencies in the public and private sectors must focus their attention on the needs, interests, and satisfaction of their customers or clients,

Table 5.1 Attributes of the Library as Warehouse or Utility

Attribute	Warehouse	Utility
Needs assessment	Intuitive	Systematic
Clearly defined mission statement	No	Yes
Budget requests	Unjustified	Justified
Written collection and service policy statements	No	Yes
Short and long term planning	Rarely	Continuous
Change and innovation	Resists	Leads
Selection criteria for collection	Positive reviews	Known user interest and needs
Staff organization structure	Hierarchical	Heterarchical
Service goals	Provide access	Customization
Level of service	Passive or reactive	Assertive
Seeks and adopts new information technologies and formats	Among the last	Among the first
Most important resource	Collections	Staff
Terminology for user charges	Fines	Service charge
Orientation of library use policy	Potential user	Immediate user
Main statistic for measuring success	Items circulated	Satisfied users

so must librarians seriously assess user and nonuser information needs. Similarly, librarians must extend their role beyond the limits of providing *access* to information. This new perspective must focus on the goal of customizing their systems, organizations, collections, and services to meet specific and known community information needs.

A summary of the two scenarios for a warehouse and a public utility are described below. Table 5.1 lists attributes of a library, followed by the implementation of those attributes in a library that exhibits warehouse tendencies, compared to a library that acts as a public information utility

Warehouse

The warehouse model for libraries values the collection. The policies and procedures are designed to maintain a strong collection for the potential user, who is not identified. A needs assessment is rarely done systematically; instead, the intuition of the staff accounts for the known needs of the clientele, i.e., the staff "just know" what the clients need and want without going through the bother of identifying needs through a systematic needs assessment. Selection decisions are made based on positive reviews in the professional media.

The warehouse typically does not have a clearly defined mission statement which articulates the purpose, role, and function of the library. Short and long-term planning is rarely done; consequently budgets tend to be unjustified, based on tradition—last year's budget. Collection development and service policies usually are not written. The result is a stagnant organization that exists on the status quo, doing the same things year after year, and resisting change. The status quo suggests that technological advances are usually ignored, or not considered until enough other libraries have demonstrated a usefulness to warrant careful investigation and consideration.

The organization is a hierarchy with little communication initiated at the top and filtered through the levels of the hierarchy. With little teamwork; the rugged individualist prevails; turf and domains become the preoccupation of the staff. An organizational attitude is that there are rules and policies to follow under all circumstances. The dominant interaction among levels of the hierarchy is for coordination and control. Upper level managers take pride in having access to specialized knowledge and seek to restrict dissemination within the hierarchy.

Service is at the passive, or, at best, reactive level. The tendency is to build a collection and maintain it for users. The desired goal for users is independence and self-sufficiency in using the collections and services. Little or no effort is made to assess client needs and to design services which will address those needs.

Since the warehouse values the collection, the success of the warehouse is measured by the number of items owned and circulated. When the circulation rules are violated, fines are charged to penalize the violator.

Research by D'Elia and Rodger (1994) defines the roles the public expects its libraries to perform. This Gallup Poll study, based on a national survey of adults, indicates that the public expects the library to serve primarily as an educational center, which "provides students, both children and adults, with the books, magazines, and other services they need to do their school work" as well as providing educational materials for independent learners and preschoolers.

Relatively less important is the library's role as a research center and information center for business and personal use. A subsequent study by D'Elia and Rodger (1995) reinforced the perception of libraries as education centers by revealing "trivial differences" between community opinion leaders and the earlier national sample on their evaluation of the roles of libraries.

The roles articulated in these studies project the library as a passive or reactive warehouse, serving individuals after they have taken the initiative to phone or visit there; we submit that the library must take a proactive role in delivering information at a time, place, and format appropriate to the needs of individuals who want it. It is our contention that this agency would function as a public information utility, as described below.

Information Utility

The information utility has a profoundly different culture from that of the warehouse. In the utility, the value structure is based on the importance of people—both the staff and the clientele. Clients are treated as valued customers whose information needs are systematically appraised through interviews, focus groups, surveys, analysis of user records, observation of the community, and the study of local newspapers and community news sources. Based upon identified user needs, services are customized for individuals and groups within the community, e.g., financial planning seminars for retired people. Staff, not the collection, is considered the most important resource of the information utility. Courteous, personalized, and assertive services can be provided to individuals, groups, and corporate agencies in the community.

Service requires planning, and an information utility has a clearly defined mission statement which articulates the purpose, role, and function of the library. The needs assessments feed into the planning process, resulting in service policies and justification for budget planning. Information resources are obtained and the information collection is built upon the known needs of clients.

Staff and clients are involved in the development of a mission statement and in the short- and long-range planning of the organization because the management structure is heterarchical, not hierarchical. Staff at all levels participate in developing and implementing a shared vision of the library. Communication is open, and a feeling of individual and collective worth and trust encourages staff to participate in decision-making, planning, and evaluation of information services.

The organization is in a constant state of change, what Tom Peters describes as "chaos" (1987, 55–56). The librarians and staff enjoy the challenges which accompany constant change. Because no individual can keep up with change, the staff works in teams, also described by Peters (1992, 471–474). Collaboration among staff is critical in the heterarchical organization which encourages teams to form around problems. Gone is the typical departmental and committee structure. While differences exist between the work of professionals and support staff, there is mutual respect and a team spirit which results in a collaborative approach to problem solving and a collegial atmosphere in the organization. This positively charged atmosphere results in the library experimenting, attempting to employ Peters' notion of "small starts," and employing new technology, often on an experimental basis (1987, 238–256).

A comparison of the attributes of the warehouse and information utility is found in Table 5.1.

Changing the Warehouse to an Information Utility

With respect to the categories listed in Table 5.1, it is likely that most libraries are somewhere between a warehouse and a utility. When this process of change and transformation is projected along the points of a continuum, the critical point in the transformation of the organization appears to be when the staff has shifted its values from a concern for collections to a concern for the public. When this transition point has been reached, it is as difficult to turn back as to go forward.

We believe the critical stage is reached when a library staff decides to conduct a systematic needs assessment of its client community. From experience, we've observed that an effective, systematic community analysis results in a change of library staff perspective that is irrevocable. Once actual and potential users of a library are recognized as the *raison d'etre* of the library through a systematic needs assessment process, the staff experiences a value shift from a collection-centered perspective to one of client satisfaction. This value shift is a fundamental requisite for a library to move from the realm of warehouse to public information utility.

As the user becomes the main focus of the staff, there is a natural tendency to respond to issues from the point of view of the user. First among them is the realization that the registration file is more important than the shelf list or catalog. Policies that discriminate against a known borrower in favor of a potential borrower are quickly perceived as absurd. Terms such as "fines" are recognized as pejorative and carry a connotation of criminality rather than the intent which is to levy a "service charge" for an exception to borrowing rights.

The registration process is perceived as a primary opportunity for conducting a needs assessment interview to determine how a borrower may best be served by the library. It is also an opportunity to present the library to the borrower from the perspective of the aphorism which states: "you never have a second chance to make a good first impression." A relatively inexpensive personal computer, plus an elementary software package for creating a relational database will allow the librarian conducting the registration interview to build a database of borrower subject profiles. A comparison with the local telephone directory will provide a beginning list of nonregistered citizens.

The registration interview would provide the opportunity to capture information from the potential borrower that will enable the creation of a subject profile to be entered into the database. Two policies may be implemented with this process: (1) the library need never again select an item without knowing the name of someone who would want to use it; and (2) the library can be confident that it is spending as much time with each borrower as with each item added to its collection. These and other client-centered policies gradually move the library from the warehouse to the information utility.

An Information Utility's Role in a Community

An information utility provides the information needed for the economic vitality of the community. New and small businesses must be nurtured to succeed. Needed is customized information service which enhances existing business and technological support systems while providing new businesses the necessary information to succeed. This interactive system should be part of a larger information network reaching various manufacturing and other enterprises, e.g., health care and other human services. Such an information system currently is under development nationally with public libraries serving as the community point of access. The role of the information utility is to create and demonstrate a customized service to marshal the technology and existing information networks to provide small manufacturing and service enterprises the information necessary to manage resources, improve products and services, and expand markets.

Community Information Infrastructure

An information infrastructure is essential for a community's healthy economy, and technology facilitates the storage, retrieval, repackaging, and transmission of information. Likewise, technology has engendered a global society which transcends traditional barriers of time and space. Most of the information needed by an individual or an enterprise to succeed is accessible through the existing and developing capacities of local, regional, national and global components of modern information networks. The role of the information utility is to marshal this information and to package it for use locally. In addition, the library as an information utility should be at the core of the community information infrastructure, providing a focal point and leadership for all individuals and agencies participating in the infrastructure.

Never before has there been so much information available, yet never before has the difficulty in retrieving the right information been so great. The increasing amount of information results in a corresponding complexity in the management of an enterprise. Increasing complexity results in a corresponding reduction in time available to access information for decision makers. Needed are librarians (or information managers) who will provide a personal link between the client's needs and the appropriate information. This new information professional takes responsibility for diagnosing the precise information needed, locating it, acquiring it, and repackaging it to fit the needs of the client.

Missing from these community information agencies is a facilitating linkage between the information and the client. Currently, the client must invest precious time and effort to visit the library to exploit its resources. The information utility will have an information manager functioning as a field agent who will save the decision maker's time by meeting with clients and delivering customized information on-site.

Our view is that such a utility can be only partially supported through public funds. After completing a community analysis, a baseline level of information service can be determined. While this baseline service may be provided free, additional service would be provided on a customized level for a fee. The result would be a public library with an auxiliary service which is self-supporting.

Conclusion

The concept of information transfer is a way of conceptualizing the work of information professionals. The information transfer model is linked to the information professions and the roles that they play in the information transfer process.

Information transfer is a type of communication. It can be defined as the communication of a recorded message from one human or human mind to another. Unlike communication which assumes that the sender and receiver of a message are contemporaries, information transfer requires a recorded message transmitted on a medium that enables senders to transmit an idea to people who are not their contemporaries. In other words, information transfer is asynchronous.

The information transfer cycle—the life cycle of information—includes these ten steps:

1. Creation
2. Recording
3. Reproduction
4. Dissemination
5. Bibliographic control
6. Organization by disciplines
7. Diffusion
8. Utilization
9. Preservation
10. Deletion

The public need for information is unquestioned. Any library or information agency needs to have only one goal: To provide customized information services to satisfy the needs of its actual and potential users. If this goal is attained, libraries and other information agencies will remain viable and vital to society. A transition from the role of warehouse to community information utility can enable the library or information agency to become an integral part of their community's long-term mission. In this role libraries and information agencies will not only survive, they will thrive.

References

D'Elia, George and Eleanor Jo Rodger. 1994. Public opinion about the roles of the public library in the community; the results of a recent Gallup Poll. *Public Libraries* 33: 24.

———. 1995. The roles of the public library in the community; the results of a Gallup Poll of community leaders. *Public Libraries* 34: 98.

Downs, Robert B. 1975. "Problems of bibliographical control." In *Essays on bibliography*, ed. and comp. Vito J. Brenni, 124–144. Metuchen, NJ: The Scarecrow Press.

Kuhlthau, Carol. 2004. *Seeking meaning: A process approach to library and information services*. Westport, CT: Libraries Unlimited.

Peters, Tom. 1987. *Thriving on chaos*. New York: Harper & Row.

———. 1992. *Liberation management*. New York: Alfred A. Knopf.

Shannon, Claude E. and Warren Weaver. 1963. *The Mathematical theory of communication*. Urbana-Champaign: University of Illinois Press.

6

The Cycle of Professional Service

Chapter Overview

Promoting effective use of information is central to the mission of libraries and other information agencies. When applying the information transfer model from Chapter 5, we can define the role of the information professional as promoting the diffusion of information and knowledge. Consequently, it is important for the information professional to customize information to fit the needs of individual and group users—to help information users understand and use information effectively. This customization requires engagement of a fundamental professional skill, diagnosis of information need. The purpose of this chapter is to explore the concept of diagnosis as part of the cycle of information service, and to suggest implications for information professionals. A theoretical model for studying diagnosis is outlined; this model first appeared in *School Library Media Quarterly* (Grover 1993) and has been updated for this chapter.

Role of the Professional

A professional of any kind possesses knowledge which enables that individual to apply professional knowledge with a service as the product. The role of any professional, e.g., physician, librarian, teacher, or financial planner, is that of diagnosing needs, prescribing a service which meets those needs, implementing that service, and evaluating the outcome of this interaction. In most professions, this process is accomplished at two levels—with individuals and with groups, as indicated in Figure 6.1 below:

This process, which we call "the service cycle," will be described below as it applies to an information professional and is based on the medical model for diagnosis. The reader is urged not to dwell on the different terms used to distinguish the diagnostic processes for individuals and groups. The different terminology is used merely to emphasize the distinction between individual and group services.

Figure 6.1. The Diagnostic Process

For Individuals	For Groups
Diagnosis	Analysis
Prescription	Recommendation
Treatment	Implementation
Evaluation	Evaluation

Diagnosis/Analysis

The professional must be able to assess the information needs of clientele at two levels: (1) analyzing the characteristics of the community served, and (2) analyzing the needs of specific individuals at the point when and where they seek information from the library media center.

The purpose of the first level of analysis, i.e., community analysis, is to provide the professional, as manager, with specific data about the community and its residents. Knowledge acquired through a systematic process of data collection and analysis will enable the information professional to understand the environment in which the library media center will operate. The school, college, or corporation, too, is a community which must be analyzed to determine the needs of the various groups which make up the community for which information service is planned. An understanding of the community and the school will provide a conceptual framework for customizing collections, services, and space allocations. This level of analysis is a first critical step in customizing library media service for individuals and groups within the school, and a great deal of literature exists on the assessment of user needs from the group perspective. Community needs assessment is discussed in more detail later in this chapter.

The second level of analysis is the one-on-one interaction with a user at the point when the decision has been made to seek information. The professional must diagnose the information needs of the user as the first step in the professional/client interaction. At this point, the professional initiates a diagnostic process with the client as well as accepting responsibility for the outcome. This interaction must begin with the basic questions of "What, why, how, when, and where" and narrow to match the professional's perceptions of such client characteristics as level of literacy, cognitive style, and social construction of reality. Once this level of needs assessment is completed, the professional will proceed to the next stage of the service cycle, i.e., prescribing or recommending the source or sources from which the appropriate information may be acquired.

Prescription/Recommendation

The professional, in a one-on-one relationship with a client, will prescribe appropriate information sources in which the desired information may be located to satisfy the diagnosed need. The professional as a manager approaches the diagnosis/prescription process from an organization perspective. That is, the process is not intended to serve the needs of a single person, but rather, the entire population within the library service area. The needs assessment is an analysis of aggregate data about the population of the service area and is used to create an organization customized in its design, collections, and services to fit the characteristics, behaviors, and idiosyncrasies of that population. Conclusions from this analysis can lead to informed decisions about such specifics as the size and scope of collections and services or the number and type of video and audio cassettes in the collection.

Treatment/Implementation

The "treatment" or "implementation" is the organization and application of the service which has been prescribed or recommended. At the individual level of service, the treatment brings the client and the needed information together. This service requires knowledge of various information sources and services which are available within the system, as well as those located elsewhere. With the advancement of more complex and sophisticated technology, the library and information professional must be aware of (1) the array of information sources available, (2) the "best use" of a particular information package for meeting client needs, (3) the preferred formats of the client, and (4) the information needs of the client. This phase of professional service relies heavily on the diagnosis in order to determine client preferences and information needs. As a manager, the library and information professional organizes a service which addresses the information needs of a group, employing knowledge of the group's characteristics to provide the information, staff, and facilities to offer the service.

Evaluation

After the information service has been implemented, the outcome must be evaluated in terms of clientele satisfaction. An unsatisfactory resolution of the original need should trigger a repetition of the entire cycle. The second cycle may amend a part of the sequence, or it may require an entirely new approach. In a reference situation, for example, the information professional would observe and query the client after presenting information to assess the appropriateness of the information provided. Likewise, a service should be evaluated and modified according to the findings of an evaluative process. Similarly, allocation of organization resources for specific purposes should be evaluated after implementation. Methods for collecting and analyzing data for purposes of evaluation can range from simple verbal inquiries to sophisticated quantitative and qualitative analyses, depending on the circumstances.

Whether applying this process of prescription or analysis, diagnosis or recommendation, treatment or implementation, and evaluation to an individual or group, a critical component is the diagnosis of the individual's need, preferences, and cognitive style. This aspect of the professional's role is extremely important, yet how do we treat that role in our professional literature? The role of the professional and what we know about the diagnostic process now will be explored.

The Diagnostic Process

Diagnosis of an individual's information need typically occurs through a communication process with the individual information user. Usually called "the reference interview," this process is a communication process during which the library user's needs can be identified and a source, or sources, of information can be recommended.

The interview must take into account the individual differences of the client, such as cognitive style and preferences for format. Unfortunately, the reference interview often is not viewed from the perspective of the user. As noted by Kuhlthau (2004), information systems typically have been guided by the bibliographic paradigm which views information use from the system's perspective.

The reference interview has been the subject of numerous studies by researchers in library and information science. Bunge's (1984) review of literature provides an historical perspective and Dervin (1986), noted below, has applied communication theory to the question negotiation process. A good description of the reference interview appears in Bopp and Smith (2001, pp. 47–68).

The issue in this chapter is the following: How can the reference interview process be improved? How can the information professional better address the unique information requirements of the individual client? How can information literacy be promoted with individuals by more effectively diagnosing information needs and using results of that diagnosis for recommending information sources?

The reference interview as described above can be converted into a diagnosis of information need used with a thoughtful approach which employs knowledge of human behavior in the individual's use of information. Diagnosis may occur at various points in a client's search and use of information. The client's perspective and proposed use of information must be carefully analyzed in order to better discern what clients consider "the right answer" to their questions or needs. In addition, the communication process is more than the verbal exchange described above. Because much communication is nonverbal, methods of involving nonverbal communication in the process must be explored. Following is a discussion of a model for the diagnostic process in an expanded definition of the concept of the reference interview.

An Overview of Information Psychology

Professional practice is enabled by application of knowledge shared by the profession; this knowledge enables the professional to diagnose information needs, recommend information sources and services, implement those recommendations, and evaluate them. The professional knowledge required of information professionals has been discussed in Chapter 4:

Information psychology—how individuals seek, acquire, organize, process, utilize, and store information;

Sociology of information—how society, and groups within society, create, produce, disseminate, organize, diffuse, utilize, preserve, and discard information;

Information organization management—how to create and manage an organization designed to support and enhance the information transfer process; and

Information engineering—how to design databases of library collections, and other information systems customized to meet the needs of a client population.

Of special interest in the consideration of diagnosis is information psychology. This study of human behavior draws heavily upon behavioral science, similar to the way that educational psychology applies behavioral theory to the learning environment. Following is a discussion of the elements of information psychology which might contribute to a better understanding of the diagnostic process.

Diagnosing Information Use Behaviors

The model for information user behaviors is found in the framework for information psychology, as noted above. The information professional may be called upon to diagnose information need at any of the following points in the behaviors of acquiring information: Awareness of need, action decision, strategies for search, behaviors in search, evaluation, assimilation, memory, and utilization. Following is a brief description of these actions:

Awareness of Need

A client determines a need for information. The need may be for educational, recreational, decision-making, or research purposes. The first stage in the information use behavioral process is becoming aware of a need for information.

Action Decision

After becoming aware of a need, a client may elect to act by seeking to satisfy that need.

Strategies for Search

Once a decision is made to search for information, clients will employ their unique strategies for locating information. A plan of action is formulated, usually very informally.

Behaviors in Search

The search strategies are enacted by the client. These behaviors might include consulting indexes, consulting with a librarian, asking a friend, etc.

Evaluation

The results of the search are evaluated by the client to determine if the search should be modified, if the search should continue, or if the search should be terminated.

Assimilation

If the results of the search are deemed satisfactory, the information may be assimilated into the client's information system, e.g., the information may be copied for further use, notes taken, or input into a word processor.

Memory

If the information is pertinent, the client may memorize the information; therefore, the information may be learned, becoming a part of the individual's knowledge.

Utilization

If learned, the information may cause behavioral changes which cause the client to use the information.

At any of the stages above, the client may consult with an information professional in order to solicit help in information seeking. The professional must identify the stage of information seeking as part of the diagnostic process, using knowledge based on the theories below in order to complete the diagnosis.

Theory Base for Diagnosis

Information psychology applies theories of human behavior to the information transfer process. Following is a discussion of selected theories which could be applied to diagnosis.

Cognitive development theories, particularly the work of Piaget (Piaget and Inhelder 1969), have application to the diagnostic process. Knowing the stage of cognitive development, e.g., stage of concrete operations (about ages 7–12), or formal operations (about ages 11–15), would enable the professional to suggest different levels of information sources. Age of an individual is an indicator of cognitive development, but Piaget points out that individuals can progress through the cognitive stages at vastly different rates.

While Piaget's work is useful for understanding the cognitive development of children and young adults, studies of the developmental stages of adults is helpful for understanding the interests and life stages of adults. The work of Levinson (1978) and Sheehy (1995), for example, suggest patterns of development experience by adults.

Research and theory on learning styles can contribute to the understanding of information needs and information processing for clients in libraries and information agencies. Brain research, especially the study of brain hemisphericity has application to understanding cognitive styles. Dominance of one side of the brain can suggest learning preferences, e.g., linear or holistic, symbolic or concrete, sequential or random, logical or intuitive, verbal or nonverbal. There are implications for preferred types of learning modes—visual, auditory, or experiential. The work of Edwards (2002), Posner (1994), and Vitale (1982, 1989) are examples of application of cognitive theory.

Psychological type also is related to information processing preferences. Based on Carl Jung's theory of personality types, the Myers-Briggs Type Indicator has been developed to indicate four basic psychological dimensions:

Energizing—how and where you get your energy

Attending—what you pay attention to when you gather information

Deciding—what system you use when you decide

Living—what type of life you adopt (Hirsh and Kummerow, 1989)

Each of the above preferences has two possible choices:

Energizing: introversion and extraversion. Introversion relates to drawing energy from a person's inner world of emotions, impressions, and ideas. Extraversion relates to drawing energy from outside oneself in the world of people, activities, and things.

Attending: sensing and intuition. Sensing is the preference for paying attention to information which is derived from the five senses. Intuition refers to the preference for paying attention to an intuitive "sixth sense" and noting what could be, rather than what is.

Deciding: thinking and feeling. Thinking relates to a preference for organizing information to decide in a logical, objective manner. This preference is similar to left-brain dominant preferences. Feeling is related to organizing information in a personal, values-oriented manner, similar to the behavior of a right-brain dominant person.

Living: judgment and perception. The judgment preference suggests a person who lives in a planned, organized way. Perception refers to the preference for flexibility and spontaneity.

Life types theory suggests tendencies toward behavior. People may consciously alter their preferences but tend to rely on their natural preferences. Type preferences can be determined by using the Myers-Briggs Type Indicator, an easily administered and scored test. A person's preferences can be used to suggest search strategies, sources of information, and planning of information service. Grindler and Stratton (1990) have applied type indicator research to teaching and learning styles, as an example of application for diagnosis.

Role theory also provides a theory base for understanding information needs in the process of diagnosis. The key concept in role theory is that roles suggest certain patterns of behavior which can be expected. Each person assumes many roles, and in that role exhibits certain behaviors which accompany those roles. Biddle (1979) gave examples:

> Children are constantly enjoined to act in a more grown-up fashion; new recruits into the armed services must learn roles of deference and deportment; the young lady who is to make her debut will adopt the style and manners of the event; predictable patterns of behavior appear within the school, the factory, the office, the sports arena . . . the summer camp. Some of us, in fact, spend a good deal of time talking about roles. Parents, teachers, psychiatrists, social workers may sometimes feel as if there are no other topics of conversation at the end of their working days. (p. 57)

Another attribute of roles is the limited context of role. No one role is exhibited by an individual at work and at home 24 hours a day. A role is a sometime thing which may be dictated by the variety of environmental factors which cause an individual to assume the role such as teacher, parent, friend, golfer, spouse, etc.

Role, then, produces expectations for behavior. The danger is that we may stereotype individuals upon identification of role. Stereotype may be defined, in terms of role theory, as " . . . the degree to which an expectation is based on hearsay rather than evidence" (Biddle 1979, 157). Consequently, application of role theory requires awareness of behaviors which have been observed and associated with role—not merely those behaviors which we believe to be associated.

Expressed in another way, role suggests behavior which is considered acceptable for membership in a certain social group. Membership in that group requires learned behaviors, knowledge, and attitudes. If a person is known to be a member of a certain group, that person may be expected to possess certain knowledge and have the ability to perform certain tasks usually associated with that group. For example, membership in the school library media profession assumes certain knowledge, attitudes, and skills which can be attributed to all who assume that role. By identifying an individual by role, one can make certain assumptions about that individual's information needs for that role.

While role theory may be applied to people who are members of various groups, the individual still possesses a unique perspective which is solely that individual's. Symbolic interactionists have studied the constant interaction between the individual and that person's interaction with groups. Therein lay the challenge in diagnosing information need: The individual information user represents a confluence of individual preferences and abilities for information processing, combined with a set of roles which predetermine which information is needed and to prescribe an information package which addresses the preferred information processing style of the individual.

Information theory has been developed for library and information professionals. Among those theories with implications for the diagnostic process are the theories of Kuhlthau and Dervin. Kuhlthau's research on the search process contributes both to the development of theory in information psychology and to diagnosis; her work has defined the search process as follows:

> ... it is a complex learning process involving thoughts, actions, and feelings that takes place over an extended period of time, that involves developing a topic from information in a variety of sources, and that culminates in a presentation of the individual's new perspective of the topic. (Kuhlthau 1989, 19)

Kuhlthau's findings regarding the feelings, thoughts, and actions of students during the search process can be very helpful to information professionals so that they can more effectively diagnose information needs and strategies, depending on the student's progress in the search.

Dervin and Dewdney's application of communication theory has resulted in the application of "neutral questioning" to the reference interview. Their perspective is "that information does not have an independent existence but is rather a construct of the user" (Dervin and Dewdney 1986, 507). Dervin and Dewdney proposed open-ended questions to attempt to understand the purpose and use for the information requested by the client; their approach was to understand how the user will "make sense" of the information.

Implications for Practitioners

Information professionals work with individuals and with groups. In order to diagnose information need, the practitioner must be able to apply relevant behavioral theories to the diagnostic process to recommend appropriate information sources or services to the individual.

This chapter has articulated several theories which can be applied to the diagnostic process, including cognitive theory, learning theory, brain hemisphericity theory, life types theory, role theory, and information theory by way of suggesting elements of a model for diagnosing information need. The challenge is to sharpen the diagnostic process through application of these theories.

As discussed above, the diagnosis of an individual's information need typically occurs during a "reference interview," a conversation between the information professional and the client. This communication process might be considered data-gathering in order to expand the concept, just as a physician gathers data on a patient before diagnosing treatment for an illness. For example, a physician interviews a patient regarding symptoms of the malady ("How are you feeling? When did you first notice this problem? Have you ever experienced this condition before?") The physician may also observe the patient, e.g., condition of skin, eyes, throat, etc., and may routinely administer appropriate tests (blood pressure, blood test) during the diagnosis.

Likewise, an information professional might employ other data-gathering mechanisms to enhance diagnosis. Questions might be expanded to elicit more information about the individual's information processing style. Observation of age and information use patterns based on past experience might be applied to determining preferred information style. As an example, Vitale applied results of brain research to indicators of hemispheric dominance which can be observed or determined through interviews with children. Indicators include eye dominance, hand dominance, hand position, muscle testing, body symmetry, and eye movements. For example, the left side of the brain controls the right side of the body, and the right side of the brain controls the left side of the body; a left-handed child is usually right-brain dominant, but a right-handed child may be either left- or right-brain dominant. Vitale (1989) reported research which enables one to determine dominance through observation as follows:

> If a right-handed child holds his pencil in a straight position with the wrist straight and the pencil aimed toward the shoulder, the left hemisphere is probably dominant. If a right-hander rotates his hand or aims the pencil at a right angle to the body, he is probably right-hemispheric. (p. 36)

Vitale provided numerous additional observational tests for determining hemispheric dominance and learning styles. Likewise, Vitale suggested questions to explore learning preferences. Following is an example:

> *Question: I want you to see your favorite ice-cream cone in your head. Where do you see it?* (Be sure child is familiar with the object you ask him to visualize.)

> Interpretation: If the child points between the eyes or a little to the right, I have found it indicates he is a visual learner. If he points to the top of his head or puts his whole hand on his head, he probably is a haptic learner. Both of these responses indicate a right-hemispheric learning style. (Vitale 1989, 42–43)

The diagnostic process for individuals, as noted above, relies upon knowledge from several disciplines in the behavioral sciences. This chapter has discussed briefly the contributions of learning theory, cognitive theory, life type theory, brain theory, information theory, and role theory to enhance the diagnosis of information need. These fields are but a beginning. Other areas for further investigation might include various fields of psychology and sociology, social psychology, linguistics, physiology, cultural anthropology, ethnography, cybernetics, and others.

The Environmental Context

This environmental context which influences the information transfer process includes the following aspects:

- **Culture**—language, philosophical, and moral values, history, and all those valued characteristics as they influence the individual's information processing style;

- **Geography**—aspects such as climate and physical environment which can influence information processing;

- **Political structure of society**—the system for governance and underlying values regarding the role of government in the society served by the information agency; in a school library media center, the school's governance system as it influences the flow of information to individuals;

- **Legislation and regulations** issued by legislative and regulatory agencies of the government which govern access of information to individuals, e.g., copyright, intellectual freedom;

- The **economic system** under which the individual functions;

- **Technology** as it is utilized by the client and as it influences information transfer;

- **Information policy**—policies regarding secrecy, censorship, privacy, the public's right to know, government responsibility to inform, and other policies which influence the transfer of information to individuals.

These environmental variables are portrayed in the Information Psychology model displayed in the Appendix. This model is an attempt to define the diagnostic process and to suggest ways to study and refine this fundamental professional task. Additional exploration and application of behavioral and social theory will enable information professionals, and other information professionals, to enhance their roles in promoting effective information use.

Community Analysis

The discussion to this point has focused on diagnosing the information needs of individuals; however, the information professional works with groups as well. Consequently, we must take some time to consider the challenge of customizing services to groups of people served by a library or information agency.

As we saw with individual clients, customizing of information services requires a knowledge of the clientele, in this case communities. To customize services to communities we must systematically collect data about the community in order to infer the information needs; however, a community is a very complex organization. How do we grapple with this complexity? The community analysis model described here divides data collection into four parts; but first let's define "community analysis."

Defining "Community Analysis"

In this book, we will use the definition of "community analysis" developed by Greer and Hale (1982) as they analyzed the information needs of more than two dozen communities around the United States:

> Community analysis is a systematic process of collecting, organizing and analyzing data about the library and its environment. It is designed to assist the administrator in choosing from among alternative patterns of satisfying residents' information needs and interests. (p. 358)

This process of assessing a community's needs applies to any definition of a community—a municipality, a university, a corporation, a government agency, a school system. Likewise, the model for community analysis outlined here can also apply to any definition of "community."

The Community Analysis Research Institute Model

During the 1970s and 1980s, the Community Analysis Research Institute (CARI), founded by one of the authors, conducted numerous analyses of communities and presented more than 100 community analysis workshops throughout the United States. As a product of the community analyses conducted early in this process, the Community Analysis Research Institute (CARI) Model for community analysis was created.

The CARI model established four units of analysis for communities:

1. Individuals
2. Groups
3. Agencies
4. Life styles

Each of these units will be described briefly.

Individuals

This aspect of community analysis requires assessing needs and examines a community through the demographics of a community. A look at census data results in an analysis of such variables as the population of the municipality and the ethnic makeup of the community, the socioeconomic makeup. Following are characteristics which are informative in the analysis of individuals within a population, and this information can be attained from recent census data for municipalities:

- Age characteristics
- Family structure, including households and children, marital status

- Education characteristics, including school enrollment and years of school completed

- Economic characteristics, including employment status, occupation, industry, and income

The examples above for municipalities can be adapted easily to other kinds of communities as well. The communities of colleges, schools, private enterprise, and government agencies also can be analyzed in the same way. For example, a school library media specialist would pay attention to the number of faculty and students, the size of academic departments, the ethnic composition of the student body, the numbers of students in classes. In addition, the school librarian should pay attention to the demographics of the community as an influence on the school system. All the elements of a community analysis for a municipality could be considered but in less depth. The school librarian would look for indicators to support the needs of the students and teachers.

Academic communities would need to look at data similar to that of schools—numbers of students in departments, schools and colleges within the university, number of majors and minors, and other distinguishing characteristics of the student body and faculty. What makes this college or university unique? How does this uniqueness influence library and information services?

In many types of special libraries, the information professional works alone or with a small cadre of professionals and technical staff among a much larger organization which is supported by the library. For example, a law library in a government agency or law firm is staffed by information professionals with knowledge of the law and expertise in library and information resources and services.

Regardless of the type of community, the analysis of *individuals* is intended to break down a complex organization to look at the components of people who make up that organization. That is the purpose of analysis of the demographics of a community.

Groups

A second variable in the CARI model for analyzing communities is *groups*. The information professional conducting an information needs assessment must identify the various groups in the community and their characteristics and information needs.

The definition of "groups" for our purposes is "a formal or informal organization which meets and functions regularly." Unlike an agency, a group does not have an office or telephone for contact. Examples of groups in a community would be service organizations (Lions Clubs, Rotary, etc.), service fraternities and sororities, and clubs. In smaller communities, the local newspaper may include news of clubs and meeting schedule.

To identify systematically and analyze groups, it can be helpful to categorize them. For example, a matrix might be constructed using these categories:

- Recreation
- Social

- Church-related
- Cultural
- School
- Hobbies
- Ethnic
- Age-related
- Environmental
- Political
- Project oriented
- Commercial
- Vocational
- Occupational

In a school community, the groups would include school student organizations, e.g., marching band, debate club, science club, photography club, and other organizations which cater to student interests. Other groups might be faculty teaching teams, in a larger system the principals may meet as a group, the assembly of department chairs in school, the Parent Teachers Association, the school board.

Academic communities, like schools, would have clubs by interest groups, e.g., Math Club, Psychology Club, Fellowship of Christian Athletes. Other groups would include administrative groups, e.g., Deans' Council, advisory groups to schools and colleges, fraternities and sororities, faculty senate or union, and various committees on campus. Special library communities will also have informal organizations within the staff for organizational, administrative, educational, and recreational purposes.

Groups may have information needs that can be addressed successfully by an information professional; however, the informality of the group can hinder attempts to learn of the group's purpose and information needs. The groups may be elusive; since they do not have phone numbers, it may be difficult to identify the leaders in order to engage in a conversation about interests and information needs. However, many groups have a Web site, and this source can be effective in making contact, and study of the Web site can help determine information needs.

Agencies

While groups are usually informal organizations, *agencies* are formal parts of a larger organization, and these agencies provide a service or a product. For example, a community will have such agencies as a police and fire department, public library, human resources department, recreation department, schools, and numerous other agencies which have a mission within the municipality. A community analysis requires assessing information needs by identifying and analyzing missions and characteristics of agencies serving the community.

Other agencies which are very important to a municipality are the businesses established within the community. As with public agencies as noted above, each private enterprise in a community has a mission which it must fulfill to stay in business. Some enterprises may be large enough to staff their library or information services, but many are small enough that they cannot afford an in-house information staff; consequently, the public library may be the best source for small business's information needs.

Agencies may be categorized as follows to create a checklist for a community analysis:

- Government
- Religious
- Health
- Cultural
- Education
- Business
- Informational

The above list is not comprehensive, and readers may wish to add to it for their own communities.

Agencies in a school district or school building would be those offices which serve the students and faculty in a specialized way. For example, the school nurse, psychologist, library, athletic department, music department, are examples of agencies within the school which serve a mission for the school.

Academic agencies would include the offices of departments, schools, and colleges within a university. Agencies might include the printing services, public affairs office, budget office, library, technology support, health center, advising offices, and any other service within the college or university to serve the students, staff, and faculty.

Agencies in the special library organization, like those of schools and academe, would be the offices within the organization which provide services to the organization. Some of the same examples would be appropriate, e.g., human resources, printing, budget office, etc.

Because agencies provide a service, they are often information intensive. Current and accurate information is needed by agencies to serve the organization effectively. Information professionals can provide that information if the information needs of agencies are effectively identified.

The first challenge is the identification of agencies in your community. Since they are formal organizations, a telephone directory is a good source to check first. Working with agencies can serve the general public (or the school/academic/special clientele) indirectly by serving the agency, which in turn may serve the public better because the agency has the information needed for better service or products.

Life Styles

The fourth category of our community analysis model is "life styles." This term refers to the unique "culture" of the community—its history, values, customs, traditions, topography, climate, leisure activities, and other attributes that make this community unique. Let's examine these characteristics:

- History: What does the history of the community tell us about the community as it is today?

- Values: What are the primary concerns and values of the community residents? What are the most important elements in the lives of the residents?

- Customs: What traditions or rituals are a regular part of the residents' life?

- Topography: What topographical features are prominent in the community? How do these features influence traffic and everyday living?

- Climate: How does the climate influence activities and life in the community?

- Leisure activities: How do people spend their leisure time? Which activities are most common?

- Transportation: How do people move from one place to the other? Is the library or information service easily accessible to all potential clients?

- Communication: Is the communication infrastructure supportive of easy and frequent communication among the community residents? Are there blockages to effective communication?

- "Community-ness": Is there a sense of community? Do the community members see themselves as part of this community? To what extent is there community pride?

- Economic life: How would you characterize the economic level of residents? Is the community affluent? "Hanging on" economically? How does the economic condition affect life style?

- Social issues: What are the dominant social concerns of the community members? What issues appear to hold their attention at the present time?

These components of "life style" can influence the types of information services offered in a community of any type—municipality, academic environment, school library, or special library clientele. What are the implications in your community for each of the factors above?

The four perspectives of a community analysis outlined above will enable the information professional to identify the unique qualities of a community and to identify agencies and groups who are leading contributors to the life style of the community. It is a systematic approach for collecting data for making decisions abut information services to be offered. Next, we'll examine the process for collecting data.

Data Gathering Techniques

As noted at the beginning of this section, a community is a complex organization, whether a municipality, a university community, a school, or a special library community—law firm, hospital, government agency, or other agency. The Community Analysis Research Institute community analysis model provides a framework for identifying and collecting data for analyzing information needs in a community. However, where does one find the information in each of the four categories—individuals, groups, agencies, and lifestyle? Please be aware that these categories are helpful when analyzing a community, the categories are not mutually exclusive; the discussion of sources for data gathering which follows combines the groups to show the overlap and to emphasize the merging of categories.

Individuals

When studying the individuals in a community, the following questions should be considered:

- Who are the typical library/information users? Where are they?
- What are the occupations or job categories of the community?
- Who are the typical nonusers of the library and information services?
- What variables account for nonuse of library/information services?
- What has been the rate of growth or loss of population?
- Are there areas with special characteristics? What are they?

This information can be found readily in existing agencies, e.g., the community library, the city planning agency, the school offices, local chamber of commerce, zoning board, or utility companies.

Colleges and universities would have some of this information in administrative offices at the college/university or at the system level. Special library agencies also would house some of this information in the administrative offices.

Groups

Since groups are informal, identifying groups in a community can be more challenging than agencies, which are listed in a phone directory. Newspapers within the community are a good source of groups, clubs, and various organizations. Directories may be available in print or on Web pages. Another good source, and perhaps the best, is people; talk with community residents to determine which are the most popular clubs and other organizations. From these random conversations with various elements of the community will come a general understanding of the names and relative popularity and activity of groups within the community.

Agencies

The sources of information for agencies is similar to that of groups. Walkarounds (or drivearounds), newspapers, especially the yellow pages, directories, and people in the community are all good sources of information regarding the dominant and most active agencies in the community.

Lifestyle

Lifestyle includes a wide swath of any community's heritage and uniqueness. In order to study lifestyle, this topic is divided into components with suggested sources.

History. A community's history can be explored by addressing the following questions:

1. What has been the influence of historical events and conditions on today's life styles in the community?

2. Where did the early leaders of your community come from during its development, and what contributions are still evident?

3. What are the chief conditions, circumstances, resources, or factors of location, which determined this community's development to its current state?

4. What were the important steps in the economic development of the area?

5. What movements have swept through this community at one time or another? What impact have these movements had?

These historical questions can be explored through reading of histories, reports, and documents of the community and can be found in libraries, local museums, archives, and public records. Talking with longtime residents of the community can be very informative in answering these questions.

Topographical Features

Physical and geographical features can influence the lifestyle of any community. The following questions can guide exploration of this topic:

1. What climatic and geographic characteristics suggest certain life styles and influence patterns of behavior?

2. What issues are provoked by the existence of topographical features?

3. Where are the identifiable neighborhoods or clustering of community residents?

The geographical features can be identified by personal observation, study of maps, and analysis of planning agency documents.

Transportation/Traffic Patterns

Location of the community can influence access to it and delivery of library/information services. The following questions are pertinent:

1. To what extent do traffic patterns influence the behavior of community residents?

2. What groups are most affected by traffic patterns, barriers, and changes?

3. How do people get from one place to another?

4. Is the library or information center located conveniently?

5. Do transportation pattern clash with library hours?

This information can be attained by driving/walking around, consulting the security office or police department, or contacting the planning department of the agency or community.

Putting the Information to Work

A diagnosis or community analysis is a vital component of information service which meets the needs of clientele. If needs are not met, the library or information agency is not doing its job, and it can be marginalized or even cut. The data collected must be used to set priorities for planning new information services, reaching unserved populations, and discontinuing unwanted and unneeded services that now exist.

Diagnosis and analysis of communities can determine the types of services and levels of services that can be offered. The following categories of information use are helpful to think about the possibilities:

- Teach or learn: The educational function of information
- Enjoy: The recreational function
- Appreciate: The cultural function of information
- Decide: The informational function of information
- Create new information or knowledge: The research function
- Find or locate: The bibliographic (or identification) function of information

In addition to the types of services (based on function), an information professional can consider three levels of service:

- Passive level of service, which provides the resources (books, journals, computer software, etc.) for use with no help from the professional staff.
- Reactive level of service, which provides professional assistance when the information user requests help
- Assertive level of service, which anticipates the needs of clientele based upon the results of a systematic community analysis

Since this is an introduction to the information service field, we'll not go further into design of service. However, it is important to note that both community analysis and service planning and implementation is a complex process which requires more thought and work than thinking "We should provide service X to our users because Library Y started it, and it's a cool idea." What works for Library Y may not address needs of Information Center Z. That's why customizing services is so important.

Conclusion

Information in today's society requires a high level of service in order for libraries and information agencies to be successful within their communities. A key to this success is the ability to assess information needs, design information services to meet those needs, implement the services, and evaluate the service to "fine tune" it. The diagnostic interview and community analysis are essential tools which enable information professionals to customize services as needed by information users. Techniques presented in this chapter are key ingredients to the success of information professionals in our knowledge society.

References

Biddle, Bruce J. 1979. *Role theory: Expectations, identities, and behaviors*. New York: Academic Press.

Bopp, Richard E. and Linda C. Smith. 2001. *Reference and information services: An introduction*. Englewood, CO: Libraries Unlimited.

Bunge, Charles A. 1984. Interpersonal dimensions of the reference interview: A historical review of the literature. *Drexel Library Quarterly* 20: 4–22.

Dervin, Brenda, and Patricia Dewdney. 1986. Neutral questioning: A new approach to the reference interview. *Reference Quarterly* 25: 507–513.

Edwards, Betty. 2002. *Drawing on the right side of the brain*. New York: Jeremy P. Tarcher.

Greer, Roger C. 1987. "A model for the discipline of information science." In *Intellectual foundations for information professionals*, ed. H. Achleitner, 3–25. New York: Columbia University Press.

Greer, Roger C., and Martha L. Hale. 1982. "The community analysis process." In *Public librarianship: A reader*, ed. J. Robbins-Carter, 358–366. Littleton, CO: Libraries Unlimited.

Grindler, Martha C. and Beverly D. Stratton. 1990. Type indicator and its relationship to teaching and learning styles. *Action in Teacher Education* 12: 3134.

Grover, Robert. 1993. Diagnosing information needs: a proposed model. *School Library Media Quarterly* 21: 95–100.

Hirsch, Sandra K., and Jean Kummerow. 1989. *Lifetypes*. New York: Warner Books.

Jean, Piaget, and Barbel Inhelder. 1969. *The psychology of the child*. New York: Basic Books.

Katz, William A. 1992. *Introduction to reference work*. Vol. 2. New York: McGraw-Hill.

Kuhlthau, Carol C. 1989. Information search process: A summary of research and implications for school library media programs. *School Library Media Quarterly* 18: 19–25.

———. 1991. Inside the search process: Information seeking from the user's perspective. *Journal of the American Society for Information Science* 42: 361–371.

———. 2004. *Seeking meaning: A process approach to library and information services*. Westport, CT: Libraries Unlimited.

Levinson, Daniel J. 1978. *The seasons of a man's life*. New York: Alfred A. Knopf.

Posner, Michael I. 1994. *Images of mind*. New York: Scientific American Library.

Sheehy, Gail. 1995. *New passages: Mapping your life across time*. New York: Random House.

Vitale, Barbara M. 1982. *Unicorns are real; A right-brained approach to learning*. New York: Warner Books.

———. 1989. *Free flight: Celebrating your right brain*. Rolling Hills Estates, CA: Jalmar Press.

7

The Information Infrastructure

Chapter Overview

The information infrastructure consists of the personnel, technology, policies, organizations, agencies, and processes which underlie the information transfer process in society. The term "infrastructure" is used purposefully to encompass the cohesiveness of our information support system; without using an all-encompassing term, narrow concepts emerge. In this chapter we examine the information infrastructure in order to visualize the role of information professionals and their influence on the creation, diffusion, organization, and utilization of information and knowledge.

Definition of "Information Infrastructure"

In 1993 a federal Information Infrastructure Task Force issued a report, "The National Information Infrastructure: Agenda for Action." In the executive summary, the national information infrastructure is described as ". . . a seamless web of communications networks, computers, databases, and consumer electronics that will put vast amounts of information at users' fingertips" (http://www.ibiblio.org/nii/NII-Executive-Summary.html).

The report noted that development of the information infrastructure could "help unleash an information revolution that will change forever the way people live, work, and interact with each other." Among the changes proposed were the following:

- People could live almost anywhere they wanted, without foregoing opportunities for useful and fulfilling employment, by "telecommuting" to their offices through an electronic highway;
- The best schools, teachers, and courses would be available to all students, without regard to geography, distance, resources, or disability;
- Services that improve America's health care system and respond to other important social needs could be available on-line, without waiting in line, when and where you needed them. (Executive Summary)

While this report sketches a picture of the national information infrastructure in broad strokes and suggests its benefits to society, the definition of "information infrastructure" cries for clarification. It is often depicted as only the Internet and the technology components which enable the transmission of vast amounts of information and knowledge at high speed. This definition is similar to describing the American transportation infrastructure as a system of superhighways. While the interstate highway system is a vital component, it is only one part of a much more complex system.

Some authors have defined "national information infrastructure" more broadly, as this example demonstrates:

> The NII may be viewed three ways: as a **policy** for **national** information infrastructure development; as federal **programs** to enhance and support this development; and a wide range of **applications** which demonstrate the tangible uses and benefits of the **technologies**. The policy has been articulated in a series of NII reports; the program is supported through major government R & D and grant efforts; the applications focus on a variety of applications in schools, libraries, hospitals, government, and businesses. (McLoughlin 2001, 23)

While we agree that the information infrastructure is composed of the elements listed above, we offer the following definition for use in our discussion of the information infrastructure:

> The information infrastructure is a **global** network of **people, organizations, agencies, policies, processes, and technologies** organized in a loosely coordinated system to enhance the creation, production, dissemination, organization, storage, retrieval, and preservation of information and knowledge for people. The primary objective of this network is the diffusion of knowledge for a society.

Technology is frequently the focus when the information infrastructure is discussed. Nevertheless, we want to focus—not on technology—but on the users and human element of the information infrastructure. The core of the information professions must be focused on people as users of information, and the secondary focus is on the design of organizations and services to deliver the information. Libraries are but one element of the information infrastructure. Managing a library or database is a significant but specific activity. Other information professions are defined by the kinds of information systems managed within the information infrastructure, e.g., archives, museums, networks, Web sites, and records in a variety of formats. Recall that a brief overview of the information professions was outlined in Chapter 1.

Technologies will change, but what's important is how people process information—the most significant aspect of the information professions. Some of the current Internet search engines provide people the opportunity to find their own information. Professionals give value added to save time for searchers.

Because of the international Internet network, we want to emphasize the *global* nature of the infrastructure. The information infrastructure of the world is a vast system which includes news organizations, universities, corporate researchers, satellite transmissions systems, think tanks, newspapers and magazines, radio and television stations and networks, government agencies, publishers, libraries, schools, and other organizations and agencies engaged in research and mass distribution of information and knowledge. In a knowledge society, software producers and professionals are also a part of this infrastructure. The network is so vast that it employs a sizeable segment of the adult population. This infrastructure extends much beyond the technology itself and policies, agencies, and processes which govern its use.

Similarly, communities have an information infrastructure, i.e., the people, organizations, agencies, policies, processes, and technologies organized in a system to enhance the transfer of information to members of that community. Public, university, school, and special librarians should take responsibility for determining the players in their communities and how they can be advanced through an effective information system. The library should be a leader in the development of a community information infrastructure for any environment—municipality, school, college or university, law firm, health facilities, public agency, or private sector enterprise. Since we have identified the major elements of the information infrastructure, we'll begin exploring it by looking at another example of an infrastructure in order to construct a model for examining the information infrastructure.

A Model for Studying the Information Infrastructure: The Transportation Infrastructure

Since the information literature describes the information infrastructure in somewhat narrow terms, as described above, the authors sought to construct a more inclusive model to delineate the information infrastructure, and we began with an examination of another, well-known infrastructurem, that of transportation. This is especially appropriate since the Internet is often referred to as the "information super highway." We'll examine transportation by studying the definition, conveyances, support industries, and other essential elements of the system.

Definition and Systems

Transportation is defined as "the movement of goods and persons from place to place and the various means by which such movement is accomplished" (*Encyclopaedia Britannica* 2006). The United States boasts a highly developed system, which includes ground, air, and water transportation. The land transportation system includes highways, roads, bridges, railroads, subways, and paths for bicycles and pedestrians. The transportation subsystems below are adopted from those found in a recent edition of *World Book* ("Transportation" 2005).

Conveyances and Channels

The transportation industry consists of passenger and freight carriers, equipment manufacturers, and related industries which provide fuel and various services and facilities. The related industries play a vital role in transportation as do government agencies. Equipment manufacturers produce the vehicles necessary for transportation—airplanes, trains, automobiles, buses, and trucks. They also supply the equipment needed to operate the vehicles. This equipment includes railroad tracks, airplane communications systems, replacement parts, and maintenance equipment.

Passenger and freight carriers include bus lines, mass transit companies, airlines, railroads, trucking companies, and shipping firms. Private companies own and operate the bus lines, airlines and intercity, and most of the railroads in the United States. However, local and federal government agencies regulate most mass transit services of all kinds.

Support Industries

Related industries support the carriers and including the manufacture of vehicles, road construction, the servicing of vehicles, and car sales. Production of fuel is a vital supporting industry. Also significant in the efficient management of a transportation system is the information system which schedules passengers, monitors progress of vehicles, and generally provides support for efficient transportation.

Government Influence

Government regulations deal primarily with transportation safety, fuel economy, the emission of pollutants by vehicle engines, and the business practices of transportation companies. Governments at the state and national levels establish safety rules for the various methods of transportation. Governments also set and enforce standards for vehicle emissions and regulate the business practices of transportation companies.

Personnel

A variety of personnel are required to operate the transportation system, ranging from the unskilled (custodians of the vehicles) to highly trained and skilled operators (airline pilots). Also needed are the highly educated engineers who design the systems and vehicles, architects of the structures which house vehicles, computer specialists who design and program supporting information systems, and plant managers for the manufacturing of vehicles, fuel, and other supporting products. Service providers are trained to provide customer-friendly service on planes and trains.

Table 7.1 lists elements of transportation infrastructure, with an overview of similar elements in the information infrastructure.

Elements of the Information Infrastructure

As shown in Table 7.1, the information infrastructure can be analyzed in much the same terms as the transportation infrastructure. However, the information infrastructure has been altered radically by the infusion of technology, especially computer technology, after World War II. The transfer of information has been influenced significantly by the advance of digitization, a paradigm shift comparable to the shift to air travel in the transportation infrastructure. This shift in the means for storing and transmitting information can be compared to the epic shift from handwritten manuscripts to printed books. With the implementation of computers, the

Table 7.1 The Transportation and Information Infrastructure

Characteristic	Transportation Infrastructure	Information Infrastructure
Definition	Conveys goods and people	Transfers ideas from one individual or group to another
Systems	Land, air, water	Publishing, broadcasting systems, cable systems, satellite communication, the Internet, libraries, government agencies
Conveyances	Trains, buses, cars, airplanes, boats carry people and goods	Books, magazines, television, radio, audio recordings, video recordings, e-mail, software carry information and knowledge
Channels	Rails, roads, highways, bicycle pats, rivers, lakes support conveyances	Publishing, newspapers, broadcasting systems, cable systems, satellite communication, the Internet, libraries, government agencies support information and knowledge transfer
Support Industries	Manufacturers of conveyances, fuel, road materials	Printing industry, software producers, hardware manufacturers
Government Influence	Safety regulations, economic regulations, emission standards, business practices	Information policy, laws, regulations
Personnel	Custodians, conveyance operators (pilots, train engineers, sea captains, etc.), engineers (designers), architects, plant managers, service providers, police, gas station attendants	Engineers, technicians, information professionals, office workers, support personnel

creation, production, and dissemination of information has been changed forever. Because of this cataclysmic change and the subsequent complexity of the information infrastructure, we'll first outline a brief history of the information infrastructure.

Since the information infrastructure must focus on people who use information, information psychology is at the core, just as the core of the education infrastructure is educational psychology. What we know about learning through educational psychology influences how we address the structure of processes of the educational system. Likewise, information psychology is the comparable core of the information professions; the most significant research we can do relates to the information transfer process for individuals. Each of those processes of information transfer must be examined to determine how the organizations, people, and public policies work to establish information infrastructure of the nation. Components of the national infrastructure also can be developed at the local level. Libraries would be at the core of the local information infrastructure. Libraries have a major role in educating those who don't have a college education and aren't curious. The role of libraries has expanded with the advent of new technologies, rather than contracted.

A Model for Analyzing the Information Infrastructure

The information infrastructure has exploded with the infusion of digital technologies into an existing infrastructure long dominated by the book publishing industry. With the invention of the printing press in the fifteenth century, the publishing industry was begun. The printing press enabled the duplication of the printed words in a volume impossible before that time. The work of Gutenberg caused a revolution in the production and distribution of knowledge. A similar revolution has occurred in the last five decades with advances in broadcasting and the last two decades with advances in computer technology.

First, let's examine the information infrastructure which developed to support the publishing industry; second, let's review the changes wrought by the broadcasting industry; finally, let's impose the newer technologies which are influencing a transformation of the publishing industry.

A model for examining the information infrastructure is the information transfer model (see Chapter 5), which can be used to define elements of the information infrastructure by addressing the following questions:

1. What are the patterns of information and knowledge creation?
2. What are the systems for recording new information?
3. What are the mechanisms for the mass production of information?
4. What varieties of systems are employed in the dissemination of information?
5. What systems for bibliographic control of the records are being produced in society?
6. What is the paradigmatic structure for the organization of information by subject fields?
7. What are the patterns of diffusion of knowledge?
8. How is information used in society?
9. What systems exist for the preservation of information?
10. How does public policy impact the information transfer process?

Each of these elements of information transfer will be discussed below and applied to the information infrastructure.

Patterns of Information or Knowledge Creation and Recording

As noted in Chapter 5, knowledge creation occurs through both conventional research processes and through less formal but usually structured processes, both of which require peer review before acceptance as social knowledge. With the advent of the Internet, less review is required before information or knowledge may be accepted as legitimate in some forms of publication.

Popular information and knowledge is created every day through the reporting of news. Radio and television stations, newspapers, magazines, and some Web site managers collect news, edit it, and record it for reading and broadcasting via network television or radio, publication, or Web site. Larger news organizations, e.g., *The New York Times*, NBC News, *60 Minutes*, *Newsweek*, and *Time* have rigorous processes for checking the accuracy of news stories, although those processes sometimes are questioned for their veracity. Reporters research a news event, interview eye witnesses and primary participants, and submit the stories for review by editors. There is a systematic, rigorous process for assuring the airing or publication of accurate, timely, unbiased information. However, one could argue that, over the last decade, bias and political views have seeped into supposedly unbiased reporting on the television and radio networks.

The system for reviewing information for packaging and distribution was established in large part by the book publishing industry. In this process, authors submit their manuscripts to a publishing company, which has staff editors who solicit manuscripts and review them. Publishers of nonfiction, especially publishers of scholarly works, routinely submit manuscripts to subject area experts for review. These experts determine if the knowledge contained in the publication is current and accurate; if research is presented, these experts determine if the results use recognized or conventional methods for producing the new knowledge. In the case of original research, has the dominant research paradigm been used and applied in a manner satisfactory to the mainstream of thought in that area? Are the results in keeping with conventional thinking in the field? One might argue that this process supports the "status quo"; however, the strength of this system is to screen new works for faulty research methods and unfounded generalizations.

The key component of this process is peer review, researchers and experts in the field of study reviewing the work of peers in the field.

A similar review process is conducted for scholarly publishing, beginning with funding of a research proposal. Researchers in all fields of academe must face the prospect of funding research from internal sources within the university, or by such external sources as government grants, foundations, professional societies, or partnerships with corporate agencies. The viability of a project is assessed by the potential funding agency, and few projects can be funded. When a project is funded and completed, more review is conducted when the results are recorded, reported, and submitted for publication. A review by peers determines if a research report is accepted for publication and dissemination by professional journals, many of which are now electronic.

Regardless of the format of a journal, paper or electronic, the peer review process by researchers in the field will determine which journals will publish results of a research project. This review process assesses the scope of the project, the importance of the project, the appropriateness of the research methods, the analysis of data, the relevance of the conclusions, and the general importance of the findings. The report may be submitted to the author(s) for revision before acceptance for publication. While this rather comprehensive review process assures the funding and publication and dissemination of relevant research, the process tends to promote conventional thinking and conventional application of research methods. Such review may stifle creative thinking and applications in new and different ways. Consequently, significant research may be refused by funding agencies and publishers before finding acceptance.

With the increasing cost of journal publication, smaller, specialized research journals have evolved into online publications published on the Internet by private publishers or by professional organizations or universities. Subscriptions may be charged, or publications may be offered free of charge. Nevertheless, information is available to a broad and interested audience, and the journal may be as respected as a paper publication if the rigor of the review process is maintained.

Similarly, monographs can be published on the Web sites of individuals, circumventing the review process. However, an increasing number of scholarly journals are converting to the electronic format, and new journals are being created online. The scholarly electronic journals use the same process as the paper journals, i.e., an editor coordinates the distribution of manuscripts to readers who critique the manuscript, and the editor (or an editorial board) makes decisions for publication based on the evaluation of knowledgeable reviewers. Typically, the evaluators do not know the identity of the author(s), and the author does not know the identity of the reviewers. To maintain the integrity of a scholarly publication, the peer review process is critical whether the journal or monograph format is paper or electronic.

Consequently, the information infrastructure for the creation of knowledge includes the people who collect information, e.g., newspaper, magazine, television, and radio reporters; researchers in universities, think tanks, and corporate research offices; editors of paper and electronic magazines, newspapers, professional and scholarly journals; and editors of television and radio news.

Mass Production of Information

As described above, scholarly research and publication tends to be recorded in electronic or printed journals. However, more popular knowledge can be recorded and mass produced in a variety of ways—newspapers, magazines, books (paperbacks can be issued days after an event), radio, television, and Internet versions.

Until the 1920s most new knowledge was disseminated through the print media—newspapers, magazines, journals, pamphlets, and books. During the 1920s radio was an innovation which found its way into many homes in the Western world. Radio enabled reporters to interview news makers and to distribute information widely. Then, as recording technology increased in quality, oral information could be recorded for later broadcast. Another medium for recording and distributing knowledge in the first half of the twentieth century was the news reel, which was shown before movies. Current world events were recorded, edited, and shown in movie theaters.

After World War II television, invented in the 1920s, found a market in American homes. While entertainment was the focus of early television, news and education programs were also popular and were often broadcast live. As the recording of audio and video was perfected with the invention of video tape, programs could be recorded and played back with a quality comparable to a live broadcast.

While broadcast radio and television revolutionized the recording and dissemination of information and knowledge, the Internet also revolutionized radio, television, newspaper, and journal publishing. Created as a communication network for researchers in the mid-1960s, the personal computer and wide band telephone and cable networks provided a confluence of technologies which supported an explosion of Internet utilization around the world.

During the 1990s the Internet invaded the communication industry, providing Internet users the capability of creating their own broadcast channel for journals, small newspapers, even books. Anyone with the know-how could create a Web site to promote her/his views on a favored topic. Gone was the elaborate review process of network television and radio, newspapers, journals, magazines, and the book trade. This network, the Internet, evolved through the creation of a complex network of telephone and cable lines, satellite transmission, and sophisticated computing capability.

The term "information infrastructure" is often used as a term to describe the Internet infrastructure and does not include the publishing, recording, and broadcast industries as part of the large and complex information infrastructure which is a prominent player in contemporary society and its economy. The information infrastructure includes, then, the press workers and supervisors; the television and radio staff behind the scenes who monitor and maintain the on-air programming; the writers who prepare scripts for the broadcasts; the on-air personnel who read the copy the provide the presence on the air; the producers and directors who plan and implement the programming schedules; and the sales and marketing staff who sell advertising time and market programs to the public.

Dissemination of Information

The publishing industry mass produces knowledge packages—books, journals, magazines, pamphlets. However, the dissemination or distribution system requires a vast network to move the publications from the publishers to the consumers. Corporate publishers distribute their products primarily through bookstores, news stands, and libraries. Marketing of books and magazines is itself a giant industry, which includes advertising in the media, appearance of authors on television and radio, newspaper interviews, and book reviews in popular and professional publications.

Government Publications

One of the most prolific publishers and disseminators of information is the U.S. government. The executive and legislative branches of government do countless studies and gather information to support bills which are proposed as laws. Countless hearings are held and studies commissioned as background for hearings on legislative matters. Agencies in the executive branch of government produce reports of their work. The U.S. government has its own publishing system, the United States Printing Service. Generally speaking, a "government document" is any publication that is printed at government expense and by the authority of a government agency, whether at the local, state, national, or international levels.

The U.S. government through its executive agencies publishes many government documents as part of its service to provide information to citizens. A description of the government publications system, the U.S. Government Printing Office can be found in such guides as Sears and Moody (2000), Morehead (1999), and Robinson (1998). The U.S. government disseminates its information through bookstores and through government depository libraries. As with commercially produced books, periodicals, and ephemeral material, the U.S. government, state, and local government materials are disseminated through school, public, academic, and special libraries and information centers.

During the 1990s as the Internet became more accessible to the public, and search mechanisms became more sophisticated and dependable, the U.S. government revamped its approach to government information by publishing information electronically through compact discs and online. Now online access is the quickest access point to government information through the U. S. Government Printing Office Web site (http://www.gpoaccess.gov/index.html).

Libraries

Major distribution centers are libraries of various types—public, school, college and university, and specialized. The library profession has developed a systematic process for the review of printed and electronic resources through such professional review journals as *The Booklist*, *Choice*, and other review publications. Private publishers have also joined in providing reviews with such journals as *Horn Book*, *Library Journal*, and many other specialized sources. With the volume of books published annually, no library can purchase all of the titles, and professional reviews are necessary in order for librarians to select, purchase, and make available those resources in various formats that will meet the needs of the library's clientele.

Since the development of public libraries during the first half of the nineteenth century, libraries have played an increasing role in the dissemination of information and knowledge to the general public, to school teachers and students, to college and university faculty and students, and to such specialized audiences as medical professionals, corporate agencies, and public agencies. As part of this dissemination process, libraries have developed systems for acquiring, organizing (cataloging), storing, retrieving, circulating, preserving, and discarding information resources. These processes will be discussed in detail in a later chapter.

The Broadcast Industry

Joining the publishing industry in the dissemination of information in the twentieth century were television and radio networks, cable television, and satellite transmission. Invented during the 1920s, television gained a wide audience during the economic boom that followed World War II. During the 1950s television networks were established, and the manufacture of affordable television receivers made possible the entertainment revolution which saw a rapid diffusion of television to more than 90 percent of the U.S. population by 1965, only 20 years after the conclusion of the Second World War.

Television was soon seen as a medium rich in the transmission of information as well as entertainment. News organizations formed for radio during the 1920s and 1930s quickly expanded to include television, and the news services which provided brief newscasts at movie theatres soon found a new audience in television. The availability of daily news programs via television competed with daily newspapers as a forum for the presentation and analysis of news events. While newspapers and news magazines were not rendered obsolete, their coverage of news was influenced by this new medium of television. Newspapers sought to provide the depth of coverage comprehensiveness of coverage that television and radio could not provide in a 30-minute or 60-minute daily format.

By the 1980s satellite transmission of news invaded the competitive news environment of television and radio. Cable News Network (CNN) entered the news competition in 1981, declaring 24-hour coverage of news with a worldwide network of reporters and transmission centers. Suddenly, the reporting of news was immediate; there was no longer a delay for the recording of news events for shipping to a network site in the U.S. for editing and transmission through a network. Reporters were able to report live and on-site as newsworthy events were occurring. The viewer was placed in the role of interpreting events as they occurred without the intermediary of a news reporter or editor.

The Internet

During the 1990s and into the twenty-first century, satellite transmission was joined by the Internet, electronic mail, and electronic books and periodicals to make vast changes in the traditional dissemination pattern for information packages of various kinds. As satellite transmission revolutionized broadcast news, so the Internet revolutionized the recording and dissemination of information and knowledge.

Suddenly the publishers of books, magazines, and newspapers were no longer the gateways to the publication and wide distribution of information packages. No longer were networks the filters and gateways to news via radio and television networks. The Internet enabled technologically savvy people to create Web sites and to make available to the world their writings and their views on any topic. The external editing and refining process was now at the discretion of the Web site creator. Everyone with the expertise to create a Web site was able to publish an electronic newspaper, magazine, journal, or book from their computer work-station. The communication channel between creator of information and the consumer was shortened dramatically. The authority, accuracy, and objectivity of the information were left to be judged by the consumer, without any required external influence.

As a result of satellite transmission and of wide implementation of the Internet, the consumer of information has a more active role in the evaluation and use of information. The consumer has a wide range of choices in selecting information sources, in assessing the value of those sources, and in the use of information found. Indeed, consumers can easily, if they desire, become creators of information through a Web site. Consumers have been liberated from the broadcast and publishing industries, if they desire to choose other formats as a source of information.

An example of Internet "democratization" or consumer control of idea dissemination is a "Wiki." A Hawaiian word for "quick," Wikis allow "open editing." Users can access and edit a Web page. For more information, see "What is Wiki" (http://www.wiki.org/wiki.cgi? WhatIsWiki Accessed 1/17/07). The result of open editing is a continuously changing, and sometimes biased and inaccurate, accounting of ideas and events, without the formal review process traditionally associated with the publishing of books and journals.

Bibliographic Control of Records

An important segment of the information infrastructure provides for the organization of the information produced. In librarianship, the organization of records is accomplished through bibliography and "bibliographic control."

(See also "Bibliographic Control" in Chapter 5, "Information Transfer in the Information Professions.") Several important publications, as well as libraries with national scope, contribute to bibliographic control efforts.

"Bibliographic Control" Defined

"Bibliography" has been defined by Theodore Besterman (1940) as ". . . a list of books arranged according to some permanent principle" (p. 2). This general definition applies to the two basic types of bibliography as summarized by Shoemaker (1967):

What is bibliography? Dozens of definitions reflect the various forms and emphases. Two major divisions are the study of books as physical objects (analytical bibliography) and the study of books as ideas (enumerative or systematic bibliography). Today these two divisions are concerned with other vehicles of ideas as well as books. Microfilms, motion pictures, tape recordings, phonograph records and other objects can be studied bibliographically (p. 4).

The term "bibliographic control" is the term sometimes used to express the ultimate goal of bibliographies—to have a record of all publications. Downs and Jenkins (1967) have addressed the impossibility of achieving bibliographic control:

> Perfect bibliographical control would imply a complete record of the existence and location of every book, every document, every article, even every written thought. The probabilities of ever reaching such a utopia are remote. (p. 1)

National Bibliographies

Bibliographies have long been a key factor in the information infrastructure. National bibliographies were created in the early twentieth century to provide a systematic record of books published in a country. After World War II, United Nations Economic, Scientific, and Cultural Organization (UNESCO) promoted national bibliographies for the new countries emerging with the disintegration of the British Empire. Although the United States has never had a comprehensive national bibliography, the *National Union Catalog* of the Library of Congress came close to being that record. The Library of Congress became the closest thing to a national library, and its cataloging of new publications has been as comprehensive as a bibliography could be in an expanding world of publishing during the twentieth and twenty-first centuries.

Private Sector Publishers

Participating in the effort to provide bibliographic control was the publishing industry. Among the leaders in this movement were R.R. Bowker, who published *Books in Print, the United States Catalog, Weekly Record,* and *Publishers' Weekly*. *Weekly Record* was part of *Publishers' Weekly*, the first attempt to provide a listing of books published weekly. H.W. Wilson began publishing *Cumulative Book Index* in 1900. In 1948 Wilson started publishing monthly cumulations in *Book Publishing Record* and its companion publications *Publishers Trade List Annual* and *Books in Print*. These publications were efforts to list accurate bibliographic information of new books published by "main line" publishers. Professional associations like the American Library Association published review sources which systematically engaged professionals in the review of books for consideration for purchase by libraries. Private publishers like R.R. Bowker Company also published respected book reviews like *Library Journal* and *School Library Journal*. Large public and university libraries created and sometimes published catalogs and bibliographies of books in a selected field of study. These efforts have been more common, and are discussed in the section which follows.

OCLC

As noted, the concept of "bibliographic control" was a goal considered unattainable by the 1960s. In the twenty-first century, it is even more unattainable. More feasible and more common among libraries and information agencies is the practice of providing bibliographies in subject fields. The important function of bibliographical control within the information infrastructure now is accomplished only by national libraries and agencies like the Online Computer Library Center (OCLC).

Founded in 1967, OCLC describes itself as "...a nonprofit, membership, computer library service and research organization dedicated to the public purposes of furthering access to the world's information and reducing information costs" (http://www.oclc.org). A worldwide organization, more than 50,000 libraries in approximately 100 countries and territories subscribe to OCLC services to locate, acquire, catalog, lend, and preserve library materials.

A major bibliography produced by OCLC is WorldCat, a worldwide union catalog created and maintained collectively by more than 9,000 member institutions, reputed to be the largest and most comprehensive database of its kind. Resources listed in WorldCat span much of recorded history and most forms of human expression, including electronic books, wax recordings, MP3s, DVDs, and Web sites (http://www.oclc.org/worldcat/default.htm, accessed May 29, 2006).

Library of Congress

The Library of Congress and British Library are other examples of gigantic national government-sponsored organizations which identify and catalog large segments of the book and nonprint media production of their respective nations.

The Library of Congress serves as the research arm of the United States Congress. It is also the largest library in the world, with more than 130 million items. The collections include more than 29 million books and other printed materials, 2.7 million recordings, 12 million photographs, 4.8 million maps, and 58 million manuscripts (http://www.loc.gov/about/, accessed 5/29/06).

The Library of Congress Online Catalog contains approximately 14 million records representing books, serials, computer files, manuscripts, cartographic materials, music, sound recordings, and visual materials. The Catalog also displays searching aids for users, such as cross-references and scope notes. The catalog records reside in a single integrated database; they are not separated according to type of material, language of material, date of cataloging, or processing/circulation status.

The Catalog includes Romanized records for Chinese, Japanese, and Korean language material cataloged since 1984, Hebrew and Yiddish cataloged since 1988, and Arabic and Persian cataloged since 1991. These catalog records appear in the Library of Congress Online Catalog in the Roman alphabet and with English language subject headings. (http://catalog.loc.gov/help/contents.htm, accessed May 29, 2006)

As the volume of publications increased, many university and large public libraries still attempt to collect virtually all titles in a field. Although the Library of Congress and some of the Association of Research Libraries (ARL) have appropriately defined their mission to collect virtually all American publications, most other libraries should be dedicated to a particular audience, and subject bibliography should be the foundation for collection development.

British Library

The British Library was founded in 1972 when the British Library Act was passed by Parliament (http://www.bl.uk/about/history.html). Under this Act, the several institutions were administratively combined to form the British Library: the library departments of the British Museum, the National Central Library, and the National Lending Library for Science and Technology. In 1974 the British National Bibliography and the Office for Scientific and Technical Information joined the United Kingdom's (UK) new national library. Two additional institutions subsequently became part of the Library increasing the breadth of its collections: the India Office Library and Records (1982) and the British Institute of Recorded Sound (1983).

The best known component was the library departments of the British Museum. The Museum's Department of Printed Books was founded in 1753, the year of the foundation of the Museum itself. Over the intervening 200 years, the library of the British Museum had grown into one of the largest in the world, sustained by its privilege of legal deposit whereby it was entitled to a copy of most items printed in the United Kingdom, books, periodicals, newspapers, maps, and printed music. A product of this collection policy is the national bibliography, which records the publishing activity of the United Kingdom and the Republic of Ireland. Included are printed publications and, more recently, electronic resources.

New books and serials have been recorded in the British National Bibliography (BNB) since 1950. The BNB is the single most comprehensive listing of UK titles. UK and Irish publishers are obliged by law to send a copy of all new publications, including serial titles, to the British Library.

The Library of Congress and British Library are two examples of national libraries that attempt to maintain bibliographic control of the intellectual production of their respective countries. Examples of other national libraries are Bibliotheque Nationale (France), Det kongelige bibliotek (Denmark), National Library of China, Die Deutsche Bibliothek (Germany), National Diet Library (Japan), and the National Library of Australia.

Subject Bibliographies

Let us turn away from the impossible goal of bibliographic control to examine the process engendered by systematic or subject bibliography, the listing of items by topic for the convenience of the user. Originally, bibliography was descriptive and it evolved into subject bibliography in the latter part of the nineteenth century when subject headings were added to indexes. Subject bibliography was, and is, intended to provide the best material, or most appropriate for a particular audience. As noted above, bibliographers initially were concerned with the identification and description of books, and the concept has been extended to include other media as well. One occasionally encounters the term "mediagraphy" for a bibliography of videos, sound recordings, or other media. More recently, the term "webography" is sometimes used for a listing of Web addresses for the use of an information consumer seeking a certain type of information. Web masters often provide a series of links to related topics on a Web site, another example of the bibliography used for a new medium of information storage.

Subject bibliographies are customized to an audience. Entries are selected with the user in mind, and bibliographic terms reflect the special language (jargon) of the expected users. Search engines are not dealing with context. Unless information professionals do the research to determine audience needs, technology drives the results of a search, and the searcher must weed out pertinent results. The implication for libraries is the more urgent need for value-added service; search engines may produce 100,000 hits on one term, and clients are unable to sort through that much information. The information professional should be able to refine the search, and that can be done only after a diagnosis of need is completed.

As our society moved beyond the collection of books and journals into the technology-based information stage, the concepts of subject bibliography have become more relevant because information consumers are searching for specific topics and concepts, not books or periodical articles. Google, Yahoo, and other search engines are using the framework for subject bibliographies in their systems. The evolution of subject bibliography is straightforward and applies directly to the development of libraries, indexes, and abstracting services.

Google is doing the same thing that has been driving the library and information field since it was founded, applying a new technology to the tasks of the profession. Unfortunately, most current search engines and automated indexing systems have ignored the descriptive bibliography framework for usable standardizing techniques which provides guidelines developed by librarians and familiar to many in the general public and useful in effective information retrieval.

Given the extraordinary potential of automated indexing and searching technologies, and with the ability to diagnose information needs through the work of educated professionals, we should be able to attain the expectations of a classic writer on bibliographies, Verner Clapp (1951, 17), who wrote that a bibliography should:

- Assemble all the material relevant to the subject of the search.

- Provide comprehensive coverage to the extent that comprehensive coverage is needed, yet permit selectiveness where that is required.

- "Leap over barriers of nationality, language and alphabet."

- Reconcile the differences in points of view on a subject found in more than one discipline, "often manifested merely in differences of terminology."

- When needed evaluate, characterize, or criticize the sources of information which it lists in order to narrow down the search or to produce a synthesis or provide a synopsis.

- Signal new contributions to learning, calling them to the attention of workers in other fields where these contributions might be employed, adapted, or developed.

- Be organized to "present to the inquirer the minimum of delay and difficulty, either in the choice of bibliographical services to be used in the search for particular kinds of information at particular levels of analysis, in the prosecution of his search, or in redundant searching in needlessly multiplied and overlapping services." In other words, keep the user in mind, and try to make her/his work easy.

Clapp's last point is perhaps most important: In preparing any kind of bibliography, keep the information user at the forefront and determine his/her needs!

Organization of Information and Knowledge

General Organization

Librarians have provided leadership in the organization of knowledge and information. Melvil Dewey led the way with his Dewey Decimal Classification System (DDC), which is used in schools and many public libraries. Large public libraries, college and university, and some special libraries use the Library of Congress (LC) system for classifying or organizing collections.

Before discussing Dewey and LC, it is helpful to be clear on two terms: "classification" and "notation," which are defined below:

- "Classification" provides a system for organizing knowledge. Classification may be used to organize knowledge represented in any form, e.g., books, documents, electronic resources.

- "Notation" is the system of symbols used to represent the classes in a classification system. In the Dewey Decimal Classification, the notation is expressed in Arabic numerals. The notation gives both the unique meaning of the class and its relation to other classes. The notation provides a universal language to identify the class and related classes, regardless of the fact that different words or languages may be used to describe the class. (Introduction to Dewey Decimal Classification, www.oclc.org/dewey, p. 1)

Dewey Decimal Classification System (DDCS)

Created by Melvil Dewey and first published in 1876, the DDC is a general knowledge organization tool published in print and electronic versions by OCLC. DDC has been translated into more than thirty languages.

The DDC basic classes are organized by disciplines or fields of study. Ten main classes or divisions together encompass the entire world of knowledge. Each main class is further divided into ten divisions, and each division into ten sections (not all the numbers for the divisions and sections have been used).

The ten main classes are:

- 000 Computers, information & general reference
- 100 Philosophy & psychology

- 200 Religion
- 300 Social sciences
- 400 Language
- 500 Science
- 600 Technology
- 700 Arts & recreation
- 800 Literature
- 900 History & geography

Class 000 is the most general class, and is used for works not limited to any one specific discipline, e.g., encyclopedias, newspapers, general periodicals. This class is also used for certain specialized disciplines that deal with knowledge and information, e.g., computer science, library and information science, journalism.

Each of the other main classes (100–900) comprises a major discipline or group of related disciplines.

Class 100 covers philosophy, paranormal phenomena, and psychology.

Class 200 is devoted to religion. Both philosophy and religion deal with the ultimate nature of existence and relationships, but religion treats these topics within the context of revelation, deity, and worship.

Class 300 covers the social sciences, including sociology, anthropology, statistics, political science, economics, law, public administration, social problems and services, education, commerce, communications, transportation, and customs.

Class 400 comprises language, linguistics, and specific languages. Literature, which is arranged by language, is found in 800.

Class 500 is devoted to the natural sciences and mathematics. The natural sciences (500) describe and attempt to explain the world in which we live.

Class 600 is technology. Technology consists of utilizing the sciences to harness the natural world and its resources for the benefits of humankind.

Class 700 covers the arts: art in general, fine and decorative arts, music, and the performing arts. Recreation, including sports and games, is also classed in 700.

Class 800 covers literature, and includes rhetoric, prose, poetry, drama, etc. Folk literature is classed with customs in 300.

Class 900 is devoted to history and geography. A history of a specific subject is classed with the subject.

Since the DDC is arranged by discipline, a subject may appear in more than one class or discipline. For example, "clothing" has aspects that fall under several disciplines. The psychological influence of clothing belongs in 155.95 as part of the discipline of psychology; customs associated with clothing belong in 391 as part of the discipline of customs.

Arabic numerals are used to represent each class or division in the DDC. The first digit in each three-digit number represents the main class, as displayed above. For example, 500 represents science. The second digit in each three-digit number indicates the division. For example, 500 represents general works in the sciences, 510 is mathematics, 520 is astronomy, and 530 is physics. The third digit in each three-digit number indicates the section. 531 is used for classical mechanics, 532 for fluid mechanics, and 533 for gas mechanics. The DDC uses the convention that no number should have fewer than three digits; zeros are used to fill out numbers.

A decimal point, or dot, follows the third digit in a class number. To the right of the dot the classification continues to the degree of classification needed to classify an item. For example, the following example demonstrates a hierarchy from the applied sciences general heading (600) to a specific category of animal husbandry, cats and dogs:

- 600 Technology (Applied sciences)
- 630 Agriculture and related technologies
- 636 Animal husbandry
- 636.7 Dogs
- 636.8 Cats

Now in its twenty-second unabridged edition, published in 2003, the Dewey Decimal Classification system is revised frequently to reflect changes to the body of human knowledge. The DDC has proven to be a relatively easy system for library users to understand and use. A problem rests with the constraint of ten categories for all knowledge. With the explosion of knowledge, especially in the sciences and technology, the system can expand to accommodate these changes, but the expansion is accompanied by extremely long numbers. A system better designed to accommodate the growth of knowledge and the classification of specialized areas of knowledge is the Library of Congress system, which has been adopted by larger universities and special libraries.

Library of Congress System

The Library of Congress (LC) Classification System, like the DDC, assigns letters and numbers to subjects. The LC system has 26 classes, compared to 10 in the DDC. Capital letters designate classes, which are subdivided by two capital letters and numbers, which can be expanded using decimals. Using a combination of letters, numbers, and decimals, LC allows for the assignment of precise classification of subjects. Because of its expansiveness, LC is much preferred for large and/or specialized collections of materials.

The major classes in LC follow:

A – General Works
B – Philosophy. Psychology. Religion
C – Auxiliary Sciences of History
D – History (General) and History of Europe
E – History: America
F – History: America
G – Geography. Anthropology. Recreation
H – Social Sciences
J – Political Science
K – Law
L – Education

M – Music and Books on Music

N – Fine Arts

P – Language and Literature

Q – Science

R – Medicine

S – Agriculture

T – Technology

U – Military Science

V – Naval Science

Z – Bibliography. Library Science. Information Resources (General)

As with the Dewey classification system, LC is divided into subclasses. The technology class, T, is divided as follows:

Subclass T   Technology (General)

Subclass TA Engineering (General). Civil engineering

Subclass TC Hydraulic engineering. Ocean engineering

Subclass TD Environmental technology. Sanitary engineering

Subclass TE Highway engineering. Roads and pavements

Subclass TF Railroad engineering and operation

Subclass TG Bridge engineering

Subclass TH Building construction

Subclass TJ Mechanical engineering and machinery

Subclass TK Electrical engineering. Electronics. Nuclear engineering

Subclass TL Motor vehicles. Aeronautics. Astronautics

Subclass TN Mining engineering. Metallurgy

Subclass TP Chemical technology

Subclass TR Photography

Subclass TS Manufactures

Subclass TT Handicrafts. Arts and crafts

Subclass TX Home economics

Each subclass is further divided. An example is subclass TR, photography, shown below:

Subclass TR

TR1-1050   Photography

TR250-265 Cameras

TR287-500 Photographic processing. Darkroom technique

TR504-508 Transparencies. Diapositives

TR510-545 Color photography

TR550-581 Studio and laboratory

TR590-620 Lighting

TR624-835 Applied photography. Including artistic, commercial, medical photography, photocopying processes

TR845-899   Cinematography. Motion pictures

TR925-1050 Photomechanical processes

The Library of Congress Classification System has proven to be a versatile, expandable, and easily understandable system which can be applied to both large and small libraries and collections, including highly specialized collections.

Creative Cataloging Systems

The Dewey Decimal Classification System and Library of Congress System are the two most frequently used classification systems in the world. However, they are general standardized systems. The advantage is that a person can go from one library in Illinois to another in California, and one of those systems probably will be used. In fact, the systems are used worldwide.

The strengths of these systems, their general applicability and their universality, are also their weaknesses. For small, specialized collections, neither of these systems may be appropriate. For example, a church library would have most resources in the 200s. A law library using LC would have most items KF. Why shouldn't a small, specialized collection develop a unique system which fits the needs of its clientele by creating special subject headings and an alphanumeric cataloging system which makes sense to the users? If the library is proprietary and won't be part of a network which exchanges resources via interlibrary loan, a special, customized system may be very appropriate.

An example is an information center developed and used by the authors for a client in the health field. We developed a classification scheme based on the organization's activities and needs, using its vocabulary. The organization funded project proposals in six areas, and those areas became the focal point for the classification system. A seventh general category was added. The seven classes were:

1. General grant making—knowledge a grant maker must have

2. Primary care

3. Health promotion

4. Disease prevention

5. Health data

6. Public health

7. Rural health

The system was flexible enough to accommodate changes which occurred as the project funding changed. Topics like "history of the organization" were added as needed. Each information package (book, journal, CD, video, etc.) was given a number. For example, a compact disc on general grant making might be assigned a distinctive number as follows:

1   =   General grant making

CD   =   Nonprint format designation

2006   =   Year of acquisition

025   =   Accession number

T   =   An alphabetic character which is the first word of the title, "Trends"

If a periodical is processed, the volume and issue number is included. Videos and nonprint items have a format designation after the initial class number. This customized classification system enabled distinctive numbers for the same title in different formats. Clients found the system easy to use, the key test for any information classification system.

Cataloging Electronic Resources

Michael Gorman (2003) has pointed out the irony which the library and information community faces with the technological advances which have affected the organization, storage, and retrieval of information:

> The great irony of our present situation is that we have reached near-perfection in the bibliographic control of "traditional" library materials at the same time that the advent of electronic resources is seen by some as threatening the very existence of library services, including bibliographic control. (pp. 82–83)

"Metadata" are the data associated with electronic records as they are created. Metadata is the unseen record of a document's creation—date, time, and general description of the document. A current issue in the library and information profession is how this information can be used to gain bibliographic control of electronic information resources. This issue is discussed in more depth in Chapter 10.

Organization by Subject

Bibliography by subject field is a much more feasible way of gaining control of a subject field's output of new knowledge. Libraries of all sizes and types frequently produce bibliographies on subjects to meet the needs of their clientele. Public libraries may produce bibliographies on subjects such as child care, how to quit smoking, or preparing for retirement. College and university libraries may produce bibliographies on conducting research in a subject field. School libraries may prepare bibliographies to help students complete class assignments, e.g., drug abuse, the American Civil War, or writing a research paper.

More complicated and comprehensive subject bibliographies exist in nearly every discipline and profession. For example, in the library and information field, H.W. Wilson's *Library Literature* has been a standard source for many years. In other disciplines, professional organizations have produced significant bibliographies for scholars and professionals in their fields. Examples include the Modern Language Association's *MLA International Bibliography of Books and Articles on the Modern Languages and Literatures* (usually referred to as the "MLA Bibliography"), American Psychological Association's *Psychological Abstracts*, and American Chemical Society's *Chemical Abstracts.*

Other scholarly and professional organizations produce reputable indexes and bibliographies which serve to provide bibliographic control of their subject fields for the benefit of scholars, students, and practicing professionals. The National Science Foundation and other government agencies have subsidized some of these bibliographies, demonstrating the government's intent to maintain subject bibliographies as important elements in the nation's information infrastructure. Government-sponsored subject bibliographies include *Agricultural Index* and *Index Medicus*. Private publishers have produced two leading subject bibliographies in the legal field, *Lexis/Nexis* and *Westlaw*.

Once published only in paper format, nearly all such subject area bibliographies provide access to subject areas through online databases. Such electronic resources are more current than paper indexes and more accessible to the public.

Patterns for Diffusion of Knowledge

While "dissemination" of knowledge, discussed above, refers to spreading knowledge and making it *accessible* to an audience, "diffusion" refers to the transfer of knowledge from one individual or group to another individual or group (see also Chapter 5, "Information Transfer in the Information Professions"). The following definition is found in Chapter 2:

"Diffusion" is the transmission of knowledge from one individual or group to another individual or group in such a way that the recipients absorb or transfer the knowledge into personal action. Learning must occur for diffusion to be successful. Schools and colleges are social institutions which are part of the knowledge infrastructure designed by society to diffuse knowledge from one generation to another.

Information and knowledge that is diffused is learned. It is perceived by an individual or group as beneficial and accepted as part of their store of knowledge. The diffusion process usually is taught in a formal setting—a school, college, church, organization, or other social agency. These agencies are part of the information infrastructure.

The American school system is an example of a social agency responsible for the diffusion of knowledge in American society. The purpose of the schools is to inculcate American youth in the culture of American society so that they will become productive members of society. Taught in schools are the values, history, literature, and basic knowledge generally considered essential for a productive citizenry. In recent years, that body of knowledge has been expanded to include technology skills as well as the language arts, family and consumer science, music, history, math, science, business education, foreign languages, physical education, social studies (including psychology, sociology, and geography), and technology education.

Some of the subjects in public schools have changed little over time, e.g., mathematics, history, literature, music, foreign languages. Others have evolved considerably. For example, "technology education" has replaced "vocational education" and expanded to include such topics as computer applications, desktop publishing, computer assisted drafting and design, video broadcasting, and even robotics and an introduction to engineering at the high school level.

Similarly, groups within the larger national society, subsocieties, likewise provide for the diffusion of knowledge peculiar to the group. Each subsociety which is responsible for new knowledge in a field, e.g., a profession, a discipline, a religion, a service organization, has formal and informal means of diffusing that knowledge. For example, religious denominations have

Sunday schools, seminaries, and parochial schools to teach the doctrine of that denomination, with supporting literature and learning resources. Service organizations and hobby groups likewise provide education into the history and values of their groups, although the education is informal and often casual.

In the library and information field, undergraduate programs in library and information science teach basic knowledge for people entering the job market in information provision. Professional degrees at the master's level are accredited by the American Library Association; there are approximately fifty-six such schools in North America. Doctoral programs prepare researchers in library and information science, and about twenty-five such doctoral programs exist in North America.

Library service should have a goal of supporting knowledge diffusion. In other words, libraries are a vital part of the information infrastructure, and the role of library and information professionals is to facilitate both the dissemination and diffusion of knowledge. In the dissemination process, information professionals maintain collections of resources. In the diffusion process, information professionals work with individuals and groups to help them learn by providing guidance and information skills instruction. For example, cataloging books is a dissemination service. Reference service or information skills instruction are examples of diffusion of knowledge in library and information service. Essential to creating and offering effective educational services is an understanding of learning theory and educational methods. A trend in the profession has been the evolving role of the librarian and information professional to engage with the client in supporting learning through the use of information resources. This educational function is a central function of librarians in schools, colleges, and universities.

In summary, the diffusion of knowledge includes the teaching of accepted knowledge in formal institutions, including public and private schools, colleges, universities, and other agencies which are part of the information infrastructure. Diffusion of knowledge results in knowledge usage for some purpose—a manifestation that this knowledge has become part of the individual's or group's knowledge base. Library and information professionals can facilitate the diffusion process by customizing services to address the needs of clientele. However, knowledge is inert unless it is applied or put to use, the next stage of the information transfer cycle.

Information Utilization in Society

Information use is possible only after information or knowledge has been diffused—learned by the information client, as described in the previous section. Contemporary Western society has been called an "information age" or a "knowledge society." After a brief discussion of the link between diffusion of information and information use, we'll return to the importance of information use in today's society.

The Link between Diffusion and Information Use

It is generally agreed by learning theorists that learning results in changed behavior. In other words, we may say that we've learned to use a new software program. That new knowledge can be demonstrated by successfully using new features of a word processing program. For example, you may wish to use the index feature of your word processing software. You read the documentation that accompanies the software and read carefully the "help" information provided. When you have comprehended this information, you are able to use that new knowledge to construct an index. Therefore, we can say that "information use" is the application of knowledge to problems or issues in our world.

Similarly, learning new attitudes can be demonstrated by changed behavior. A person who claims to have learned to appreciate classical music will demonstrate that learning by freely choosing to listen to Bach or Mozart instead of country music or the "classic" rock 'n' roll of Elvis Presley or the Beatles. Learning means that people change their behavior to achieve something.

Information use contributes to the evolution of progress in science, the social sciences, humanities, and the arts. Almost any endeavor is a consequence of information use. In the Middle Ages knowledge wasn't used, and the result was maintenance of the status quo. Progress of a society is the result of applied new knowledge. In the United States, new inventions are often readily adopted by Americans when the public sees the benefits of use. Television was diffused in approximately two decades, a very rapid diffusion of an innovation. Accepting an innovation requires new knowledge, and library and information professionals provide a vital service in the facilitation of learning. Again, libraries are an important element of the information infrastructure.

Information Use in a Knowledge Society

In our everyday manner of speaking, "information" and "knowledge" are used interchangeably. In this discussion, we'll distinguish the differences. In our daily lives we are bombarded with information from the time we wake up to the time we fall asleep at night:

- We may awaken to a radio alarm which is playing music or perhaps the news.

- The television or radio may be on in the background as we brush our teeth, have breakfast, get dressed, and prepare for the day.

- Our car radio may be tuned to the news as we drive to our work, or we hear a five-minute news summary interspersed with our favorite music station.

- Our favorite newspapers may be book marked on our Internet browser, and we may receive regular postings of news, stock reports, sporting events, and weather "narrow cast"—delivered—to our computer workstation.

- We subscribe to paper newspapers, journals, magazines, and music CD clubs which are delivered to our homes.

- For entertainment we purchase DVDs (digital video discs) CDs with our favorite movies and recording artists to plan on our car and home audio and video entertainment centers.

- Our television feed from cable or satellite provides offers us scores, or perhaps hundreds, of channels providing more news, sports, entertainment, educational, and hobby information than we can digest or use.

As John Naisbitt declared in his landmark 1982 book *Megatrends*, "We are drowning in information, starved for knowledge" (p. 24). From the information we are bombarded with via the broadcast media, the Internet, print publications, and from our colleagues, we must select the knowledge that we need to lead happy, productive lives.

Information professionals are educated to know the sources of information, the "keys" or indexes and catalogs that enable us to identify sources of information. We know the sources of reviews of new media, and we know how to evaluate various packages of information—books, journals, and Web sites. We can help clientele who may feel overwhelmed with the information they receive daily to sort through the morass and to develop strategies for making the task manageable in their lives. We can help people to use information effectively in their work and in their leisure.

Preservation of Information

Information packages, like most commodities, must be preserved, or they decay and must be destroyed. Why is preservation an important issue, and what should be preserved? Randy Silverman, preservation librarian at the University of Utah was asked those questions for another publication (Fowler 2005, 88–93).

We should be concerned with preserving records of an agency for these reasons:

- As a part of American culture, companies and institutions of all types play a role in their community, state, and nation. The long-term memory of the agency enables us to understand achievements of the organization within the context of history.

- Historical records are part of the institution's heritage. As Silverman notes, "Sometimes there is a fear that records retention for the corporate memory will mean there is a documentation of failures, too. But you have to have a sense of how you've grown and how you got there. You don't have to publish failures but you should keep it for the company's use." (Fowler, p. 89)

- Fiscal and legal mandates require retention of some records for periods of time, e.g., audits and tax records.

Because the archival function is inherent in the role of any information agency, an information professional has a responsibility for preserving those documents (regardless of format) which have historical value for the agency's clientele.

The preservation problem for books and journals is summarized succinctly by Teper (2005):

While they are an excellent long-term vehicle for conveying information, one of the great ironies of print collections is that the vast majority of them are composed of organic materials. In other words, the media that carry the bulk of the information in our collections are subject to a natural process of decay. While some adhesives are now plastic-based, many binders continue employing animal-based adhesives, especially in less technologically advanced countries. Pages and boards continue to be primarily wood products, and most of the papers used in the non-Western world still contain high levels of unpurified wood pulp—the root of the brittle books crisis. When bound in a sewn fashion, the thread in most sewn volumes is composed of natural fibers. All these materials decay.

Preservation of paper products requires a study of the different kinds of paper, their chemical properties, and the ways that books, magazines, photographs, papers, and other original documents can be placed in acid-free bindings and stored in facilities where temperature and humidity are controlled. While this type of preservation has been studied, and techniques have been developed, the same is not true for digital information. Technologies change, and the capacity to decode stored information is very challenging.

The availability of electronic information is today taken for granted. With the rapid growth of the Internet and the World Wide Web, millions of people have grown accustomed to using these tools as resources to acquire information. Digital information is rapidly becoming a principal medium to create, distribute, and store content, including text, motion pictures, and recorded sound. Increasingly, digital content embodies much of the nation's intellectual, social, and cultural history. The Library of Congress has taken a leading role in a national effort to archive and preserve digital information. In 2000, Congress appropriated $100 million for a national digital-strategy effort, led by the Library of Congress. The Library of Congress was chosen because of its mission to "sustain and preserve a universal collection of knowledge and creativity for future generations." The Library of Congress Digital Preservation Program focuses on policy, standards, and technical components necessary to preserve digital content. The intent is to present recommendations to the U.S. Congress regarding the most viable options for long-term preservation (http://www.digitalpreservation.gov).

In conclusion, the preservation of information packages is very much a part of the information transfer process, and information professionals play a role in determining which information sources should be preserved, the techniques for preservation, and the proper application of those techniques.

A Model for the Technology and Information Infrastructure

Earlier in this chapter we proffered a definition of "information infrastructure":

> The information infrastructure is a national network of people, organizations, agencies, policies, and technologies organized in a loosely coordinated system to enhance the creation, production, dissemination, organization, storage, retrieval, and preservation of information for the people. The primary objective of this network is the diffusion of knowledge for a society.

Based on that definition and the analysis of the information infrastructure, and using the information transfer model as a framework, we offer the model in Table 7.2 to facilitate the study and analysis of the information infrastructure.

Table 7.2 An Information Infrastructure Model

Information Stage	Organizations	Professions	Occupations
Knowledge creation and recording (research)	Universities Think tanks News organizations Corporate researchers Government agencies	Professors Scientists Journalists Information professionals Web masters	Support staff
Mass production	Book publishers Research journals Newspapers TV and radio stations Web sites Media producers	Editors Publishers TV & radio producers & staff Web masters Electronic publishers	Press workers TV & radio staff Technicians
Dissemination	Professional organizations Libraries Book stores Government bookstores and Web sites TV and radio stations	Administrators Librarians Reviewers Book store staff Web masters TV & radio producers & on-air staff	TV & radio staff Sales staff Marketing staff
Bibliographic control	Libraries Bibliography publishers Webographies	Librarians Publishers Editors Web masters	Library technicians Editorial assistants
Organization by subject field	Libraries Professional organizations Publishing companies Government agencies	Librarians Indexers Subject specialists	Library technicians Information technicians Editorial assistants
Diffusion of knowledge	Schools Colleges and universities Churches Private enterprise Libraries Social organizations	Faculty Clergy Managers Librarians Information professionals	Teaching aides Library technicians Staff Members of organizations
Information use	All organizations	All members of professions	All staff in organizations led by professionals
Preservation of information	Libraries Archives Museums	Librarians Archivists Curators	Technicians Museum, library, & archives staff

Role of Information Professionals

What are the roles of the information professionals in this infrastructure? Professionals with a Master of Library Science Degree (or its equivalent) can appropriately create, organize, and manage any of the agencies that are in the information infrastructure. The development and articulation of this information infrastructure is the intellectual contribution that the information professions should be making to academia. Currently the information infrastructure is limited to discussions of the Internet—so narrow that it's like the discussions of bibliographic control, which deteriorated into storage and retrieval issues. When the discussion conceptualizes the issue to only a fragment of the whole, much is lost.

The information transfer model enables library and information professionals to think of ways they can become actively involved in the information transfer process. It is a way of thinking about the library and information profession.

Each of the categories of the information transfer model is listed below with suggestions for an information professional's involvement.

- Knowledge creation and recording—Information professionals can assist researchers by (1) helping them to identify keys to the research literature in the field—indexes, bibliographies, catalogs, and leading researchers; (2) If the researcher is engaging in interdisciplinary research, the information professional can help identify special or subject area encyclopedias or textbooks which provide an overview of the field of study.

- Mass production of information—Information professionals can provide leadership in the work that is done in the publishing, broadcasting, and Web mastery fields.

- Dissemination of information—Information professionals traditionally have excelled in this portion of the information transfer process by acquiring, organizing, and circulating information and knowledge, primarily as periodicals and books. With the many formats available today, the role of information professionals likewise has expanded to include expertise in the newer media for disseminating information, including the Internet.

- Bibliographic control—librarians are heavily engaged in the cataloging and classification of knowledge and information. Organization of books, periodicals, videos, compact discs, and various forms of computer-stored information, is a vital role of information professionals. This organization includes the application of special vocabularies and unique organizational schemes for subject fields.

- Diffusion of knowledge—Librarians throughout the history of the profession have assisted clients who were engaged in learning. The role of librarians in public libraries, schools, universities, colleges is more important than ever because of the growing number of people returning for continuing education, to "retool" for a new occupation, to learn at a distance. The role of the librarian is to help the learner to locate appropriate resources and, through knowledge of the information transfer process, to help clients understand the information they are encountering.

- Information use—As noted in the model above, all information professionals should be engaged in helping individuals and groups to use information effectively, a result of effectively diffusing information and knowledge. Contemporary society requires that people stay current in their use of information.

- Preservation of information—All information agencies and information professionals should be engaged in the evaluation of information and preservation of that information which has lasting value for the organization and clientele of that organization. Information professionals must be aware of the information needs of clientele now—and in the future.

Summary

The information infrastructure consists of the personnel, technology, policies, organizations, agencies, and processes which underlie the information transfer process in society. The term "infrastructure" is used purposefully to encompass the cohesiveness of the information support system.

The information infrastructure is a critical aspect of society, both as an intellectual area for research and study and as an operational area. The information infrastructure is like the body's vascular network—the information infrastructure is like the system of veins and arteries, and information is the blood. An aneurysm can disrupt the whole body the way a failure of a component of the information infrastructure can disrupt the whole information network in society. Understanding the information infrastructure is a crucial, fundamental foundation for study in the information professions, yet it is doubtful that information professionals have seen the responsibility to develop the infrastructure.

As late as the 1950s, the goal of librarians was to be "bookmen" and women—a preoccupation with the acquisition, storage, organization, and dissemination of books. In the 1960s the information profession sought to include other media—films, audio recordings, and other forms of instructional materials. Some schools which prepare librarians changed the name of the school to "Library Services" but did not focus on the receiver of information. Development of the Internet has furthered the advancement of the information infrastructure and the role of library and information professionals. It's no longer reasonable for anyone to assume that librarianship is concerned solely with information packages and with technology. Information management implies working with people to promote and enhance the vast information infrastructure.

References

Besterman, Theodore. 1940. *The beginnings of systematic bibliography*. 2nd edition, revised. New York: Burt Franklin.

Clapp, Verner W. 1951. "The role of bibliographic organization in contemporary civilization." In *Bibliographic organization; papers presented before the fifteenth annual conference of the Graduate Library School July 24–29, 1950*, ed. Jesse H. Shera and Margaret E. Egan, 3–23. Chicago: The University of Chicago Press.

Downs, Robert B. and Frances B. Jenkins. 1967. "Introduction." In *Bibliography: Current state and future trends* (Illinois Contributions to Librarianship, no. 8), 1–3. Urbana: University of Illinois Press.

Fowler, Susan G. 2005. *Information entrepreneurship; information services based on the information lifecycle*. Lanham, MD: Scarecrow Press.

Gorman, Michael. 2003. *The enduring library: Technology, tradition, and the quest for balance*. Chicago, IL: American Library Association.

Introduction to Dewey Decimal Classification. http://www.oclc.org/dewey (accessed January 31, 2007).

Library of Congress. Digital Preservation. Available at http://www.digitalpreservation.gov (accessed July 8, 2007).

McLoughlin, Glen J. 2001. "The national information infrastructure: The federal role." In *internet policies and issues*, Vol. 3, ed. B. G. Kutais. Huntington, New York: Nova Science Publishers.

Morehead, Joe. 1999. *Introduction to United States government information sources.* 6th ed. Englewood, CO: Libraries Unlimited.

Naisbitt, John. 1982. *Megatrends: Ten new directions transforming our lives.* New York: Warner Books.

OCLC (Online Computer Library Center). http://www.oclc.org (accessed January 31, 2007).

Robinson, Judith Schiek 1998. *Tapping the government grapevine: The user-friendly guide to U.S. government information sources.* 3rd ed. Phoenix, AZ: Oryx Press.

Sears, Jean L. and Marilyn K. Moody. 2000. *Using government information sources: Electronic and print.* 3rd ed. Phoenix, AZ: Oryx Press.

Shoemaker, Richard H. 1967. "Bibliography (General)." In *Bibliography: Current state and future trends* (Illinois Contributions to Librarianship, no. 8), ed. Robert B. Downs and Frances B. Jenkins, 4–10. Urbana: University of Illinois Press.

Teper, Thomas H. 2005. Current and emerging challenges for the future of library and archival preservation. *Library Resources & Technical Services* 49: 32–39.

The British Library. http://www.bl.uk/about/history.html (accessed June 3, 2006).

The National Information Infrastructure Agenda for Action Executive Summary. http://www.ibiblio.org/nii/NII-Executive-Summary.html (accessed January 17, 2007).

Transportation. *World Book Online Reference Center.* 2005. World Book, Inc.5 Jan. 2005. http://www.worldbookonline.com/wb/Article?id=ar564680.

Transportation. 2006. In *Encyclopædia Britannica.* Retrieved June 23, 2006, from Encyclopædia Britannica Premium Service: http://www.britannica.com/eb/article?tocId=9113701.

U. S. Government Printing Office Web site. http://www.gpoaccess.gov/index.html.

What is Wiki. http://www.wiki.org/wiki.cgi?WhatIsWiki (accessed January 17, 2007).

8

The Processes and Functions of Information Professionals

Chapter Overview

The purpose of this book is to explain the role of information professionals in today's society—what they do and why they do things as well as *how* they do things. First, the information professional must pay close attention to the needs and interests of the information user. This is the focus of our philosophy in this book. With that focus in mind, we identified in Chapter 1 and described in Chapter 4 the four features common to practice in the information profession:

- The information professional works with individuals, who have unique information requirements and a unique style for finding and using information. We refer to this study as "information psychology."

- The information professional works with groups of individuals and these groups have definable and unique information needs and patterns for use. We have given this study the designation "sociology of information."

- The information professional manages an organization comprised of staff, budget, and facilities. We call this "information organization management."

- The information professional organizes and maintains an information storage and retrieval system to meet the needs of the organization's clientele. For this function, we use the term "information engineering."

This chapter concentrates on two of these areas—information engineering and information organization management. We will examine the elements of building and maintaining an information base (information engineering) as well as the philosophy and processes associated with providing information services to a clientele (information organization management).

The Importance of Customization

All information professions spend a portion of their time working with individual clients. For example, a librarian in a public library will answer questions of businessmen who are asking for a description of a certain company in which they wish to invest. Alternatively, a school library media specialist who works with a fifth grade teacher to plan a science unit that will study bears and include development of student skills in gathering and organizing information. In both examples, the information professional identifies the need of the client and attempts to address that need by identifying and providing appropriate information sources.

The school library media specialist, in the example above, might also work with the entire fifth grade class, teaming with the teacher in the science unit. Likewise, a university librarian might prepare an instructional unit for an advanced education teaching methods class about to embark on a library research project. In each case, the group has identifiable characteristics (fifth grade and upper division education students) and are fulfilling a role which has certain predictable elements. Identifying the role of a client gives librarians an instant understanding of the group's social characteristics and helps librarians focus their efforts to locate appropriate information and to instruct the members of the group.

Different cultures have unique and predictable patterns for the creation, recording, mass production, dissemination, organization, diffusion, utilization, and preservation/destruction of information. We call this the "information transfer" process. Considerable research is necessary to understand the information transfer patterns of various social groups. It is possible to investigate the information transfer patterns of those with whom we are unfamiliar by interviewing members of those groups to identify these patterns. Among the differences that exists between the information professions is the types of groups with whom information professionals work.

Information professionals design and manage the organization of services and resources for the delivery of information to individuals and groups who are the agency's clientele. This professional must manage a budget, the collection, staff, and facilities.

Information professionals are charged with the responsibility for a collection—books, journals, reports, audio and video recordings, microforms, CD-ROMs, data-bases, Web sites, and electronic books are examples of the wide variety of formats now available. Professionals are responsible for identifying appropriate items for an agency's clientele, selecting resources, and organizing them, storing them, retrieving them, and preserving them. Knowing the characteristics of the individuals and groups using these resources is important in order to select and organize the resources in a manner that will be most convenient for the clientele.

The Processes of Building a Collection of Resources

Building a collection or database, like planning an information service of any kind, requires knowledge of the clientele served. Chapter 6 details the steps required to understand the needs of individuals or groups. A professional possesses knowledge which enables that individual to diagnose needs, prescribe a service or database which meets those needs, implement that service, and evaluate the outcome of this interaction. We call this process "the service cycle."

The professional must be able to assess the information needs of clientele at two levels: (1) analyzing the characteristics of the community served, and (2) analyzing the needs of specific individuals at the point when and where they seek information from the library or information center. An understanding of the community and the school will provide a conceptual framework for customizing collections, services, and space allocations. This level of analysis is a first critical step in customizing information service for individuals and groups. For more detail on needs assessment, see Chapter 6.

The professional processes for building a collection of information resources are the following: identification, evaluation, selection, acquisition, organization, storage, retrieval, circulation, preservation, and discarding. Each is discussed below.

Identification and Evaluation

The process of building a collection or database begins with identifying the possible information resources that could be added to the collection. The identification process can begin with clients who have used or heard of an information resource that would be useful in their work. Clients often can provide adequate information (title, author, or description of content) to be able to identify the resource. Quite often, the title or author is close, but incorrect. Imagination comes into play to try various variants of the requestor's suggestion to "get it right."

An effective needs analysis provides the best information for building a collection. Understanding the needs of the clientele enables the information professional to know current needs and to anticipate future needs. Knowledge of these needs enables the information professional to go to reliable tools which provide specific titles for the identification and evaluation of resources for the collection. These tools may be reviewing services or services which alert the information professional that titles have been published.

The library profession is engaged in publishing a number of reliable selection aids. For example, the American Library Association (ALA) has published *Booklist* since 1905, a source of recommended books and media for libraries. A division of ALA, the Association of College and Research Libraries, has published *Choice*, monthly reviews of books and other media for academic libraries, since 1964.

Other well-known and reliable sources for identification of newly published resources include the following:

Library Journal is published biweekly by the R.R. Bowker Company, a long-standing publisher in the library/information field. Each issue contains pertinent articles for professionals and hundreds of reviews by librarians.

American Reference Books Annual, an annual and comprehensive review of reference books of use in many types of libraries. The most comprehensive review source for reference titles.

Publishers' Weekly is a publication which lists the new books published by the American publishing industry. This service does not review new titles, but it is an alerting service to new titles on the market. As such, it is a reasonably comprehensive source for identifying new publications in the United States.

Interviews with practicing librarians reveal that technology has influenced the identification of resources. In the past, librarians and other information professionals perused book and media reviews and often referred to reviews or descriptions on slips provided by a subscription service. These slips were distributed to selectors in the library. Publishers' catalogs and fliers received in the mail were consulted. The process was manual and cumbersome.

Now libraries subscribe to online slip services which send slips electronically with descriptive information on new resources. Now book reviews are available online, and librarians receive e-mails and faxes about new books. In addition, publishers still get fliers and paper catalogs. As one librarian said, "To select a dozen titles which took a couple of days previously, now can be done in 10-15 minutes" (Joyce Davis Interview).

Selection

After titles have been identified, evaluated, and determined to be available for purchase, a purchasing decision must be made; this decision process is identified as selection. Review sources, like those listed above, can be valuable resources for determining the suitability of specific titles for a collection. However, the reviews themselves must be evaluated to determine the authority of their evaluation for the clientele for which considered. Reviews tend to be general evaluations, taking into consideration the quality of writing, format, illustrations, indexing, and accuracy. A title may receive a very positive review, but the title may be inappropriate for the needs of the clientele. Knowing the needs of the clientele is critical to the selection process.

The selection process may include addressing the following questions:

- Does this information source address one or more of the issues of interest to the clientele?
- Are the issues addressed in a manner appropriate for the clientele?
- Is more than one viewpoint presented?
- Is the information current?
- Is the information accurate, according to latest research?
- Are the values presented those of the prevailing paradigm, or are they presenting an alternative view?
- Are other information sources available to present a similar perspective on the issue? If so, how is this information source unique?
- How does this information source contribute to the current collection of the information agency?
- Is purchase of this information source defensible in cost?
- What is the final decision? Purchase? Delay a decision? Do not purchase?

As noted in the "identification" section above, reviews and other information is now available online, and reviews may be e-mailed to colleagues or to faculty in universities or schools to solicit opinions of knowledgeable clientele. One librarian observed, "More and more people are not doing the reviewing; they are using preselection services by publishers" (Sharon Coatney interview). This practice raises questions about the efficacy of this process in satisfying the known needs of the libraries clientele.

Acquisition

After a selection decision is made, steps must be taken to acquire the information sources identified and selected. Format of the information is a key factor in the acquisition process. Vendors are companies that purchase resources from a variety of sources and provide "one stop shopping" for libraries and information agencies to purchase books, periodicals, and nonprint information sources. Vendors purchase items wholesale and can usually offer products at a reduced price from the retail prices. Examples of such vendors are Baker and Taylor, Bro-Dart, McClurg for books and such vendors as Blackwell for periodicals.

Vendors attempt to meet librarians' needs by putting reviews online and indicating reading levels. The service provided is usually fast delivery, with the additional benefit of providing cataloging, the next process to be discussed.

Organization

Organization of information resources includes three major activities— classification, cataloging, and database design. Each will be discussed in this section.

Classification

The organization of resources may be done by using one of the standard *classification* systems, Dewey Decimal Classification (DDC) or Library of Congress (LC) for books, journals, and electronic resources. See Chapter 7 for a discussion of these two systems.

Cataloging

The *Rules for Descriptive Cataloging* published by ALA provides the protocols for effectively describing each item to be added to the collection. Cataloging information can be purchased, making the cataloging process much more efficient and cost effective than original cataloging. However, such systems apply general rules for classification, and exception decisions made locally must be addressed locally. To save time, it is advisable to "follow the rules" and to use decisions made by DDC and LC. Most libraries and information centers do "copy cataloging" through OCLC or by using the classification and cataloging provided when items are purchased. When items are received, the processing may include putting in a security strip, putting on a dust jacket, or other preparations before making an item available to be put on the shelf for use by clientele.

If working with a special collection with a unique classification system (see the example in Chapter 7), an information professional may use the cataloging information for subject headings and apply an original classification for the call number or the designated address for the item to be stored. The classification system used for books should be used for any information packages so that clients can find all resources on a topic shelved together.

Using a separate system for organizing and storing items by format can be a hindrance to the user. Here is where the issues of "organization" spill over into issues of "storage."

Databases

If creating a new database customized to meet local needs, the questions to address include the following:

- Who will use the database? A general clientele? Specialized clientele? Both?

- Should the vocabulary be general or specific to the specialty area? (Related to question above.)

- Is there an existing thesaurus of terms, or is there an index that can be used as a guide?

- Are there clients who would be knowledgeable enough and available to serve as consultants as decisions are made?

A major decision is whether to use an "off the shelf" database like Access, or whether to create a new database. For most information professionals, they will select a software package and use it, or they may have a staff person (if the organization is large enough) to provide the programming expertise to create a database. However, most libraries and information centers do not have the luxury of such a programming specialist, and the "off the shelf" solution is the way to go.

If a database is purchased, it must be set up on proxy server and listed in the library's catalog and added to the library's list of databases. For electronic journals and books, license agreements must be checked to be sure that the licensing terms are followed. As one librarian said, "New technology actually complicates the processes. Companies provide special services for electronic sources, and acquiring them is more complex because the industry is so new. There is not a work flow as with printed sources" (Dalene Hawthorne interview).

Storage and Retrieval

Storage of resources is a decision that can influence client use and ease of retrieval. Should all formats be stored according to the classification scheme, or should they be separated by format? If the former solution is chosen, all information packages, regardless of format, will be stored or shelved together. As a result, the browsing client will "stumble upon" CDs, books, journals, and video recordings in the same general location. If a decision is made to shelve journals or nonprint media in other locations, that decision, too, can facilitate browsing by format. In any case, the items of different format are brought together in the catalog of the library or information center.

The areas most frequently separated in libraries are periodicals and government publications. Periodicals may be shelved in a special location to facilitate supervision, answering client questions, and circulation. They present special circulation problems. In fact, many libraries do not circulate periodicals because loss of one journal issue means that the "run" of issues has been interrupted, and service has been affected. In addition, journals and nonprint media are expensive, and the professional staff may decide that the loss of such items cannot be justified financially, and that warrants closer supervision of the collection.

Government publications present additional issues. Both state and federal government publications are issued a Superintendent of Documents (SUDOCS) classification number, and many libraries choose to use the SUDOCS number to catalog and to store government publications of all types. Since the government's classification scheme is much different than either LC or DDC, the choice to use SUDOCS to classify and store government sources requires a separate storage area. One can also argue that government publications are a specialized area and deserve specially trained information professionals to address the special attributes of the government publication system. Indeed, a special division of the ALA Government Documents Roundtable (GODORT) was established for this reason.

If resources are stored electronically, access to computers is another issue which the professional must consider. Who will have access to public terminals? How will the terminals be monitored—or will they be monitored? How will support be provided to users of the terminals and resources?

Circulation

"Circulation" is concerned with the way in which information resources are available to clientele. As mentioned earlier, a library's lending policies are a local reflection of an information policy. Here are some issues related to circulation:

- Will clientele be able to take items from the facility?
- Must items be used in-house? In a certain area within the building?
- If items can be circulated outside the facility, how long may they be checked out?
- Is there a penalty for returning items after the due date? If so, what is that penalty?
- Are certain items not circulated? (For example, "reference" items? Electronic resources?)
- Are certain items circulated only for a short period? (For example, reserved items circulate only over night or only for 1 hour).

These questions must be addressed with the needs of the clientele in mind and the mission of the information center.

Preservation

When resources have been in the collection for a time, a decision must be made:

1. Should this resource be replaced with a more recent edition?
2. Should this item be discarded?
3. Should this item be repaired and preserved for future use in the collection?
4. What are the constraints of space and construction costs?

These are important questions for the future users of the information center. To address these questions, the information professional must contemplate the mission of the library or information center and address these questions:

- What is the role of the information center in preserving information resources for the organization's clientele?

- Does another nearby library (or one which has electronic resources for easy access) retain the same title so that clients who desire the resource may have access through another source?

- Does the information center have the storage space to retain this resource?

- Does the anticipated use of this resource justify the expense of preserving and storing it?

Discarding

If the review of resources (see "preservation") indicates that preservation of a resource is not justified, the item should be discarded. No library can justify keeping all items purchased in perpetuity. Some items must be discarded to make space for others. Items that must be discarded should be clearly marked that they have been discarded. Sometimes libraries will sell discarded books at a community book sale as a way to fund raise. Still others destroy old books and journals.

A professional must fight the urge to keep everything. For some, throwing away books, journals, or other media is tantamount to a sacrilege. However, one must think in business terms. Keeping every item in a collection has a cost, the cost of maintaining items through rebinding and for maintaining the space to retain items. The overhead for heating, cooling, and cleaning space costs money, and the cost of taking up space for the purchase of new, current materials. Keeping items when they are not needed is not free.

Summary of Processes

The processes above are those associated with building and maintaining a collection of information resources. These professional processes are required for building a collection of any formats and making that collection available to clientele. A key factor in each process is keeping in mind two concepts: (1) the mission of the information agency, and (2) the information needs of the clientele. All decisions focus on these two points.

The processes which are used by information professionals have been changed significantly by the introduction of new technologies. As one librarian stated, "Technology has taken people out of the back room and put them on the front lines" (Joyce Davis interview). Decreasing the time and expertise required to catalog resources has diminished the number of people engaged in cataloging and processing, enabling libraries to use those positions to serve the public directly.

Other changes are wrought by the increasing availability and use of electronic resources. Librarians license electronic books, journals, and databases—the library does not own these resources. Each lease is handled separately, although some vendors have entered this arena and offer services which facilitate the processing of leasing of these resources. Nevertheless, the acquisition of electronic resources has changed the work flow—the processes—required when new resources are added to a library's collection.

The Functions of Information Agencies

In Chapter 6, the importance of a needs analysis is emphasized as the basis for providing information services. The authors have conducted more than thirty analyses of communities for public, school, special, and academic libraries. These community analyses resulted in the following categories of information use:

- Teach or learn: The educational function of information
- Enjoy: The recreational function
- Appreciate: The cultural function of information
- Decide: The informational function of information
- Create new information or knowledge: The research function
- Find or locate: The bibliographic (or identification) function of information

These uses of information lead to the functions of information agencies, as identified above in parentheses. We will discuss each function in more depth below. However, the reader should be aware that the information profession tends to blend or cumulate the services or functions. For example, "reference service" is often the general term used when the service is teaching information skills (educational function), teaching appreciation for good literature (cultural function), providing information for decision making (informational function), assisting the researcher (research function), and helping to locate information (part of the bibliographic function), including the preparation of bibliographies, Webographies, pathfinders, and other finding aids. The recreational function, also, may be considered part of reference services. In the section which follows, we will dissect the functions in order to examine more carefully the various uses of information and the implications for the work of information professionals.

Educational Function

The educational function of libraries and information agencies supports learning. This function is one of the oldest forms of service provided by the profession. It is the reason that public libraries were founded in the early 1800s, to serve as a school for the "ordinary person." Schools, especially secondary schools, were out of reach for all but the wealthy. Public libraries were funded in Massachusetts and supported by tax money in order to provide citizens an opportunity to extend their formal schooling through public libraries.

Although the first public libraries were scarcely more than a collection of textbooks and readers, with no professional service to the readers, it was a beginning. Melvil Dewey was a proponent of libraries as schools in his treatise on the profession:

Therefore, our leading educators have come to recognize the library as sharing with the school the education of the people. The most that the schools can hope to do for the masses more than the schools are doing for them in many sections, is to teach them to read intelligently, to get ideas readily from the printed page. It may seem a strong statement, but many children leave the schools without this ability. They can repeat the words of the book, but this is simply pronunciation, as a beginner pronounces another language without getting any clear idea of the meaning. Could the schools really teach the masses to read, they would be doing a great work. The children of the lower classes have to commence work at a very early age, and it is impossible to keep them in the schools long enough to educate them to any degree. The school teaches them to read; the library must supply them with reading which shall serve to educate, and so it is that we are forced to divide popular education into two parts of almost equal importance and deserving equal attention: the free school and the free library. (Dewey, 1876, pp. 22–23)

The educational role of the library has expanded considerably since this article by Dewey. The educational function is still a primary function of most libraries—public, academic, school, and special. Clientele come to the library or electronically access the library to learn on their own. However, this is but one use of the educational function.

In recent years, librarians and other information professionals have become more engaged in the teaching/learning process. Leading the way have been school and college/university librarians who have collaborated with faculty to teach students information skills. Sometimes called "bibliographic instruction" or "information literacy," information professionals teach people information skills. See the section "Information Literacy" in Chapter 10 for further discussion of the educational function.

The educational function engages learners as individuals in small groups, in formal classes, and in large groups. Libraries in those institutions charged with education have the greatest role in the educational function of information. School library media centers and college and university libraries are very engaged in fulfilling the educational mission of their agencies.

ACRL, the Association of College and Research Libraries, publishes and updates regularly guidelines for college and university libraries. The most recent guidelines, "Standards for Libraries in Higher Education," was approved by the ACRL Board of Directors in 2004. These standards provide the following guidelines for instruction in academic libraries:

> As an academic or instructional unit within the institution, the library should facilitate student success, as well as encourage lifelong learning. By combining new techniques and technologies with the best of traditional sources, librarians should assist primary users and others in information retrieval methods, evaluation, and documentation.

In addition, librarians should collaborate frequently with classroom faculty; they should participate in curriculum planning and information literacy instruction as well as educational outcomes assessment. Information literacy skills and user education should be integrated across the curriculum and into appropriate courses with special attention given to information evaluation, critical thinking, intellectual property, copyright, and plagiarism ("Standards for Libraries in Higher Education" 2006).

Public libraries engage in the educational function and work to complement schools. Some public libraries promote education through collaboration with other agencies, e.g., the local literacy council, adult education, book discussion groups, and by providing a high interest/low vocabulary book collection. Public libraries also provide resources to support home schooling.

The school library has an integral role in education. "The school library is part of the overall goal of achievement and must support every area of the curriculum. The library is as responsible as the classroom. We teach more than information literacy goals; we teach all of the goals" (Sharon Coatney Interview). In addition to the prominent role of school library media specialists in student learning, there is a growing function to provide staff development for the school's faculty.

Cultural Function

The cultural function of libraries was at the heart of the founding of the ALA, which adopted Melvil Dewey's suggested motto: "The best reading for the largest number at the least cost" (Vann 1978, 77). In his essay on the profession, Dewey (Ellsworth and Stevens 1976, p. 22) wrote: "He [the librarian] must see that his library contains, as far as possible, the best books on the best subjects, regarding carefully the wants of his special community." The term "best reading" reflects the essence of the cultural function of information, i.e., providing clientele the best examples of our cultural heritage as represented in literature, history, music, dance, and various art forms.

Butler (1933) held that if the librarian ". . . holds the classic point of view he will regard as his highest contribution to social welfare the delivery of the world's best books to his readers. Or, since many of these readers will be unable to appreciate the highest excellence, he can satisfy himself by giving tem the best that they can understand" (pp. 85–86). By further explanation of the cultural function, Butler (1953) issued this challenge to librarians:

> His first duty is not to demonstrate to his readers that the pronouncements of science are true, or even to assist them in making new discoveries of fact. He must serve primarily as an archivist of culture and aid his readers to find whatever they require as far as this has been put upon the record. If, in the course of this duty, he can also serve for the moment as an informal teacher, he will deserve well off of society. (p. 90)

The pervasive value system of library and information agencies is to select the "best" available information resources because budgets do not allow for the purchase of every item desired. Consequently, if the acquisition budget is limited (and nearly all but the few libraries in affluent communities or corporations have such limitations), the information professional must be selective in choosing the resources for a collection. In a corporate setting, the clientele may be instrumental in determining which are the best journals, databases, and books to procure for the collection. Law libraries will collect the electronic and print books and periodicals which are the most reputable and useful in the view of the attorneys and other legal practitioners—paraprofessionals and judges.

In public and school libraries, the cultural function may be questioned as librarians attempt to lure readers, viewers, and listeners of all ages to use the collection for cultural, educational, and recreational purposes. At this point, the term "culture" must be expanded to include the popular literature, music, and art forms of the day. While few will question the addition of works by William Shakespeare, Mark Twain, T.S. Eliot, or Robert Browning to a collection because they are recognized as authors of "classic" literature, should popular authors like Dan Brown (*The Da Vinci Code* 2003*)*, John Grisham (*The Firm* 1991, *The King of Torts* 2003, and others), or Agatha Christie (popular mystery series) be included in library collections for adults and youth?

The latter examples are popular culture—that literature, music, and art which is popular for a time. One can argue that the popular culture of a generation may endure and become culture in the classic sense. Shakespeare's plays, for example, were very popular with the people of the seventeenth century in Great Britain. The strength of his characters, his adroit use of language, and strong story lines have endured and will be studied as part of the English language cultural heritage in future generations.

Similarly, the classical symphonies of Mozart and Bach, like Shakespeare, were popular in their day and have become classical musical pieces for future generations. Jazz music, a product of the early twentieth century, apparently is an enduring art form which is appreciated and studied in music schools throughout the world.

The cultural function includes the sharing of cultures of various ethnic groups—the music, motion pictures, literature, and customs of immigrants and of other international cultures. Increasingly we are citizens of a global society, and libraries are repositories for representative artifacts of the cultures of our world.

The cultural function includes a variety of formats—books, periodicals, audio recordings of various formats, and video recordings. Consequently, information professionals must be aware of the technologies which record various cultural products and be prepared to select, organize, store, and preserve a variety of formats.

Another reason for including popular culture in library collections is the popular appeal which current authors, artists, and musicians have to attract clientele to use libraries. Their reason may be cultural, educational, or recreational. The latter function will be discussed next.

Recreational Function

The recreational function is synonymous with "enjoyment." It is concerned with the use of information resources during leisure time. These resources include novels, poetry, periodicals, and nonfiction to support interests, audio recordings, video recordings, and games, including electronic formats.

Recreational use of libraries might be controversial for some members of the public and for some information professionals. The recreational function was not one of the original functions of libraries. It was not mentioned prominently in the literature of the profession until the latter part of the twentieth century. The inclusion of paperback books as acceptable items for library collections was not generally accepted until after World War II. The expendable nature of the paperback format violated the social norm that books were treasures to be valued as artifacts.

The rationale often given is that the recreational function is a way of reaching people who may not otherwise use the library, or who cannot afford to buy the resources, or simply don't want to pay for them if they are "only" recreational. Once in the library, the librarians may steer clientele to other resources and services that will benefit the individual. We believe that the reason to include recreational resources is to meet the recreational needs and wants of clientele—that recreational needs are as important to quality of life as educational or cultural or informational needs. Another point is that today's recreational materials may be tomorrow's "classics."

Research Function

The research function equates to creating new social knowledge. While we often use the term "research" to indicate that a user of information is "doing library research" to write a paper or report, the context of "research" is really to assist in the educational function, helping a person to learn.

The use of "research" here is that systematic, formal process which requires (1) a literature review to determine the state of the art in an area of inquiry, (2) a careful articulation of research questions or hypotheses, (3) a systematic plan and effort to collect data, (4) analysis of the data, (5) a report of the results, including generalizations extrapolated from the data. This research may be the formal, carefully articulated and conducted study which conforms to the scientific paradigm of a discipline or field, or it may be the problem-oriented, practical research conducted by members of a profession. The latter research intended to solve professional problems is often called "action research." Both types of research contribute new knowledge to a discipline or field of study.

The information professional ideally may be involved at any of the above stages of research: (1) assisting with the key search terms and collaborating with the researcher to conduct a thorough, effective literature review; (2) relating the literature review to the construction of research questions or hypotheses; (3) collaborating with the researcher in planning the research data collection; (4) collaborating in the analysis and interpretation of the data collected; (5) collaborating on the writing of the research report. This type of collaboration currently is the standard in many special libraries, especially in the medical and legal fields; it requires the information professional to have the necessary research expertise gained by an advanced degree in a field—the rationale for university librarians to have a master's degree in library and information science, along with a master's degree in a subject field. Similarly, law librarians may be required to have a Doctor of Juris Prudence (JD) Degree, or a research library may require a Doctor of Philosophy (Ph.D.).

Engagement in the research process depends on the environment of the information agency. School librarians are rarely engaged in the research function, except in those rare cases when a teachers or principal may request help as they conduct "action research" to solve a professional problem or to fulfill an assignment in a graduate class. However, school librarians and other information professionals may themselves engage in action research to address professional problems, and then publish the results.

In academic libraries, librarians are on call and can be consulted by faculty to assist with research through in-depth consultation. Information professionals in research libraries and archives often engage with researchers for a long period of time. For example, an archivist often works with researchers by appointment, and a librarian might work five hours or more with a researcher on one question (Heather Wade interview).

Informational Function

The information function provides information for decision making. Providing information to people instead of teaching them *how to use* information sources is not a new concept in the library and information profession; however, implementation of information service has been slow to evolve.

Samuel S. Green (1876) was one of the first librarians to write about information service. He emphasized the importance of working with people to meet their needs: "A librarian should be as unwilling to allow an inquirer to leave the library with his question unanswered as a shopkeeper is to have a customer go out of his store without making a purchase" (p. 327).

Although oriented to service, Green warned librarians not to go too far with service: "Be careful not to make inquirers dependent. Give them as much assistance as they need, but try at the same time to teach them to rely upon themselves and become independent" (p. 328).

Today, in this age which bombards us with information daily, hourly, our professional values are different. The ALA Reference and User Services Division (RUSA), it its "Guidelines for Information Service," provides this goal:

> The goal of information services is to provide the information sought by the user. Information service should anticipate as well as meet user needs. It should encourage user awareness of the potential of information resources to fulfill individual information needs.

The information function is usually called "reference service" or "information service" in today's libraries and information centers. The reference or information service function of the library was formally introduced by Melville Dewey at the Columbia University library in the 1880's. It is worth noting that this was the first instance of a paradigmatic shift in managing libraries. By creating a reference department and assigning staff to this function, Dewey deliberately designated some of his resources specifically for the benefit of the clientele rather than the housekeeping of the collection.

"Reference" service is found in nearly all libraries. Reference service includes the teaching of information skills (really the educational function), "ready reference," and regular reference service. Ready reference is the term used for questions that can be answered very quickly by consulting one or two information sources. Bopp and Smith (2001, p. 7) give these examples of ready reference questions:

- An address
- The spelling or definition of a word
- A date or place of an event
- Something about the life or career of an individual

Bopp and Smith (2001) describe reference service as including the following:

- Ready reference questions
- Bibliographic verification, which provides accurate information about published and mass distributed information sources in all formats—authors, publishers/producers, date of release, etc.
- Interlibrary loan and document delivery, a service which identifies locations of resources in other libraries and provides for the delivery of these information items to a client.
- Information and referral services, which identify community agencies and individuals who can supply wanted information.

In most information agencies, some type of information service is provided, sometimes for a fee. If a service requires an extraordinary amount of a professional's time, the client may be charged—especially in special libraries. Even some public libraries have charged fees for their services when that service was beyond the "standard" service for clientele.

In corporate, government, legal, medical, and other libraries and information centers, the provision of direct information may include reports as part of the service to clientele. For example, an information professional may be asked to conduct a search of all of the laws adopted during the last 10 years in a state and to synthesize a brief report of each law's content. The synthesizing and summarizing of complex information is an important skill which is especially valuable for managers and executives in all types of agencies. Professionals with the ability to locate and summarize information quickly, concisely, and accurately are very valuable to an organization. As the amount of information available becomes greater, these skills will be even more in demand.

These services cross functions, according to our definitions, but they were launched to meet specific needs of individuals. Not included were such services as conducting online searches with or without the consultation with a user. As technology becomes more sophisticated, especially with the integration of "smart" computers (or artificial intelligence), the ability for computers to diagnose the information needs of clientele will be a major contributor to the advance of information services in the future.

Bibliographic Function

An important information function is that of organizing information for storage, retrieval, and use. In library and information agencies, the organization of information for client use is accomplished through bibliographies, indexes, pathfinders, and other finding aids. As noted in Chapter 7, "bibliography" has been defined by Theodore Besterman (1940) as ". . . a list of books arranged according to some permanent principle." The same definition can be used for a listing of audio recordings, video recordings, Web sites, or information in any format.

Once again, to implement the bibliographic function effectively, the information professional must know the needs of clientele. Then a finding aid can be developed to address those needs.

A distinct variation of the bibliographic work of most librarians is the bibliographic function of the archivist. A finding aid prepared by an archivist is equivalent to the title page of a book. Unlike the cataloging information used by nearly all librarians today to catalog books and other formats, such descriptive cataloging information is not provided to an archivist, who must study a collection of items (for example, manuscripts, photographs, realia), understand the collection and its importance, organize, then develop a finding aid (Heather Wade Interview). Standards for describing archives have been developed by the Society of American Archivists and include the following: Creator information, an abstract of collection, an explanation of the organizational scheme, and inclusive content notes—a succinct bibliographic history.

Levels of Service

A model for outlining levels of service was introduced by Greer and Hale (1982) and uses the following terms:

Passive

"The passive level of service consists of a process of choosing, acquiring, and organizing materials on the library shelves for the user to discover" (Greer and Hale, 1982, p. 359). The information professional does not attempt to assist with the understanding or use of the information. For example, in information center provides a collection of books or journals, or it creates a database for use by clientele with no assistance.

Reactive

A level of service in which professional assistance is provided on request of the clientele. An example is the traditional "reference service" provided in most libraries. Another example is the provision of finding aids (bibliographies. mediagraphies, or Webographies) upon request. "The bulk of the material chosen and programs offered is based on the librarian's best judgment of relevance. Input from the community is welcomed when it arrives, but it is not collected systematically" (Greer and Hale, 1982, p. 359).

Assertive

This level of service addresses the known information needs of clientele as identified by an information needs analysis. This level of service anticipates information need. An example is the delivery of information to clientele without their asking. For example, a university librarian e-mails a faculty member a newly arrived journal article for a literature review the professor is preparing. On the other hand, a school library media specialist, knowing the calendar of subjects to be taught to seventh grade history students, arranges a meeting with history teachers to plan a history unit which integrates the teaching of note-taking skills.

The keys to an assertive level of service are 1) systematic collection of community data from which needs and interests are inferred, 2) development of a customized collection, and 3) dissemination of information to meet the inferred and expressed needs. The central

Table 8.1 Information Services and Levels of Service

Function	Passive Level	Reactive Level	Assertive Level
Educational	A collection of resources is provided.	Services are provided when requested by clientele.	Based on a needs assessment, client needs are anticipated and service is provided.
Cultural Research Recreational Informational Bibliographic			

focus of this level of service is the community and its people. (Greer and Hale, 1982, pp. 359–360)

These levels of service can be applied to the various information functions or services described earlier in this chapter. Those services can be provided at different levels, as depicted in Table 8.1 above.

The matrix above is a model for considering the variety of services which can be offered in a library or information agency. The analysis of need and development of services in response are the essence of the library and information professions.

Putting It All Together: The Role of the Professional

Butler's (1933) philosophy describes well the role of the information professional:

> The library is no mission station for the promulgation of an established literary gospel that is eternally true. The librarian's duty is not to entice men, against their wills if it need be, to convert themselves to his way of thinking. He is merely society's custodian of its cultural archives. The responsibility which he assumes with his office is to exploit those archives for communal advantage to the utmost extent of his ability. Therefore, a major phase of the library's service to any individual reader will be to assist him to an effective method for achieving his own private purpose, so long as this is not anti-social, and to safeguard him from listing his labor in activities which are futile with reference to his own immediate desire. For all this, there must be a sympathetic understanding of the individual's motive and mental ability. Effective librarianship is largely a matter of accurate psychological diagnosis. (pp. 105–106)

Butler's comments about libraries and books is generalizable across various types of information agencies—libraries, archives, information centers, private enterprise, and government agencies. All information service begins with knowledge of the clientele, their roles, and information needed for those roles. When information needs have been identified, information services can be planned to address those needs at three levels—passive, reactive, and assertive. The services can be classified into six categories of information function—educational, cultural, research, recreational, informational, and bibliographic. It is this process of diagnosing information need, planning and implementing services, and evaluating the impact of service that comprise the essential role of the library and information professional.

References

American Library Association Reference and User Services Association. *RUSA service guidelines: guidelines for information services.* http://www.ala.org/ala/rusa/rusaprotools/referenceguide/guidelinesinformation.htm. (accessed January 17, 2007).

———. 1905-. *Booklist: Includes reference books bulletin.* Chicago, IL: American Library Association.

American Library Association. 2006. "Standards for libraries in higher education." http://www.ala.org/ala/acrl/acrlstandards/standardslibraries.htm (accessed July 4, 2006).

Balay, Robert, ed. 1996. *Guide to reference books.* 11th ed. Chicago, IL: American Library Association, 2020.

Books in print with book reviews on disc (CD-ROM). New Providence, NJ: R.R. Bowker. Monthly.

Brown, Dan. 2003. *The Da Vinci code.* New York: Doubleday

Butler, Pierce. 1933. *An introduction to library science.* Chicago: The University of Chicago Press.

Coatney, Sharon. Interviewed July 3, 2006. Ms. Coatney is a retired school library media specialist and acquisitions editor for Libraries Unlimited.

Davis, Joyce. Interviewed June 27, 2006. Ms. Davis is Dean of Libraries and Archives, Emporia State University, Emporia, Kansas.

Dewey, Melvil. 1906. "Origin of the A. L. A. motto," *Public Libraries* 11: 55, IN VANN, SARAH K., ED. *Melvil Dewey: His enduring presence in librarianship.* Sarah K. Vann, ed. 77. Littleton, CO: Libraries Unlimited, 1978.

———. 1976. "The profession." In *Landmarks of library literature, 1876–1976*, ed. Dianne J. Ellsworth and Norman D. Stevens. 21–23, Metuchen, NJ: The Scarecrow Press.

Eisenberg, Michael B. and Robert E. Berkowitz. 1990. *Information problem solving: The big six skills approach to library and information skills instruction.* Norwood, NJ: Greenwood Publishing Group.

Gale Directory of Databases. Volume 1. *Online Databases. Volume 2. CD-ROM, Diskette, Magnetic Tape, Handheld, and Batch Access Database Products.* Farmington Hills, MI: Gale Group, 1993- . Semiannual. Also available online.

Green, Samuel S. 1976. "Personal Relations between Librarians and Readers." In *Landmarks of library literature, 1876–1976*, ed. Dianne J. Ellsworth and Norman D. Stevens. Metuchen, 319–330. NJ: The Scarecrow Press

Greer, Roger C. and Hale, Martha L. 1982. "The community analysis process." In *Public librarianship, a reader*, ed. Jane Robbins-Carter, 358–366. Littleton, CO: Libraries Unlimited.

Grisham, John. 1991. *The firm*. New York: Dell.

————. 2003. *The king of torts*. New York: Bantam Dell.

Hawthorne, Dalene. Interviewed June 29, 2006. Ms. Hawthorne is head of systems and technical services at Emporia State University, Emporia, Kansas.

Library Journal. New York: Cahners, 1876-. 20 issues per year.

Wade, Heather. Interviewed June 29, 2006. She is Archivist, Emporia State University, Emporia, Kansas.

Wynar, Bohdan S., ed. 1970-. *American reference books annual*. Englewood, CO: Libraries Unlimited.

9

The Infrastructure of the Information Professions

Chapter Overview

Entering a profession is entrance to a professional community which has a distinctive culture. That culture consists of a body of knowledge, a value system, a body of literature, professional organizations which promote the culture and update professionals, and a means for recognizing members of the field. This chapter introduces the infrastructure of the library and information professions. A brief history of the information profession is followed by descriptions of information professional organizations, journals, lists, Web sites, educational programs, standards, codes of ethics, and systems of recognition by the public.

Characteristics of a Profession

An important concept to consider is the difference between a professional and a technician or paraprofessional. As we advance through the Knowledge Society, the role of knowledge workers increases—the number of people engaged in the use of knowledge as their work increases. Professionals are knowledge workers, and so are paraprofessionals and technicians. But what is the difference in their work?

In summary, a professional is a person who masters and applies a body of knowledge in a specific area of inquiry. For example, an attorney has mastered the body of knowledge associated with the practice of law; a psychologist has learned and practiced the general or specific knowledge related to human behavior. However, the definition of a profession is more complex. A profession can be characterized by the following:

- History
- A Body of Knowledge or Theory
- An Educational System
- Professional Associations

- A Code of Ethics
- Standards of Practice
- A Body of Literature
- Recognition by the Public

In other words, a profession has a unique culture, and a professional school is a purveyor of that culture, which includes the history of the field. A brief history of libraries and librarianship follows.

History

The history of the library and information professions can best be studied by reviewing the development of libraries, services, and professional education. As libraries evolved to meet the changing needs of society, the need for specially trained professionals also evolved. Following is an historical sketch of the field's evolution.

Libraries

In our historical account, we trace the history of libraries back 5000 years and categorize ancient libraries into four groups: (1) government, (2) religious, (3) commercial, and (4) private or family libraries. Each will be described briefly, leading to a discussion of the functions of libraries.

Government libraries collected the treaties, legislation, and genealogy of the royal family, lines of succession, and other recorded documents pertinent to governance, in a variety of formats, e.g., clay tablets, papyrus scrolls, or parchment. The information sources were arranged physically by subjects, often in different rooms. The major role of the librarian was to catalog or arrange the items for retrieval. We can generalize that a civilization progressed when it developed a written language and archived records from its past. Primitive societies lacking an alphabet were unable to create a record of events as they developed. The consequence was a lack of access to the past beyond the human memory. Without archives of their past, they could not advance beyond the knowledge that could be remembered, and they tended not to advance to a sophisticated state.

Religious libraries contained rules for the education of the clergy. The creed of the religion was recorded and stored—the beliefs, sacred writings, and rituals of the religion or sect.

Private libraries archived the private papers, records of property holdings, and the relationships between the family and rulers or government of the day.

Commercial libraries stored and organized the records of commerce, including bills of lading and business papers and records of various kinds.

These same four categories continued to reflect the archival function of libraries throughout history. For example, the medieval library model was the monastery library, a treasure intended to be valued equally for the collection of rare manuscripts that were copied carefully and traded and the enlightenment that its collection provided.

Early libraries were reserved for use by the royalty and the privileged classes. The Romans created "public libraries" but not as we know them today. They were available for the use of the wealthy classes but maintained publicly instead of by individuals. At the time of Caesar's death, 39 public libraries were open to the upper echelon of Roman society.

Libraries were not widespread until the Industrial Revolution and the subsequent rise of cities, industry, and printing. It was during this time that libraries assumed a new role, or the education function. One factor in this change was the creation of universities in the late Middle Ages/early modern age.

In the United States, Harvard University and its library were established in 1636. Yale University was established shortly after (1640); William and Mary College followed in 1693. The creation of the first Ph.D. program at Harvard in the 1860s required library collections to support research. Another significant change was the introduction of majors and elective courses in college curricula, allowing faculty to teach topics related to their interests. This innovation placed a strain on academic libraries to support an expanding university curriculum. In response, the library became the laboratory for the social sciences and the humanities.

In 1731, Benjamin Franklin established the Library Company of Philadelphia, the first public subscription library. It exists today as an independent, nonprofit research library. In the eighteenth and nineteenth centuries, mechanics institutes and mercantile libraries were founded to provide opportunities for workers to educate themselves and occupy management positions in expanded industries. Many of these institutions remain in service today.

In the 1830s, New York Governor DeWit Clinton promoted the passage of enabling legislation to create school district libraries. This legislation was later amended to allow public funds for the development of these libraries. These publicly funded libraries were intended as public libraries, the first instance of government money used for libraries. In the 1850s public libraries were founded in the major cities of Boston, New York, Philadelphia. The Boston Public Library was the first such library established for the common person.

As with the mechanic and mercantile libraries, a major motivator for the development of the public library was to support formal education and self-learning. While community leaders wanted to support self-education, libraries also sought opportunities to acquire the best books—the cultural function of libraries. Although collecting for the purpose of educating clientele and enhancing the culture of patrons, the librarians continued to place a high value on the collection, so the values of the archival function were maintained, i.e., books were treasures that must be preserved.

Recreational reading as a library service was frowned on until the beginning of the twentieth century, at which time it came into its own with the paperback book industry in the 1930s. With the invention of video and audio recordings, public libraries expanded their recreational services through a collection of movies and "books on tape."

Early research libraries developed in the late eighteenth and early nineteenth centuries were an answer to the military's need for new materials and products. These special libraries supported innovation and the creation of new products.

The information function began with the urging of Melvil Dewey and Samuel S. Green, who encouraged assertive librarians who would work with clientele to help them use libraries and their resources. The information function became more prominent in the late twentieth century with the increase of computer and telecommunication technologies to exploit the Internet and is now a dominant function of information agencies.

In summary, library and information service has evolved in services to clientele. Initially, service was passive and the book was a treasure to be guarded. With the awareness of the book as an educational and cultural tool, the passive function of libraries evolved into more reactive service, which was recommended by Melvil Dewey and Samuel Green (see Chapter 1). Assertive service, along with the informational and recreational functions are more recent developments and require a much better educated information professional.

The Library Profession

Until the 1900s, people managing libraries were part of the intelligentsia—the clergy, professors, historians, and other educated citizens. As with Benjamin Franklin; these were people who respected books and reading. A good part of the development of libraries was due to the work of printers and publishers, whose interest was to encourage book use. The combination of scholar, librarian, and printer was a common phenomenon after the invention of moveable type in the mid-fifteenth century.

Concurrent to these developments in libraries in the latter part of the nineteenth century was the development of the social sciences. The population in the United States was growing, as were the associated social problems—increased crime, changing family relationships, abandoned children, health issues, and mandatory education. Needed were professionals to teach, manage schools, manage hospitals, and to resolve the emerging social problems. The demand for professional services fostered the development of disciplines and the professions to address these social problems. With the growth of social sciences came specialists, professions as we know them. When the privileged classes discovered the need for special knowledge to manage emerging social problems, the professions developed with libraries to support them.

In 1853, library leaders in the United States met to discuss the emerging field of librarianship. The successful meeting of almost 100 people led to the conclusion that they should meet again. The Civil War and other events intervened and the next meeting did not occur until 1876. It was the Centennial year of the Declaration of Independence and associated celebrations gave impetus at that meeting to the creation of the American Library Association. Immediately, the fundamental components of a profession began taking shape through conversations about standards of service, a code of ethics, professional journal and other elements of a professional infrastructure.

In 1887, Melvil Dewey founded the Program of Library Economy at Columbia University. The program consisted of undergraduate courses that taught how to manage a library, including how to organize and maintain a collection of books. Pratt Institute, Syracuse University, and other professional schools were created shortly after. Early in the twentieth century, library education programs evolved from a few courses to an undergraduate major and eventually, a graduate masters program. The Williamson Report (1923) urged a fifth-year degree, which began to emerge in the 1930s. Beginning in 1950, the fifth-year bachelor's degree in library science was converted to a master's degree.

Figure 9.1. Knowledge Requirements of Library
and Information Professionals

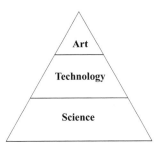

Further Reading

Because the rich history of libraries and the library profession cannot be summarized adequately in a few pages, we recommend further reading in these sources listed in the bibliography: Battles (2003), Casson (2001), Dickson (1986), Gates (1990), Harris (1995), Johnson (1965), Shera (1976), Vann (1978), and Wiegand (1996).

Body of Knowledge

A body of knowledge is central to a profession. The professional is expert in an area of knowledge that can be applied in a professional practice. A teacher has studied learning theory and techniques for applying pedagogy to learners, usually specializing in pedagogy for an age group. In addition, a teacher has mastered the subject matter to be taught, including the rudimentary knowledge taught in elementary schools. The information professional has mastered a body of knowledge related to the creation, dissemination, diffusion, organization, preservation, and recording of knowledge. We submit that the body of knowledge is the four fields which are described above—information psychology, sociology of information, information organization management, and information engineering.

A graphic representation of the knowledge required by a professional is shown in   Figure 9.1 above.

Science

As indicated in Figure 9.1, an information professional's knowledge base rests on "science"—a theory base constructed from the results of research in the profession and related fields. Since library and information science is based on knowledge of human behavior, the social sciences are prominent sources for this knowledge. Chapter 4, The Science Supporting the Information Professions, defines the theory base on which knowledge of professional practice is built and identifies the four fields which comprise the theory base for information science:

1. Sociology information—how knowledge and information are created, reproduced, and disseminated to society.

2. Information psychology—how do individuals seek and acquire information.

3. Information organization management—how information organizations are organized and managed.

4. Information engineering—how databases are developed, organized, and maintained for a particular purpose.

These four fields comprise the science base for practice of the information professions, and they provide the base from which the technology is derived.

Technology

The second level of knowledge is "technology," the theory or science which is applied to the practice of library and information professionals. Professionals apply these practices, or "techniques" to their everyday work. This level of knowledge, referred to sometimes as "substantive" level theory, is practical knowledge which can be used on a daily basis by information professionals. For example, "technology" includes:

- the application of psychology to the client interview, resulting in specific "tips" or behaviors which can be useful in helping a client identify the information s/he needs,

- the organizational schemes used to organize collections of resources, e.g., Dewey Decimal Classification System and the Library of Congress system,

- the techniques that are used to assess information needs of a clientele,

- the skills that are needed to use effectively hardware and software for the development of information services.

This knowledge, combined with the theory or science, can be applied together in the practice of a profession, what we call the "art" of a profession.

Art

"Art" is the application of "technology" and "science" to a particular professional situation. It is the synthesis of a professional's wisdom and experience, as well as information science and technology, to a professional problem. All of a professional's accumulated knowledge and experience is used to solve a professional problem or to help a particular client. For example, when an information professional is asked an information question, that professional utilizes knowledge of the information psychology, the techniques of question negotiation, a knowledge of information resources available for use, and the cumulated experience and knowledge personally available in order to address questions like this: "How can I find information to write a report on NAFTA Treaty?"

The art of the information professions is learned through study, practice, and experience. In a professional education program, this art can be fostered through the practical experience of class projects and field experiences. On the job, art is developed each day and with each professional activity. Continuing education activities can extend the art as well as the science and technology, and professional associations are one easily available source of continuing education.

Professional Associations

Professional associations are the keepers of professional culture. Associations are engaged with both preprofessional education through their interactions with schools that prepare professionals, usually in an advisory role. Professional organizations provide forums for the exchange of knowledge in the field and for dissemination of new knowledge related to practice. Professional associations contribute professional newsletters and journals which publish news of the organization and record accomplishments, trends, research, and innovative practices in the profession. Associations encourage networking among professionals through listservs; local, state, regional, national, and perhaps international conferences. Associations provide opportunities to present new practices, research, and issues at conferences. Through committee work, new policies and procedures for practice are developed, implemented, and evaluated. Professional organizations are involved with accreditation and the maintenance of professional standards, including the articulation, publication, and distribution of ethical codes. In short, professional associations are at the very heart of a professional culture.

In the library and information profession, numerous professional organizations can provide professional support for practitioners. These organizations have national, sometimes regional, and sometimes state chapters. Several of the leading professional information organizations are described in Appendix B.

Literature of the Field

The knowledge which a professional must learn in order to practice in a profession is recorded and available through a body of literature, which is organized, stored, indexed, and retrievable using the terms specific to the field of specialization. The information profession has many journals which record the research and current thinking, new techniques, and issues related to the practice of the information professions. Included are such journals as those listed in Appendix C. Indexes which provide access to the journals in the field are discussed below. Each professional organization has a newsletter, most of which are published online; the purpose of these newsletters is to inform members of changes in the organization, information about conferences, lists of publications available, and other news about the organization. Because all national associations have newsletters in some format, no attempt is made to list the newsletters of ALA divisions or professional organizations.

Indexes

Access to the field is provided through indexes. The major indexes for gaining access to the library and information literature is through the following indexes:

Library Literature & Information Science Full Text is a database which indexes English and foreign-language periodicals, selected state journals, conference proceedings, pamphlets, books, and theses, and more than 300 books per year. Updated daily, this database indexes more than 400 periodicals as far back as 1984, and provides full text of articles from 150 journals as far back as 1997. *Library Literature & Information Science Retrospective: 1905–1983* is a database which provides 80 years of citations from the indexes *Library Work* (1905–1911), *Library Journal* (1912–1920), and *Library Literature* (1921–1983). The citations are to articles and book reviews published internationally in more than 500 periodicals, plus books, book chapters, and theses. Annotations summarize content of articles.

Library Literature & Information Science Index delivers the same indexing offered in *Library Literature & Information Science Full Text*, but without the links to full text articles. It is updated daily on WilsonWeb and monthly on WilsonDisc, and it is available in print.

LISA: Library and Information Science Abstracts is an international abstracting and indexing tool designed for library and information professionals. LISA abstracts more than 440 periodicals from more than 68 countries and in more than 20 languages 1969 to the present. Published by CSA, the database is updated every two weeks, and the index is available in hard copy (http://www.csa.com/factsheets/lisa-set-c.php, accessed July 15, 2006).

Guides and Encyclopedias

For an overview of a field, guides and encyclopedias are useful. Following are sources to consult for an overview of the library and information science professions. *The Whole Library Handbook* is a one-volume encyclopedia now in its 4th edition of library history, demographics, folklore, humor, current events, and popular wisdom. Contents include bits of trivia, humor, essays, and reprints of important journal articles. It is authored by George M. Eberhart, senior editor of *American Libraries.*

World Encyclopedia of Library and Information Services (1993), Third Edition, is a one-volume reference source on libraries and librarianship worldwide. Some 340 articles by more than 300 contributors from all parts of the globe, convey the history, structure, concepts, practice, research, training, institutions, and people of its fields.

Gates' *Introduction to Librarianship. Third Edition* (1990), presents a concise and informative history of libraries from antiquity to the end of the nineteenth century along with the formation of the library profession and library education.

The dearth of guides and current encyclopedias may be attributed to the complexity of the library and information field, the rapid change in our society, and the expansion of the profession during the second half of the twentieth century.

Publishers

Of course, many books are published as textbooks and professional reading by such publishers as The American Library Association, R.R. Bowker, Marcel Dekker, Libraries Unlimited, Sage, Scarecrow Press, H. W. Wilson, etc. Increasingly, journals and books are being published online, especially more specialized titles which cannot be justified financially by publishing in paper. Following is a description of leading publishers in the library and information field.

R.R. Bowker Co. was founded in 1872 with the publication of *Publishers Weekly*, followed by *The Publishers Trade List Annual*. Other major contributions to the field of library and information management include *Ulrich's International Periodicals Directory, Books in Print, Forthcoming Books,* and *AV Marketplace*. In recent years, Bowker has transformed its products to keep pace with changes in technology by publishing on CD's and online.

The H.W. Wilson Company was founded in 1898 by Halsey William Wilson. In its first year, the company published *Cumulative Book Index*, which listed newly published book titles. In 1901 Wilson decided to do for magazine articles what he had done for books by publishing *Readers' Guide to Periodical Literature*, an index that grouped articles by subject. For this and other products, Wilson sought the advice of librarians, the audience for whom the service was designed. The practice of consulting the profession which it serves is followed today.

The company now publishes numerous full-text periodicals databases, biography databases, index and abstracts databases, collection development catalogs, *Art Museum Image Gallery, Famous First Facts, Electronic Edition*, plus many reference monographs. Early WilsonLine and WilsonTape database formats have given way to WilsonWeb, a powerful Web-based information retrieval system (http://www.hwwilson.com/abouthw/history.html, accessed July 15, 2006).

Professional Education

The body of knowledge, the literature, the ethics and values, the system of literature—the culture of a profession—must be conveyed to prospective members of a profession in a systematic way. Professional schools have evolved to diffuse the knowledge and culture of professions. The evolution of the professions began in the latter half of the nineteenth century as social science knowledge was inculcated into professional practice. For example, the study of medicine, law, and theology was formalized and moved into universities. The field of librarianship, the oldest of the information professions, coalesced into a professional organization in 1853 when Charles Jewett of the Smithsonian Institution and Charles Norton organized the first librarians' convention to improve public libraries. The American Library Association was founded in 1876 when approximately 3,700 librarians from all types of libraries met in Philadelphia. In that same year Melvil Dewey's classification system was published and the *American Library Journal* was published with Dewey as editor. In 1877 the first school for librarians was instituted at Columbia College by Dewey.

Professional education in most fields evolved during the first half of the twentieth century. As societal needs demanded more education for the practice of professions, the education of professionals moved from certification at the undergraduate level to undergraduate degrees to graduate degrees. Many professional education fields began as internship programs before moving into universities. For example, large public libraries provided training for staff, and the educational programs gradually moved into nearby colleges. The program to prepare children's librarians at the Carnegie Library of Pittsburgh moved to the Carnegie Institution of Technology (now Carnegie-Mellon University) and then into the University of Pittsburgh.

Others were begun in universities and stayed there. The University of Chicago Graduate Library School, founded in 1928 with funding from the Carnegie Foundation, was the first graduate program for the practice of the information professions. Currently, the master's degree in library and information science accredited by the American Library Association is the accepted credential for professional education in the library and information field. More than fifty such programs are accredited in North America.

Accreditation

Professions have some form of authentication, i.e., some way of identifying individuals who have gained the professional knowledge of the field through an accepted system of licensure or certification. For example, the medical, law, and accounting fields have exams and/or review boards at the local or state levels to monitor the administration of exams to test standards set at the national level.

The information professions have a system of accreditation as a means of demonstrating a level of education appropriate for the field. The American Library Association has provided an accreditation process since the 1930s for librarians and other information professionals. Graduate schools who offer master's degrees in library and information science may seek accreditation by the Association for a period of 7 years, based on Standards for Accreditation adopted in 1992. Approximately fifty-six professional programs in North America are fully accredited by the American Library Association.

School library media programs may be accredited within the American Library Association accreditation process, but there is also a review process for those programs by the American Association of School Librarians (AASL) and the National Council for Accreditation of Teacher Education (NCATE). Professional programs which are a part of a college of education tend to seek this form of accreditation. In addition, states have requirements for certifying or licensing school library media specialists as part of the teacher certification or licensure process. Certification and accreditation are voluntary, while licensure is a requirement, usually of state governments.

To date, the American Library Association (ALA) has accredited programs and has not certified librarians; however, in recent years the association has explored certification and the first certification program will be for Certified Public Library Administrators (CPLA). The program is described on the ALA Web site as follows: "CPLA will certify public library administrators who have achieved proficiency in several critical management-related subjects through experience beyond the Master's of Library Science (MLS)." The Association is also considering certification of support staff.

Guidelines for Service

Professional organizations articulate guidelines which can be used by professionals as they offer services to clientele. In the library and information profession, the divisions of the American Library Association have published guidelines for service, which we will explore. Examples are the guidelines for information service published by RUSA, cataloging standards published by ALCTS, school library media guidelines from AASL, and standards from AIIP.

Code of Ethics

Professions have a system of ethics by which their members practice the profession. In the information professions, those ethics are concerned with the value system of the profession, under what conditions services are rendered and how clients are to be treated as they seek information. Common to the ethics of information professionals are the following:

- Confidentiality of conversations between the professional and the client
- Honesty and integrity in all transactions
- Provision of the highest level of service to clientele, without prejudice
- Respect of the property rights of information creators
- Acknowledgment of the contribution of the information professions to society
- Support for freedom of expression

The ethics of the information profession, as presented by the various professional associations, articulate a common thread of high standards for the profession. Ethics are an essential part of a profession, and the other elements have been described above. Examples of ethics statements are found in the Appendix A.

Public Recognition

An important factor in recognition of a profession is acceptance by the public. The result of all of the factors, public recognition is evidenced by the allocation of tax money for library and information professional salaries, by support of facilities and collections, and for the staffing and education of staff members. For some professions, this recognition is granted as the result of passing an exam; accountants must pass an exam to be declared Certified Public Accountants, and attorneys must pass the bar exam. Others professionals are certified or licensed by completing a specified course of study provided by a sanctioned institution. School library media specialists are certified or licensed by state education agencies by completing specified requirements completed at institutions of higher education in the state.

Public, academic, and some special library positions require the completion of a master's degree accredited by the American Library Association. In most states, there is no requirement for successful completion of an exam. The issue of certification or licensure for librarians has been an issue in the profession for many years, and still is under consideration at the writing of this book. Some library and information science schools issue certificates for specialized study in such areas as children's work, information management, and archives management.

Clearly, the library and information profession has a variety of ways of recognizing competence to practice in the field. The most common recognition is the requirement for an accredited master's degree in the field. While the name may be called "Master of Library Science," "Master of Science in Information Science," "Master of Library and Information Science," or a variation of those names, the accredited master's degree has been a requirement for many librarian professional positions since the 1930s. That requirement is often carried over to nontraditional information positions like those in information management, corporate intelligence, researchers of various types, librarians of various specializations (medical, legal, hospital, newspaper, map, art, etc.).

Figure 9.2. Taxonomy of the Information Professions.

AU: Please
Provide
Figure
Caption

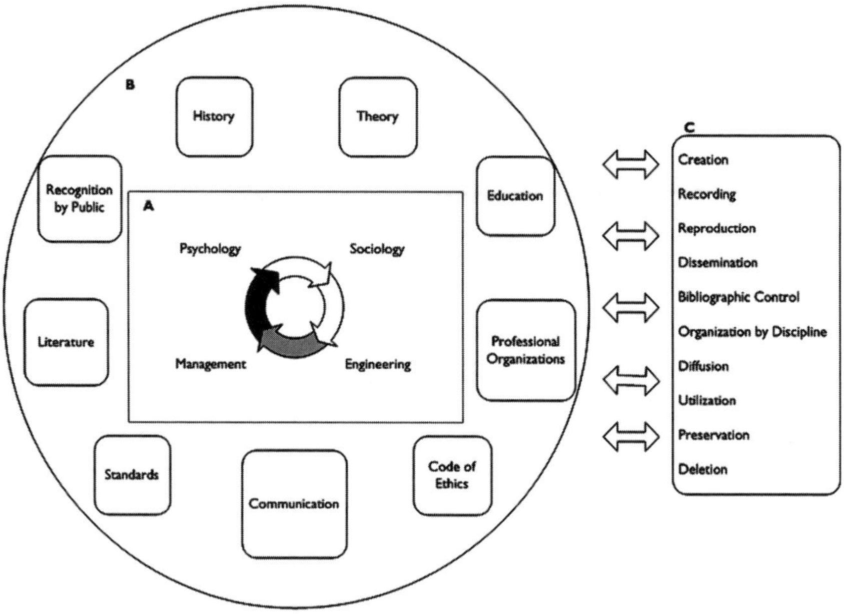

Taxonomy of the Information Professions

In this book, we have presented a number of original theories that may serve as the intellectual foundation for the practice of information professionals. We conclude this chapter by reviewing and synthesizing those theories into "A Taxonomy of the Information Professions." The Taxonomy (Figure 9.2) is a visual representation that shows the components of the core knowledge of the information professions, the elements of the information infrastructure, the functions of a profession, and their relationship to each other. This model attempts to show a dynamic system that is ongoing and ever changing. The components that relate to each other relate differently at different times and in different contexts, but there is a close relationship, as reflected in the model.

The arrows presented in Part A (the square) of the diagram show that the four fields of science are all interwoven, and each enhances the others and is enhanced by the others. These four fields are also influenced by the nine concepts listed in B. They in turn have some influence on each other. The processes identified in C are also influenced by all of the nine characteristics of B and are intimately associated with the concepts in A. These models are discussed in more detail below. For a more thorough review, the reader is referred to Chapters 4 (A), 9 (B), and 5 (C).

Core Knowledge of the Information Professions

In the center of the circle of Figure 9.2 are four topics, representing the theoretical core of the information professions (A). Psychology is the study of individual users and managers in the information professions. Sociology represents the study of the role of information and the information infrastructure in society. The management component represents study of the process of managing information agencies and maintaining information policies for enhancing information transfer in information delivery agencies in communities, regions, and societies. The engineering component of the square represents the design and management of databases containing information, whether data bits, records of aspects of societies, or collections of books. The process of designing and managing these databases is for the purposes of organizing, storing, and retrieving information.

Information Transfer in Society

The concepts listed in the vertical column on the right represent the processes associated with information transfer in society (C). These processes, discussed in depth in Chapter 5, begin with the idea that information is created by individuals, groups, or organizations. Once created, information must be recorded and reproduced so that it can be disseminated. Once disseminated, information must be organized, stored, and retrieved so that it can be utilized. Information can be preserved for future use, then deleted or destroyed when it is outdated or irrelevant. All these processes are part of information transfer.

When information is produced and not transmitted or diffused, it is of little value to the larger society and only serves the entity from which it is produced. Information is critical to the sustenance of life and action. For example, a doctor could make a diagnosis and keep it to himself; consequently, there would be no information transfer and utilization of information. The patient who does not have access to the diagnostic information is not able to ameliorate the condition.

Once recorded, data become information. The remainder of the processes in section C of Figure 9.2 are associated with the process of disseminating that information in society. Dissemination includes the production of such information packages as books, video productions, recordings, and Internet blogs. To be of value beyond the immediate and contemporary, an information system must be able to organize, store, and retrieve information. The process of organizing information for easy retrieval is called "bibliographic control," a concept originally developed to describe the organization of books but has evolved to include other forms of information. Bibliographic control enables the location and retrieval of a particular item, any particular book in a collection or concept in an essay.

Information tends to be organized in subject areas that are associated with particular areas of study in society, disciplines. Universities are organized by disciplines, which may be merged into divisions or schools, e.g., the social sciences, humanities, sciences, and fine arts (See Chapter 2). The purpose of disciplines is to give structure to the way information is produced, stored, organized, and diffused. In other words, disciplines provide a framework for producing new research and providing instruction to people in a structured, systematic manner.

Once information is assimilated into an individual's intelligence, it becomes knowledge. When information has been diffused and converted to knowledge, it is applied in a process of utilization. Utilization of knowledge is the end goal of diffusion. Utilization of knowledge provokes or inhibits change; it is the fuel that sustains the dynamics of a society.

In order to progress, societies must have access to their past, and information may be useful in the immediate present when it is produced, disseminated and diffused. It may also be useful when it is stored and retrieved at a later time from the point when produced; therefore, we need mechanisms for storing and preserving information that may have some utilitarian value in the future. The existence of archives in a society has two purposes: (1) to preserve the information in the records preserved and (2) to preserve the artifact itself.

Information that has been superseded and determined to be incorrect, outdated, or invalid may be deleted or eliminated from the public store of information.

Functions of the Information Professions

The functions of the information professions, which were presented earlier in this, are represented in the circle (B). Professions enhance the process of information transfer in society. Information is to society as blood is to an organism; information must be transferred in order for that society to remain dynamic. Similarly, blood flows to keep an organism flourishing. Lack of blood leads to atrophy and death.

Part B of Figure 9.2 portrays characteristics of professions that enable them to be of service in society. The distinguishing feature of a profession is the unique knowledge possessed by members of that profession. These characteristics in Part B are necessary for professions to maintain quality and public support for their practice. The information professions, of course, possess these characteristics as well.

Conclusion

The culture of a profession consists of a body of knowledge, a value system, a body of literature, professional organizations which promote the culture and update professionals, standards for service, recognition of membership in the profession, and a code of ethics. This chapter outlined the infrastructure of the library and information professions, including a brief history of the information profession with descriptions of information professional organizations, journals, lists, Web sites, educational programs, standards, codes of ethics, and systems of recognition by the public.

We conclude this chapter with a caveat: In addition to all of the elements of a profession, there is an additional aspect, the attitude of the professional. The intent of the educational program, code of ethics, and other characteristics of a profession *should* lead to the building of a professional who is an effective practitioner in the field. However, the true professional is more than a sum of the characteristics of the profession; the professional must be

- Motivated to be an exceptional professional—not an ordinary one who is an information professional to collect a pay check.
- Willing to go beyond the minimum effort to help clients find the information they need and want.
- Driven by the desire for excellence in all of their professional service.
- Willing to work beyond the office hours of the agency.
- Driven to move the profession forward by contributing articles to the professional journals and to mentor others.
- Wanting to be current in technology and new ideas emerging in the field.

True professionals are on a never-ending journey; they are engaged in more than a *job*. They are engaging in a continuously changing career which has untold rewards for the professional and her/his clientele.

References

ACRL. http://www.ala.org/ala/acrl/aboutacrl/whatisacrl/whatacrl.htm (accessed July 10, 2006).

ALCTS. http://www.ala.org/ala/alcts/aboutalcts/aboutalcts.htm (accessed July 10, 2006).

ALSC. http://www.ala.org/alsc/ whoweare.html (accessed July 10, 2006).

American Association of Law Librarians. http://www.aallnet.org/about/ (accessed July 10, 2006).

American Library Association. http://www.ala.org/ala/ourassociation/governingdocs/ policymanual/mission.htm#mission (accessed July 10, 2006).

———. "Certification." http://www.alaapa.org/certification/ certification.html (accessed July 10, 2006).

———. http://www.ala.org/ (accessed July 10, 2006).

American Library Trustee Association. http://www.ala.org/ala/alta/altaorg/ organization.htm (accessed July 10, 2006).

American Society for Information Science and Technology. http://www.asis.org/ about.html (accessed 7/10/06).

American Theological Library Association. http://www.atla.com/about.html (accessed July 11, 2006).

Art Libraries Society of North America. http://www.arlisna.org/ (accessed July 10, 2006).

ASCLATemplate.cfm?Section=asclaourassoc (accessed July 10, 2006).

Association of Records Managers and Administrators. http://www.arma.org/about/ overview/index.cfmhttp://www.arma.org/about/overview/index.cfm (accessed July 10, 2006).

Association for Library and Information Science Education. http://www.alise.org/ (accessed July 11, 2006).Canadian Library Association. http://www.cla.ca/ (accessed July 11, 2006).

Battles, Matthew. 2003. *Library: An unquiet history*. New York: W. W. Norton.

Casson, Lionel. 2001. *Libraries in the ancient world*. New Haven, CT: Yale University Press.

Dickson, Paul. 1986. *The library in America: A celebration in words and pictures*. New York: Facts On File Publications.

Eberhart, George M. 2006. *Whole library handbook 4*. Chicago, IL: American Library Association.

Gates, Jean Key. 1990. *Introduction to librarianship*. 3rd ed. New York and London: Neal-Schuman Publishers.

H.W. Wilson Co. http://www.hwwilson.com/abouthw/history.html (accessed July 15, 2006).

Harris, Michael H. 1995. *History of libraries in the western world*. Metuchen, NJ: Scarecrow Press.

Johnson, Elmer D. 1965. *A history of libraries in the western world*. Lanham, MD: Scarecrow Press.

Journal of Academic Librarianship. http://www.elsevier.com/wps/find/ sitemap.cws_home/sitemap (accessed July 15, 2006).

The Library Administration and Management Association (LAMA). http://www.ala. org/ala/lama/aboutlama/aboutlama.htm (accessed July 15, 2006).

Library and Information Science Research. Elsevier is an international publisher which has purchased many LIS journals. See http://www.elsevier.com/wps/find/ sitemap.cws_home/sitemap (accessed July 15, 2006).

The Library and Information Technology Association. http://www.ala.org/ala/lita/ aboutlita/org/plan.htm (accessed July 15, 2006).

Library Journal. http://www.libraryjournal.com/ (accessed July 15, 2006).

Library Quarterly http://www.journals.uchicago.edu/LQ/home.html Accessed 7/15/06

LISA: Library and Information Science Abstracts. http://www.csa.com/factsheets/ lisa-set-c.php (accessed July 15, 2006).

The Medical Library Association. http://www.mlanet.org/about/history/ mlahistory. html (accessed July 10, 2006).

Music Library Association. http://www.musiclibraryassoc.org/index.shtml (accessed July 10, 2006).

Public Library Association. http://www.ala.org/platemplate.cfm?Section=AboutPLA (accessed July 10, 2006).

Shera, Jesse H. 1976. *Introduction to library science; basic elements of library service*. Littleton, CO: Libraries Unlimited.

Society of American Archivists. http://www.archivists.org/history.asp (accessed July 10, 2006).

Theatre Library Association. http://tla.library.unt.edu/ (accessed July 11, 2006).

Vann, Sarah K., ed. 1978. *Melvil Dewey: His enduring presence in librarianship*. Littleton, CO: Libraries Unlimited.

Wiegand, Wayne A. 1996. *Irrepressible reformer: A biography of Melvil Dewey*. Chicago, IL: American Library Association.

"YALSA Fact Sheet." American Library Association.http://www.ala.org/ala/yalsa/ aboutyalsab/yalsafactsheet.htm (accessed July 10, 2006).

10
Trends and Issues

Chapter Overview

Key theories that present the foundation for library and information science are reviewed. Major issues in the library and information professions are explored, using the functions of information transfer as a framework. A review of selected library and information science (LIS) literature is used to identify current issues, including the education of library and information professionals.

Introduction

The purpose of this chapter is to identify current issues in the information professions. We will use as a framework the information transfer processes discussed in Chapter 5.

As indicated earlier in this book, the goal of the information professions is to enhance the flow of information within and among societies throughout the world, which we also refer to as promoting the process of information transfer. To accomplish this goal of enhancing the creation, reproduction, dissemination, and utilization of information requires the application of a strong academic discipline—information science—located within the broad framework of the social sciences. In this book, we have presented a number of original theories that may serve as this intellectual foundation for the practice of information professionals.

We begin this chapter with a brief review of information transfer, and we then relate issues facing today's library and information professionals to the information transfer processes. By framing issues within the theoretical framework of information transfer, the role of information professionals in a changing society is clarified.

Information Infrastructure Issues

In order to identify issues in libraries and information services, we must focus on the organizational structure required for the effective transfer of information in society, the information infrastructure. We can then have a clearer picture of the role of libraries and other information agencies in that framework. By having that clearer understanding of where libraries fit in that process, we can begin to identify the trends and issues.

In Chapter 7, we defined "information infrastructure" as follows:

> The information infrastructure is a *global* network of *people, organizations, agencies, policies, processes,* and *technologies* organized in a loosely coordinated system to enhance the creation, production, dissemination, organization, storage, retrieval, and preservation of information and knowledge for people. The primary objective of this network is the diffusion of knowledge for a society.

In the section below, we apply this definition in our discussion and utilize the information transfer model as a framework for that discussion.

The information transfer process is described in Chapter 5. To quickly review, the elements of information transfer are (1) creation of information, (2) recording and reproduction, (3) dissemination, (4) organization and retrieval, (5) diffusion, (6) utilization, (7) storage and preservation, and (8) deletion. These elements provide a model for organizing today's trends and issues.

Creation of Information

It is safe to say that the process of creating information has changed markedly in the last 20 years because of technology. Another change has been the widespread acceptance of business teams to create information with the expectation that it will lead to corporate knowledge that can add to the organization's bottom line. Major companies such as Nike and Intel employ in-house librarians who work with these teams to create new ideas from existing information. These are not the passive librarians of stereotype, but are information experts proactively engaged in their patrons' projects.

The role of the information professional in the research process has evolved from helping the researcher to evaluate information sources to determine which are more authoritative into a more proactive role, one that includes performing the research, synthesizing the results and creating a package (format and style) most likely to suit the client's needs. Today's information glut and business's desire to operate with a minimal workforce frequently results in requests of information professionals to perform this type of information creation. While this type of work typically is associated with the independent information professional, some libraries have developed service centers that charge corporate clients for research and repackaging projects.

Finally, information professionals are in the business of creating information through research, whether it is to advance knowledge in a Ph.D. program or to gather data that helps serve the information agency's clientele. Library and information science research has improved considerably over the past 20 years, when much of the effort revolved around counting volumes. However, much more research is needed to analyze and describe the trends and issues of our rapidly changing world.

Recording and Reproduction

Technology has made a major impact in the recording and reproduction of new information. The phenomenon of "digitization" in its various dimensions, e.g., digital imaging, digital preservation, digital libraries, digital archiving, has been increasingly gaining importance within the library and information professional literature. Because digital information is reproduced easily, information professionals must stay current on security measures, privacy, and copyright laws.

Dissemination

Conventional dissemination of information to users of many libraries and other information agencies has been access-oriented, focused on providing users access to information, with less regard to the users' understanding and successful use of the information. In Chapter 3 we identified levels of service—passive, reactive, and assertive. Conventional information service tends to be passive or reactive—the service is provided for the user with no help provided, or the service is provided upon request. However, to fulfill the purpose of effective diffusion and utilization in the information transfer model presented in this book, information professionals must be more engaged in the diffusion process through an assertive level of service that anticipates user needs based on a needs assessment. Information professionals must develop and maintain relationships with their clients, especially in a dynamic, global society, in order to effectively disseminate and diffuse information. People skills, or their lack, are critical to an information professional's career.

The dissemination process has been influenced by technologies such as the ones noted below.

The Internet

The Internet/World Wide Web phenomenon has created dissemination opportunities through online teaching, Internet use, and Webometrics. Online teaching is receiving scrutiny for its effectiveness to deliver courses; as might be expected, the technology that allows online teaching is only part of the equation. An information professional must be able to shift teaching styles as appropriate to the medium by which instruction is delivered. Just as using computers to replicate the card catalog was a limited utilization of technology, so is trying to incorporate everything from a face-to-face course into an online class. Some activities can make the transition and others cannot. A responsible professional is committed to continual learning and improvement to benefit the students.

In addition to online teaching, the use of virtual modes, e.g., blogs, personal Web sites, Web communities like Facebook.com, and My Space.com, are receiving a considerable amount of attention from library practitioners and researchers. Some reference desks are using IM (instant messaging) to provide ready-reference services. These relatively new forms of information dissemination present another important issue for information professionals to determine how these technologies can be used effectively for information transfer and the role of the information professional in that process, assisting users as they learn to use information technologies effectively.

Organization and Retrieval

Librarians for many years have organized and stored information resources in a variety of formats, most recently in electronic formats. The change in library services prompted by advances in technology is an organizational response to changing user needs, a response that could have economic and social significance (Bawden and Rowlands 1999).

Bibliometrics

This challenge presented by the imposition of technology to the organization and retrieval of information is addressed by research in bibliometrics, or citation analysis. Bibliometrics is concerned with the quantitative aspects of the communication of scientific information—the storage, retrieval, and dissemination of scientific information (Glanzel and Schoepflin 1994). Results of bibliometric studies can be applied to improve knowledge organization, to analyze the intellectual structure of a particular discipline, and to construct a thesaurus (Schneider and Borlund 2004). With the advancements of information technology and emergence of the virtual environment, the importance of bibliometrics "as a tool that can increase the analytical capabilities of LIS researchers" has been enhanced greatly.

Webometrics

Another important and increasingly vital issue within LIS is "Webometrics." According to Bjorneborn and Ingwersen (2004), the definition of Webometrics is "the study of the quantitative aspects of the construction and use of information resources, structure and technologies on the Web, drawing on bibliometric and informetric approaches." The term "webometrics" was first coined by Almind and Ingwersen (1997).

Webometrics deserves special attention because it gives birth to an entirely new field of specialization within the domain of bibliometrics.

Metadata

Another new phenomenon with implications for information professionals is "metadata"—data that define other data, or information that describes other information. Metadata are quite important in order to make information retrieval a successful and effective process. Digitization is necessitating the construction and use of metadata at a much broader and complex scale, so that users can get access to print and digital information with maximum ease and with minimum effort.

Metadata have become vital to address specific problems dealing with the classification and cataloging of digital resources (El-Sherbini 2001). Applications of metadata in the current context (digital, virtual, global) continue to gain importance. The rapid increase in digital repositories has increased the interest in metadata (Greenberg 2005). Metadata are in use in various communities, e.g., business, government, and education. Various metadata schemes or specifications have been developed, e.g., Dublin Core Metadata Element Set, National Information Standard Organization (NISO), and International Standard Organization (ISO).

In the U.S. legal community, metadata takes on a particularly important role as attorneys strive to comply with changes in the Federal Rules of Civil Procedure (Dec 2006) regarding discovery issues and electronically stored information (ESI). Legal information managers are only one group among information professionals who must stay current on technology and related policies. Regardless of the community in which one practices, clients count on information professionals to lead the way through complex issues such as ESI and its related metadata.

Other Issues in Information Organization

In the pre-Internet era, librarians were the unquestioned experts on information organization. The Internet challenged librarians to adapt to a 24/7 information service world and many responded proactively to this challenge by adopting various new technologies. Online catalogues, virtual referencing, and provision of books and journals in the digital format are some of the steps taken by librarians.

Organization of knowledge, as redefined by Google, is the current phenomenon to quickly retrieve information from the Internet; however, most users are unaware of basic search techniques that could increase the relevance of their search results. Another concern is that the wisdom of the universe is not entirely online, at least, not until Google's Book Search project achieves its goal of digitizing libraries around the world. Launched in 2002 under the name Google Print and renamed Google Book Search in 2005, the project involves librarians and publishers as partners in an effort to digitize the world's collection of information, making it searchable and accessible through the Internet. While the Google Book Search project is innovative, eventually it will be joined and possibly superseded by similar projects in the future. The lesson information professionals need to take away from this is to teach information skills (how to think critically) rather than technology, since information users must be able to seek information through the most reliable sources, regardless of where they are located.

Google has superseded the organization done by librarians in that its organization system is widely used by the public. From the perspective of bibliographic control, we still need classification and cataloging developed and functioning in order to build effective access points to the collection; we must organize books within a collection. Systems now pull ideas from books, but we must be able to pull books from the collections. Regardless of the package, paper or digital, the issues associated with classification and cataloging remain. How does an information professional retrieve a particular idea from a mass collection of information and knowledge? How does an information professional arrange the work of an author among the works of a group of authors? It is a knowledge management issue. While technology enables the retrieval of words and terms, the retrieval of the "right" ideas required by a user is still a vital skill and challenge to librarians and information professionals.

Other Issues in Information Retrieval

Today's computer technologies allow anyone with access to the Internet the opportunity to self-publish books, blogs, wikis, and electronic journals without the review of anyone in addition to the author. While some of this self-publishing is accepted by the discipline's peers, much of it is rife with inaccuracies, ideological biases, and lacking intellectual foundation. The information professional plays a vital role by helping information consumers sort out the information produced by knowledgeable producers from the "hacks" who are promoting their own agendas. It is increasingly the role of information professionals to engage in the teaching of information literacy skills to help information users discern the reputable information packages from the "trash."

Diffusion

As noted above in the "dissemination" section, information professionals must go beyond the concept of access to diffusion of knowledge, i.e., to help people understand information and to use it effectively. This is where information psychology plays an important role. By understanding how users seek information and recognizing the different ways people prefer to learn, the information professional can facilitate information diffusion by customizing to their clients' particular needs.

Learning Styles

Everyone has a preferred method (or methods) of learning. Some prefer to receive information in audio format; others cannot retain the message without seeing it in print. Some people process information quickly while others take much longer to absorb and understand what they hear or see. None of these styles is better than another, they are simply different. The key for the information professional is to recognize the diversity of learning styles and adapt services to maximize the client's ability to receive and retain the information package.

Information Literacy

Information literacy is a competency that enables individuals to become informed citizens of an information society. Lloyd (2003) defines information literacy as "a meta-competency that encapsulates the generic skills of defining, locating, and accessing information" (p. 87). The American Library Association (ALA) defines information literacy as "a set of abilities requiring individuals to recognize when information is needed and have the ability to locate, evaluate, and use effectively the needed information" (1989).

Another term for information literacy is "critical thinking skills," or the ability to locate evidence to support an idea and engage in logical thinking to support or refute an argument. While everyone has at least one learning style preference, not everyone has critical thinking skills. Until our clients of any age develop these skills, it is up to the information professional to have a solid grasp on the ability to locate, assess, synthesize, and evaluate information. As van Gelder (2005) noted, "critical thinking is hard," and it requires study and practice in order to master these skills. The information professional can assist clients with learning critical thinking skills and in the meantime, can model them by example.

Information literacy is becoming more important with the passage of time. As the informational content, and the medium to facilitate the production, transfer, and diffusion of information becomes ubiquitous, the need to equip one with the information literacy techniques is also becoming more important (Wallis 2005).

Knowledge Management

Knowledge management is an emerging trend in both library and information science and business management. The current emphasis on knowledge as a "key resource" vital for organizational success is a new dimension of research and professional attention.

In the business world, the importance of knowledge as a key resource has been realized and knowledge has been considered as an important pre-requisite for a successful strategy (Drucker 1993, Nonaka and Takeuchi 1995). The business world continues to lead the conversation regarding knowledge management, understanding that it requires a combination of information resources, a corporate culture of learning and a willingness to share knowledge (Widen-Wulff and Suomi 2007). The information profes-sional can and should be instrumental in their organization's knowledge management efforts.

The information professional can assist with knowledge creation, recording, reproduction, dissemination, organization, diffusion, utilization, preservation, and deletion. Thinking of knowledge management in those terms reveals that librarians have been knowledge managers throughout the history of the profession. As keepers of recorded knowledge, librarians have been supporting the knowledge transfer process in all of its phases, but they have been focused on organization, storage, and retrieval. It is now apparent that the role of librarians must be expanded to participate in all stages of information and knowledge transfer processes.

Utilization

Utilization is the outcome of diffusion. Librarians must be engaged with learning theory and with the client. The librarian must know learning theories in order to be effective as a facilitator of learning so that information can be used effectively.

Health Informatics

A growing trend is the importance of health informatics—issues relat-ing to the packaging, disseminating, and retrieving of health information. One of the contributing reasons for increasing importance of information in health sciences is growing healthcare failures, or clinical adverse events (MacIntosh-Murray and Choo 2005). Research by Murray and Choo high-lighted the importance of information and discussed the various ways in which mismanagement of information can lead to health care failures. In addition to the importance of information in health care, the exchange of "health information" in virtual communities has been practiced since the mid-1990s.

The abundant availability of health information on the Web has illus-trated the need for health librarians and information professionals to pro-mote health information literacy among health consumers (Cullen 2005). The availability of health information in a virtual environment allows infor-mation professionals to enhance the scope of information literacy to include the health information literacy.

Preservation

Preservation of electronic resources is a serious issue in the informa-tion transfer process. As storage technologies change formats, the informa-tion may be lost if the information management procedures do not include planned conversion to newer formats. For example, film and videotape as a medium is being replaced by digital technology as a storage medium for motion pictures. Unless the contents of videotapes and film are transferred to a digital storage device, or unless the original technology and its retrieval capabilities (film projectors and video players) are maintained, the films may be lost. This issue is one of concern and study by preservation specialists in the library and information professions.

Preservation issues are of concern to a variety of industries. Legal requirements of records retention for corporations are one issue; protecting corporate memory is another. Communities may wish to preserve historical items and face policy issues of whether Web site pages should be archived. Finally, governments are responsible for maintaining records of ordinances, statutes, and other legislation. Without adequate attention to digital preservation, key notes of legislative history may be lost to the detriment of a democratic society.

Deletion

Decisions by information professionals to delete information packages from a collection are a similar process to that of selecting items to purchase. The mission of the agency, needs of clientele, potential use, accuracy and currency of the information, and condition of the physical information package are all considerations when making a decision to keep or to delete an item. Appropriateness of the format or medium for the clientele, and availability of appropriate technology to access the information is also a factor. Special libraries may face additional deletion issues dictated by legal retention requirements. Beyond those, the materials' role in the corporate memory must be taken into consideration prior to final disposition.

Issues in Library/Information Education

Library and Information Science (LIS) as an academic discipline is operating in an environment that has changed drastically since the early 1990s. Part of that change can be attributed to advances in information technology that allows course delivery through interactive video and the Internet. In addition to information technology, some LIS programs schedule courses at nontraditional times in order to best meet the needs of their nontraditional students' schedules. Mergers among various academic departments and increasing emphasis on measuring departmental efficiency (in monetary terms) among various other variables have forced LIS as an academic discipline to change its curriculum, course offerings, and in some cases, core competencies.

Recent Studies of LIS Education

In the 1990s, several LIS schools started responding to the external environment by merging with other academic departments, offering a wide range of new courses, and by placing an increased emphasis on information technology. In some cases, LIS schools expanded their core competencies by changing the vary nature of their internal environment. For example, Syracuse University, the University of California-Berkeley, and the University of Washington library schools adopted a new paradigm in which the curriculum is information-centered and not library-centered.

Logan and Hsieh-Yee (2001) examined LIS education during the 1990s and identified changes, including: "responses to technological innovation and the enormous expansion of the information economy, continued awareness

of multicultural issues, recognition of importance of broader LIS focus..."
(p. 425). LIS is a discipline that is rapidly expanding its strategic reach in
order to address the various challenges that are emerging within the larger
social, political, economic and technological context.

A key study of LIS curricula was the KALIPER study a two-year project
of the Association of Library and Information Science Education (ALISE).
The purpose of the project, conducted between 1998 and 2000, was to analyze
the major curricular changes in LIS education. Considered to be the most
extensive report since the Williamson Report in 1923, the KALIPER report
found LIS a vibrant, dynamic, and a changing field undertaking an array of
initiatives.

The KALIPER study identified six trends in LIS education:

1. Although LIS schools prepare students for careers in libraries, the
   curricula "... are addressing broad based information environments
   and information problems." (Pettigrew and Durrance 2001, 174)
   Among the indicators of this trend are schools changing their names
   to drop "library" from the title in deference to "information," thus
   broadening the scope of the school and its programs.

2. Curricula continue the trend to multidisciplinarity, but the core
   courses are user-centered.

3. Increasingly LIS schools are infusing information technology into
   the curriculum.

4. Many schools are experimenting with specialization by offering certificates and specialization in such areas as information resource
   management, archival studies, information systems, school library
   media, and law librarianship.

5. LIS schools are providing a variety of formats to provide students
   flexibility. Among the options are off-campus offerings, Internet-
   based degrees, and mixed models of on- and off-campus courses.

6. Schools are expanding their programs to include related undergraduate, master's and doctoral degrees. (Pettigrew and Durrance 2001,
   173–179)

Similar trends were identified by the Delphi Study by Baruchson-Arbib
and Bronstein (2002) conducted in Israel during 1998–2000. This study examined the views of LIS experts on the future of the LIS profession in light
of the changes in information technology. Forty experts from the United
States, Canada, Western and Central Europe, and Israel participated in the
study. Researchers asked the experts questions pertaining to (a) development of traditional libraries into virtual libraries, (b) transition of libraries
from a technical to a user-centered approach, and (c) skills and competencies
needed by LIS professionals.

Among the findings:

1. The value-added services of libraries and information centers enable
   these agencies to be preserved, although they will be transformed.

2. Both traditional and virtual libraries will coexist.

3. LIS professionals have become and will continue to be trainers in
   information literacy and technology skills.

4. Trends identified by the Delphi panel of experts are similar to conclusions reached by the KALIPER study.

5. The traditional skills of LIS professionals will continue to be valued by the profession and by the Information Society.

Finally, the study concludes with the following statement:

Libraries and the LIS profession will not disappear; they will be dramatically transformed, in many instances beyond recognition, but the essence of the profession will have great value and it will survive the "Information Revolution." (Baruchson-Arbib and Bronstein 2002, 402)

It is clear from the studies cited that the library and information professions must be alert to the changes that are sparked by technology, and the role of library and information professionals will continue to evolve to be more assertive, engaged, and people-oriented, integrating new technologies into the information transfer process. In order to remain updated throughout one's career, continuing education must be a part of one's professional life.

Professional education is based on theory. For the information professions, that theory base comprises social science theory and theory generated by research in LIS. During the last two decades, researchers in LIS have borrowed from the social sciences, yet the authors submit that the information professions have not done enough with social science theory (e.g., sociology, psychology, and management theories) and more could be done by researchers to translate theory and research findings for practitioners. Likewise, we argue that practitioners are too often unwilling to read research and to apply it to their practice in the profession. Much research in LIS has been historical or descriptive, describing the state of practice. While these studies have benefited the field, more research is needed to generate theory that can be implemented in practice.

Conclusion

In this chapter, we have presented trends and issues based on the information transfer model. Although technology has influenced all segments of the information transfer process, the steps in the process remain, and the information professional has a role to play in each phase or step of the information transfer process.

Rather than making the information professional obsolete, technology provides an opportunity for the information professional to have an increasingly important role. The key to the information professional's future success is their willingness to pay attention to the theories that under-gird an expert diagnosis of information needs, planning, and implementation of services and continuous evaluation of services to ensure excellence.

"Change" is perhaps the best word to serve as a catchphrase for information professionals and for students studying to be information professionals. Be alert to changes in technology with implications for their impact on information users. The information professional must be vigilant of the environment to detect new discoveries in social science research that can better serve individuals and groups.

Furthermore, information professionals must be willing to assume a leadership role to promote the effective use of information. Knowledge of information transfer processes enables information professionals to discern trends and realize the changing role of information and information professionals in society. Leadership is needed to help others understand the role of information and information professionals and to lead the way into the twenty-first century as we immerse ourselves in a knowledge society.

With change comes the requirement for continuing professional education. We urge all would-be and practicing professionals to see their professional learning as a lifelong process. Read, attend conferences, take classes, and expand one's professional network to keep learning of new research, new technologies, and new trends that will affect your work.

We wish you, the reader, success in your professional journey into one of the most important professions of the twenty-first century!

References

American Library Association, Presidential Committee on Information Literacy, Final Report (1989), Chicago, IL.

Baruchson-Arbib, Shifra and Jenny Bronstein. 2002. A view to the future of the library and information science profession: A Delphi study. *Journal of the American Society for Information Science and Technology*.

Bawden, David and Ian Rowlands (1999). Digital libraries: assumptions and concepts. *Libri* 49: 181–191.

Björneborn, Lennart, and Peter Ingwersen. 2004. Towards a basic framework of webometrics. *Journal of the American Society for Information Science and Technology* 55:1216–1227.

Cullen, Rowena. 2005. Empowering patients through health information literacy training. *Library Review* 54:231–244.

Drucker, Peter F. 1993. *Post-Capitalist society*, 1st ed. New York: Harper Business.

El-Sherbini, Magda. 2001. Metadata and the future of cataloging. *Library Review* 50:16–27.

Glanzel, Wolfgang, and Urs Schoepflin. 1994. A stochastic model for the aging of scientific literature. *Scientometrics* 30:49–64.

Google Library Project. http://books.google.com/googlebooks/newsviews/ (accessed January 30, 2007)

Greenberg, Jane. 2005. Understanding metadata and metadata schemes. *Cataloging and Classification Quarterly* 40:17–36.

Lloyd, Annemaree. 2003. Information literacy: The meta competency of the knowledge economy? An exploratory paper. *Journal of Librarianship and Information Science* 35:87–91.

Logan, Elizabeth and Ingrid Hsieh-Yee. 2001. Library and information science education in the nineties. *Annual Review of Information Science and Technology* 35:425–477.

MacIntosh-Murray, Anu and Chun Wei Choo. 2005. Information behavior in the context of improving patient safety (hospital information management). *Journal of the American Society for Information Science and Technology* 56:1332–14

Nonaka, Ikujiro and Hirotaka Takeuchi. 1995. *The knowledge-creating company: How Japanese companies create the dynamics of innovation*. New York: Oxford University Press.

Pettigrew, Karen E. and Joan C. Durrance. 2001. KALIPER: introduction and overview of results. *Journal of Education for Library and Information Science* 42:170–180.

Schneider, Jesper W. and Pia Borlund. 2004. Introduction to bibliometrics for construction and maintenance of thesauri. *Journal of Documentation* 60:524–549.

van Gelder, Tim. 2005. Teaching critical thinking: some lessons from cognitive science. *College Teaching* 53:41–46.

Wallis, Jake. 2005. Cyberspace, information literacy and the information society. *Library Review* 54:218–222.

Widén-Wulff, Gunilla and Reima Suomi. 2007. Utilization of information resources for business success: The knowledge sharing model. *Information Resources Management Journal* 20:46–67.

Appendix A: Codes of Ethics

American Library Association

As members of the American Library Association, we recognize the importance of codifying and making known to the profession and to the general public the ethical principles that guide the work of librarians, other professionals providing information services, library trustees and library staffs.

Ethical dilemmas occur when values are in conflict. The American Library Association Code of Ethics states the values to which we are committed, and embodies the ethical responsibilities of the profession in this changing information environment.

We significantly influence or control the selection, organization, preservation, and dissemination of information. In a political system grounded in an informed citizenry, we are members of a profession explicitly committed to intellectual freedom and the freedom of access to information. We have a special obligation to ensure the free flow of information and ideas to present and future generations.

The principles of this Code are expressed in broad statements to guide ethical decision making. These statements provide a framework; they cannot and do not dictate conduct to cover particular situations.

We provide the highest level of service to all library users through appropriate and usefully organized resources; equitable service policies; equitable access; and accurate, unbiased, and courteous responses to all requests.

We uphold the principles of intellectual freedom and resist all efforts to censor library resources.

We protect each library user's right to privacy and confidentiality with respect to information sought or received and resources consulted, borrowed, acquired or transmitted.

We recognize and respect intellectual property rights.

We treat co-workers and other colleagues with respect, fairness, and good faith, and advocate conditions of employment that safeguard the rights and welfare of all employees of our institutions.

We do not advance private interests at the expense of library users, colleagues, or our employing institutions.

We distinguish between our personal convictions and professional duties and do not allow our personal beliefs to interfere with fair representation of the aims of our institutions or the provision of access to their information resources.

We strive for excellence in the profession by maintaining and enhancing our own knowledge and skills, by encouraging the professional development of co-workers, and by fostering the aspirations of potential members of the profession.

Adopted by the ALA Council June 28, 1995.

Association of Independent Information Professionals

An Independent Information Professional is an entrepreneur who has demonstrated continuing expertise in the art of finding and organizing information. Each provides information services on a contractual basis to more than one client and serves as an objective intermediary between the client and the information world.

An Information Professional bears the following responsibilities:

Uphold the profession's reputation for honesty, competence, and confidentiality.

Give clients the most current and accurate information possible within the budget and time frames provided by the clients.

Help clients understand the sources of information used and the degree of reliability which can be expected from those sources.

Accept only those projects which are legal and are not detrimental to our profession.

Respect client confidentiality.

Recognize intellectual property rights. Respect licensing agreements and other contracts. Explain to clients what their obligations might be with regard to intellectual property rights and licensing agreements.

Maintain a professional relationship with libraries and comply with all their rules of access.

Assume responsibility for employees' compliance with this code.

Approved by the membership May 5, 1989, at the Third Annual Meeting, Lowell, MA. Amended by the membership April 22, 1990, at the Fourth Annual Meeting, San Francisco, CA. Amended by the membership April 18, 1997, at the Eleventh Annual Meeting, Orlando, FL. Amended by the membership April 24, 1999, at the Thirteenth Annual Meeting, Berkeley, CA. Amended by the membership April 20, 2002, at the Sixteenth Annual Meeting, Long Beach, CA.

Source: http://www.aiip.org/AboutAIIP/aiipethics.html, accessed January 31, 2007.

ARMA International

Preamble

Information and records management is that field within the information profession responsible for managing the creation, use, maintenance, and disposition of records generated in the normal functioning of all types of organizations.

The Association of Records Managers and Administrators (ARMA International) is a not-for-profit organization representing professionals in the field of information and records management. Its primary purpose is the advancement of records and information management through education and professional development.

Purposes of the Code

This code is intended to increase the awareness of ethical issues among information and records management practitioners and to guide them in reflection, decision making, and action in two broad areas of ethical concern: society and the profession.

I: The Social Principles

Because of their responsibilities to society, information and records managers:

Support the free flow and oppose censorship of publicly available information as a necessary condition for an informed and educated society.

Support the creation, maintenance, and use of accurate information and support the development of information management systems which place the highest priority on accuracy and integrity.

Condemn and resist the unethical or immoral use or concealment of information.

Affirm that the collection, maintenance, distribution, and use of information about individuals is a privilege in trust: the right to privacy of all individuals must be both promoted and upheld.

Support compliance with statutory and regulatory laws related to recorded information.

II: The Professional Principles

Because of their responsibilities to their employers or clients as well as to their profession, information and records managers:

Pursue appropriate educational requirements for professional practice, including a program of ongoing education and certification.

Accurately represent their education, competencies, certifications, and experience to superiors, clients, co-workers and colleagues in the profession.

Serve the client or employer at the highest level of professional competence.

Recognize illegal or unethical situations and inform the client or employer of possible adverse implications.

Avoid personal interest or improper gain at the expense of clients, employers, or co-workers.

Maintain the confidentiality of privileged information.

Enrich the profession by sharing knowledge and experience; encourage public discussion of the profession's values, services, and skills.

Are actively committed to recruiting individuals to the profession on the basis of competence and educational qualifications without discrimination.

Annotated Code of Professional Responsibility

Preamble

Information and records management is that field within the information profession responsible for managing the creation, use, maintenance, and disposition of records generated in the normal functioning of all types of organizations.

The Association of Records Managers and Administrators (ARMA International) is a not-for-profit organization representing professionals in the field of information and records management. Its primary purpose is the advancement of information and records management through education and professional development.

Purposes of the Code

This code is intended to increase the awareness of ethical issues among information and records management practitioners and to guide them in reflection, decision making, and action in two broad areas of ethical concern: society and the profession.

I: The Social Principles

Because of their responsibilities to society, information and records managers:

Support the free flow of information and oppose the censorship of publicly available information as a necessary condition for an informed and educated society.

Any government or public organization operating behind closed doors or restricting access to public information is a government or an organization which does not operate in accordance with democratic principles. Information and records management professionals understand that information and knowledge are the lifeblood of a free society. Therefore, they support the broadest possible access to public information.

Support the creation, maintenance, and use of accurate information and support the development of information management systems which place the highest priority on accuracy and integrity.

The flawed creation, maintenance, or application of information can harm individuals or organizations in many ways. Information and records managers recognize that information has a life cycle and can be altered or misinterpreted at every stage of that cycle. Therefore, information and records managers undertake analyses and make recommendations regarding the appropriate creation, storage, dissemination, and use of information to insure its integrity.

Condemn and resist the unethical or immoral use or concealment of information.

Properly used, information is a powerful tool, one which can save lives, overthrow corrupt governments, or explore the universe. On the other hand, improper, illegal, unethical, or immoral use or concealment of information can wreck careers, cost lives, or destroy organizations. The information professional acts to prevent improper uses of information and refuses to affiliate with individuals or organizations that permit or promote such activity.

Affirm that the collection, maintenance, distribution, and use of information about individuals is a privilege in trust: the right to privacy of all individuals must be both promoted and upheld.

The right to privacy is a value respected by free people everywhere. Information and records managers strive to protect the individual's privacy while, often at the same time, having to reconcile that right with the right of access to information by others. The information and records manager must insure that effective policies, systems, and technologies are in place to protect information about individuals from unauthorized disclosure.

Support compliance with statutory and regulatory laws related to recorded information.

An information management program must act first in accord with the law. Otherwise, there is no proper foundation for decisions made about the creation, use, storage, or disposition of recorded information. Information and records managers must, therefore, have current knowledge of all statutes and regulatory requirements having any bearing on recorded information under their jurisdiction. This knowledge is the starting point upon which the information and records manager's ethical foundations are built.

II: The Professional Principles

Because of their responsibilities to their employers or clients as well as to their profession, information and records managers:

Pursue appropriate educational requirements for professional practice, including a program of ongoing education and certification.

Appropriate formal and continuing education is critical to enlarging one's knowledge and maintaining one's competence in any field. Because information and records management continues to be transformed legally and technologically, all information and records managers have a responsibility to attain a level of education necessary to maintain and improve their positions within their organization and the profession. Education in information and records management must continue throughout an individual's career, whether through degree programs, formal academic coursework, certification, workshops, seminars, and/or conferences sponsored by associations within the information management discipline.

Accurately represent their education, competencies, certifications, and experience to superiors, clients, co-workers and colleagues in the profession.

Misrepresentation of one's credentials is usually grounds for dismissal. Exaggeration of one's accomplishments or abilities is equally odious, is unethical, and is not to be tolerated.

Serve the client or employer at the highest level of professional competence.

Using effective information and records management principles and practices, the professional provides service at the highest level of competence. One factor differentiating a professional from other employees of an organization is that a professional is able to separate professional responsibility and judgment from personal feelings and loyalty. This serves the employer's or client's best long-term interests. Anything less demeans the practitioner and, by extension, the profession.

Recognize illegal or unethical situations and inform the client or employer of possible adverse implications.

The knowledge and values of information professionals uniquely qualify them to recognize the ingredients of ethically complex issues related to information and records management. The information and records manager pursues a reflective morality, not one limited by custom, tradition, or the moral terrain of a specific work environment. The professional has a responsibility to inform the employer or client that a given decision, action, policy, or procedure may have negative implications. The information and records manager may decide to disassociate from a client or employer who continues to pursue such a course.

Avoid personal interest or improper gain at the expense of clients, employers, colleagues, or co-workers.

Improper or illegal use of information for personal gain can take many forms. Information and records managers routinely access information during the course of their work. The information and records manager must be careful never to use or to disclose such information in a manner which will knowingly bring, or have the appearance of bringing, gain at the expense of one's employer, client, colleagues, or co-workers. Also, conflicts of interest may arise which influence the decision making process. In such cases, the information and records manager must be aware of such conflicts when recommending appropriate solutions to information and records management problems.

Maintain the confidentiality of privileged information.

Every organization has privileged information. This may include information classified for national-defense purposes or information restricted for proprietary or privacy reasons. The information and records manager has the expertise and experience to evaluate, recommend, and oversee systems, procedures, and equipment which maintain the integrity of this information—regardless of media—against unauthorized access.

Enrich the profession by sharing knowledge and experience; encourage public discussion of the profession's values, services, and skills.

The degree of professional status of any field is directly related to society's knowledge and appreciation of that field's work. Along with published research, the exchange of ideas and knowledge enriches the profession. Not every individual has the ability to stand before a crowd and speak effectively on information and records management. Every individual does, however, have the ability to communicate experiences, lessons learned, knowledge, and values. Practitioners should take whatever public-education opportunities present themselves to portray the achievements and benefits of information and records management in an accurate, engaging, and informative manner.

Are actively committed to recruiting individuals to the profession on the basis of competence and educational qualifications without discrimination.

In some organizations, nepotism or patronage may affect hiring decisions; in others, discrimination on the basis of sex, race, age, physical limitation, national origin or cultural heritage, appearance, sexual orientation, or religion may take place. Information and records managers, however, should distance themselves from such practices and act to hire and promote individuals solely on the bases of education, competence, and performance.

Copyright 1995 ARMA International, http://www.arma.org/about/overview/ethics.cfm, accessed January 31, 2007.

Society of Competitive Intelligence Professionals (SCIP)

To continually strive to increase the recognition and respect of the profession.

To comply with all applicable laws, domestic and international.

To disclose accurately all relevant information, including one's identity and organization, prior to all interviews.

To fully respect all requests for confidentiality of information.

To avoid conflicts of interest in fulfilling one's duties.

To provide honest and realistic recommendations and conclusions in the execution of one's duties.

To promote this code of ethics within one's company, with third-party contractors and within the entire profession.

To faithfully adhere to and abide by one's company policies, objectives, and guidelines.

http://www.scipstore.org/2_code.php, accessed January 31, 2007.

Appendix B: Professional Organizations

American Association of Law Libraries (AALL)

Founded in 1906, the American Association of Law Libraries promotes law libraries in law firms, law schools, corporate legal departments, courts, and government agencies. With more than 5,000 members, the Association represents law librarians and related professionals to foster the profession of law librarianship, and to provide leadership in the field of legal information.

American Library Association (ALA)

With a membership of more than 64,000, ALA's stated mission is "... to provide leadership for the development, promotion, and improvement of library and information services and the profession of librarianship in order to enhance learning and ensure access to information for all." (American Library Association 2007) ALA comprises eleven divisions, each with a type-of-library or type-of-library-function specialization. The divisions provide numerous services to members, including publications, continuing education, awards and scholarships, and conferences. The divisions are described briefly below; more information may be found on their respective Web sites.

The largest division of ALA is the American Association of School Librarians. AASL advocates for school library media programs and school library media specialists.

The Association of College and Research Libraries (ACRL), is a professional association of academic librarians and "... is dedicated to enhancing the ability of academic library and information professionals to serve the information needs of the higher education community and to improve learning, teaching, and research." (ACRL 2007)

Association for Library Collections & Technical Services (ALCTS) members are dedicated to identification, selection, evaluation, acquisition, cataloging, classification, and preservation of all kinds of library materials.

The Association for Library Service to Children is concerned with the improvement and extension of library services to children in all types of libraries and for the improvement of techniques of library service to children from preschool through the eighth grade or junior high school age.

Association for Library Trustees and Advocates (ALTA) is "dedicated to providing resources, programs, publications and services to America's public library trustees and advocates." (ALA 2007)

The Association of Specialized and Cooperative Library Agencies (ASCLA) represents state library agencies, specialized library agencies, multitype library cooperatives, and independent librarians.

The Library Administration and Management Association (LAMA) supports library leaders by offering opportunities to connect with people of similar interests, exchange ideas, collaborate on projects, publish research, mentor future leaders, and hone leadership and management skills.

The Library and Information Technology Association (LITA) explores new technology applications in libraries. Through its publications, programs, and other activities, LITA promotes, develops, and aids in the implementation of library and information technology.

The Public Library Association (PLA) has the purpose to strengthen public libraries and their contribution to the communities they serve. PLA exists to provide a diverse program of communication, publication, advocacy, continuing education, and programming for its members and others interested in the advancement of public library service.

The Reference and User Services Association (RUSA) is responsible for supporting the delivery of general library services and materials to adults, and the provision of reference and information services, collection development, and resource sharing in all types of libraries.

The Young Adult Library Services Association (YALSA) advocates, promotes and strengthens library service to teens, ages 12 through 18, and supports those who provide library service to this population.

American Society for Information Science and Technology (ASIS&T)

The American Society for Information Science and Technology seeks to improve access to information by leading the search for new theories, techniques, and applications of technology. Its membership comes from such fields as librarianship, computer science, linguistics, management, engineering, law, medicine, chemistry, and education to improve ways to store, retrieve, analyze, manage, and disseminate information.

American Theological Library Association (ATLA)

The American Theological Library Association provides programs, products, and services to support theological and religious studies libraries and librarians representing many religious traditions and denominations.

Art Libraries Society of North America (ARLIS/NA)

This organization provides a forum for ideas, projects, and programs to foster excellence in art and design librarianship and image management.

Association for Independent Information Professionals (AIIP)

The Association of Independent Information Professionals seeks to explain the role of information entrepreneurs and to provide a forum for independent information professionals to meet and exchange views.

Association for Library and Information Science Education (ALISE)

ALISE is an association of educators and researchers which promotes the scholarship of teaching and learning for library and information science.

Association of Records Managers and Administrators (ARMA)

ARMA International is the professional organization considered the authority on managing records and information—paper and electronic. Its members include records managers, archivists, corporate librarians, imaging specialists, legal professionals, IT managers, consultants, and educators from government, legal, healthcare, financial services, and petroleum agencies in the United States, Canada, and more than thirty other countries.

Canadian Library Association

The Canadian Library Association membership works in college, university, public, special (corporate, nonprofit, and government) and school libraries in Canada. Others sit on boards of public libraries, work for companies that provide goods and services to libraries, or are students in graduate level or community college programs.

The Association's five constituent divisions are:

Canadian Association for School Libraries, including the School Library Administrators' (SLAS) section

Canadian Association of College and University Libraries (CACUL), including the Community and Technical College (CTCL) section

Canadian Association of Public Libraries (CAPL), including the Canadian Association of Children's Librarians (CACL) section

Canadian Association of Special Libraries and Information Services (CASLIS), with chapters in Calgary, Edmonton, Manitoba, Ottawa, Toronto, and Atlantic Canada

Canadian Library Trustees Association, promotes and supports cooperation and communication among library trustee associations.

Medical Library Association (MLA)

Medical Library Association members reside in 43 countries and are "...committed to educating health information professionals, supporting health information research, promoting access to the world's health sciences information, and working to ensure that the best health information is available to all." http://www.mlanet.org/index.html, accessed January 31, 2007

Music Library Association (MLA)

The Music Library Association is devoted to music librarianship and all aspects of music materials in libraries. The membership includes music librarians, librarians who work with music as part of their responsibilities, composers and music scholars, and others interested in the program of the association.

Society of American Archivists

The Society of American Archivists' mission is to serve ". . . the educational and informational needs of its members and provides leadership to help ensure the identification, preservation, and use of the nation's historical record." The Society provides leadership in the development of archival policies and standards for archiving records in all formats.

Special Libraries Association (SLA)

The Special Libraries Association represents the interests of information professionals in more than eighty countries worldwide. Special librarians are information resource experts who collect, analyze, evaluate, package, and disseminate information to facilitate accurate decision-making in corporate, academic, and government settings.

Theatre Library Association (TLA)

The Theatre Library Association supports librarians and archivists affiliated with theatre, dance, performance studies, popular entertainment, motion picture, and broadcasting collections in libraries, archives, museums, private collections, and the digital environment.

Appendix C: Professional Journals

AALL Spectrum is a monthly magazine distributed free of charge to members of the American Association of Law Libraries. It publishes articles on topics of interest to law librarians, as well as news about the American Association of Law Libraries.

AIIP Connections is a quarterly publication of the Association for Independent Information Professionals. It is available in print and electronically via the AIIP Web site.

ALCTS Newsletter Online is published six times a year on the Association of Library Collections & Technical Services web site. It contains news, events, updates, current practice, and developments in the field.

ALSConnect, newsletter of the Association for Library Service to Children, is published quarterly and provides member and division news, new ideas, conference information, and member profiles.

The ATLA Newsletter is published quarterly a by the American Theological Library Association as a source of information about membership activities and job openings, as well as a forum for discussion on various issues of interest to members. It is available in paper and it is posted in on a member-restricted web page.

The American Archivist is the semi-annual journal of the Society of American Archivists. It reflects thinking about theoretical and practical developments in the archival profession.

American Libraries, monthly publication of the American Library Association, includes news of the Association, articles on current trends and issues, a calendar of association activities, and job notices.

The *Annual Review of Information Science and Technology (ARIST)* surveys the field of information science and technology, providing an overview of recent trends and significant developments. One volume is published each year.

Art Documentation is published twice yearly by the Art Libraries Society of North America. It features articles on issues of interest to art information specialists, including historiography, copyright, digital imaging, intellectual access, and database design and construction.

Broadside, newsletter of the Theatre Library Association (TLA), is published three times per year. It features articles and news items related to exhibitions and collections, information about TLA-sponsored events, book reviews, and other items of interest in the fields of theatre, film, and dance.

Bulletin of the American Society for Information Science and Technology is a bimonthly news magazine relating ASIS&T activities along with developments and issues affecting the field, pragmatic management reports, opinion, and news of people and events in the information science community.

College & Research Libraries is a scholarly research journal published by the Association of College and Research Libraries (ACRL), a division of the American Library Association. It is available online to members.

College & Research Libraries News provides articles on trends and practices of academic and research libraries. Published eleven times per year. *C&RL News* is the official news magazine of ACRL. It is available online to members.

Children and Libraries is the official journal of the Association for Library Service to Children. Published three times per year, it provides continuing education of librarians working with children, displays current scholarly research and practice in library service to children, and spotlights significant activities and programs of the Association.

Feliciter is published six times a year by the Canadian Library Association. Each issue contains opinion pieces, columns, and feature articles on professional concerns and developments, along with news of the Canadian Library Association.

The Information Management Journal is published bi-monthly by ARMA International and features articles on current topics in records and information management today, as well as marketplace news and analysis.

Information Technology and Libraries is a refereed journal published quarterly by the Library and Information Technology Association, a division of the American Library Association. It publishes articles related to all aspects of libraries and information technology, including digital libraries, metadata, electronic publishing, telecommunications, computer security and intellectual property rights, technical standards, geographic information systems, online catalogs and bibliographic systems, optical information systems, and software engineering.

The *Journal of Academic Librarianship* is an international refereed journal which publishes articles on issues pertinent to college and university libraries. Published bimonthly by Elsevier, JAL provides a forum for research and its application, policy analysis, practices, issues, and trends.

The *Journal of Education for Library and Information Science* is a quarterly publication of the Association for Library and Information Science Education. It is a scholarly journal that serves as a forum for discussion and presentation of research and issues within the field of library and information science education.

The *Journal of the American Society for Information Science and Technology*, a refereed scholarly and technical periodical, publishes reports of research and development in a wide range of subjects and applications in information science and technology.

The *Journal of the Medical Library Association*, is a peer reviewed, scholarly journal. Published quarterly, it aims to advance the practice and research of health sciences librarianship.

The *Law Library Journal* is the "official" publication of the Association since 1908. It is published quarterly and distributed to members.

Library Resources & Technical Services, published quarterly, is the scholarly journal of the Association of Library Collections & Technical Services, a division of the American Library Association. The journal supports the theoretical and practical aspects of collection management and development, acquisitions, cataloging and classification, preservation and reformatting, and serials.

Library and Information Science Research, published by Elsevier, is a cross-disciplinary, refereed journal, which focuses on research in library and information science and its practical applications and significance.

Library Journal is an independent journal which provides news reports, features, book and media reviews, and columns for library directors and staff professionals in public and other types of libraries. Articles, columns, and reviews provide current information on such topics as computer systems, books, serials, software, furnishings, publishers, distributors, and vendors in the library marketplace.

Library Quarterly, published by the University of Chicago, is dedicated to the publication of scholarship and reports of research for librarians, educators, administrators, and others involved with libraries. Topics published include sociological, statistical, bibliographical, managerial, and educational research in librarianship.

Library Trends, issued quarterly, investigates trends in librarianship for an audience of practicing librarians and educators. Each issue is devoted to a single topic of professional interest.

Library Administration & Management is the quarterly publication of LAMA, the Library Administration and Management Association division of ALA. It contains practical articles for supervisors and managers of libraries and other information agencies.

MLA News is published ten times each year by the Medical Library Association. Its purpose is to publish newsworthy information about the profession and the association.

Music Cataloging Bulletin is a monthly publication announcing policy and decisions from the Library of Congress and reporting general cataloging news that may influence music cataloging.

Notes, Quarterly Journal of the Music Library Association is published in September, December, March, and June.

Performing Arts Resources is the annual publication of the Theatre Library Association, featuring articles on resource materials in the fields of theatre, popular entertainment, film, television and radio, information on public and private collections, and essays on conservation and collection management of theatre arts materials.

Public Libraries, published six times a year, is the official journal of PLA and the only ALA journal devoted exclusively to public libraries. Each issue provides articles and columns on current topics, public library trends, and subjects of professional concern.

Reference & User Services Quarterly, the journal of the Reference and User Services Association of the American Library Association, disseminates information to reference librarians, information specialists, and other professionals involved in user-oriented library service. The print journal has a companion online edition.

RUSA Update is the quarterly online newsletter published by the Reference and User Services Association.

Special Libraries is the journal of the Special Libraries Association. It is now available in PDF as well as print.

TCB is a quarterly newsletter of the *Technical Services Section* of the American Theological Library Association. It lists new and changed subject headings and classification numbers in appropriate subject areas as well as other information of interest to religion/theology catalogers.

The Voice is the quarterly newsletter of the Association for Library Trustees and Advocates and is available with membership. An archive of *The Voice* online is available on the ALTA Web site. This newsletter highlights divisional activities and information of interest to library trustees and advocates.

YALS: Young Adult Library Services is the official journal of the Young Adult Library Services Association of the American Library Association. Published quarterly, it includes articles from the field of interest to those working with teens.

Bibliography

Achleitner, Herbert K. 1987. *Intellectual foundations for information professionals*. Boulder, CO: Social Science Monographs; New York: Distributed by Columbia University Press.

American Association of School Librarians. School Library Media Education Programs. http://www.ala.org/ala/aasl/aasleducation/schoollibrarymed/school library.htm (accessed May 30, 2007).

American Library Association. Certification. http://www.ala-apa.org/certification/certification.html (accessed May 30, 2007).

American Library Association. Code of Ethics. http://www.ala.org/ala/oif/statementspols/codeofethics/codeethics.htm (accessed May 30, 2007).

ARMA International. Code of Professional Responsibility. http://www.arma.org/about/overview/ethics.cfm (accessed May 30, 2007).

Association of Independent Information Professionals. Code of Ethical Business Practice. http://www.aiip.org/AboutAIIP/aiipethics.html (accessed May 30, 2007).

Battles, Matthew. 2003. *Library: An unquiet history*. New York: W. W. Norton.

Burke, James. 1985. *The day the universe changed*. Boston: Little, Brown.

Butler, Pierce. 1933. *An introduction to library science*. Chicago: The University of Chicago Press.

Casson, Lionel. 2001. *Libraries in the ancient world*. New Haven, CT: Yale University Press.

Cleveland, Harlan. 1985. *The knowledge executive; leadership in an information society*. New York: Truman Talley Books/E.P. Dutton.

D'Elia, George and Eleanor Jo Rodger. 1994. Public opinion about the roles of the public library in the community; the results of a recent Gallup Poll. *Public Libraries* 33: 24.

———. 1995. The roles of the public library in the community; the results of a Gallup Poll of community leaders. *Public Libraries* 34: 98.

de Solla Price, Derek. 1975. *Science since Babylon*. Enlarged Edition. New Haven, CT: Yale University Press.

Dewey, Melvil. 1976. "The profession." In *Landmarks of library literature 1876–1976*, ed. Dianne J. Ellsworth and Norman D. Stevens, 21–23. Metuchen, NJ: Scarecrow Press.

Dickson, Paul. 1986. *The library in America: A celebration in words and pictures*. New York: Facts On File Publications.

Downs, Robert B. 1975. "Problems of bibliographical control." In *Essays on bibliography*, ed. and comp. Vito J. Brenni, 124–144. Metuchen, NJ: Scarecrow Press.

Eisenberg, Michael B. and Robert E. Berkowitz. 1990. *Information problem solving: The big six skills approach to library and information skills instruction.* Norwood, NJ: Ablex Publishing.

Fowler, Susan G. 2005. *Information entrepreneurship; information services based on the information lifecycle*. Lanham, MD: Scarecrow Press.

Gates, Jean Key. 1990. *Introduction to librarianship*. 3rd ed. New York: Neal-Schuman Publishers.

Glazier, Jack D. and Robert Grover. 2002. A multidisciplinary framework for theory building. *Library Trends* 50: 317–332

Gorman, Michael. 2003. *The enduring library: Technology, tradition, and the quest for balance*. Chicago: American Library Association.

Greer, Roger C. 1987. "A model for the discipline of information science." In *Intellectual foundations for information professionals*, ed. Herbert K. Achleitner. Boulder, CO: Social Science Monographs; New York: Distributed by Columbia University Press.

Greer, Roger C. and Martha L. Hale. 1982. "The community analysis process." In *Public librarianship, a reader*, ed. Jane Robbins-Carter, 358–366. Littleton, CO: Libraries Unlimited.

Greer, Roger C. and Robert Grover. 1992. A bright future for small libraries. *Public Library Quarterly* 12: 29–39

Grover, Robert, and Jack Glazier. 1986. A conceptual framework for theory building in library and information science. *Library and Information Science Research* 8: 227–242.

Harris, Michael H. 1995. *History of libraries in the western world*. Metuchen, NJ: Scarecrow Press.

Houser, Lloyd J. and Alvin M. Schrader. 1978. *The search for a scientific profession: Library science education in the U.S. and Canada*. Metuchen: Scarecrow Press.

Johnson, Elmer D. 1965. *A history of libraries in the western world*. Lanham, MD: Scarecrow Press.

Kuhlthau, Carol Collier. 2004. *Seeking meaning: A process approach to library and information services*. Westport, CT: Libraries Unlimited.

Kuhn, Thomas S. 1962. *The structure of scientific revolutions*. Chicago: University of Chicago Press.

Lyman, Peter and Hal R. Varian. 2003. How much information. http://www.sims.berkeley.edu/how-much-info-2003 (accessed May 30, 2007).

Peters, Tom. 1987. *Thriving on chaos*. New York: Harper & Row.

———. 1992. *Liberation management*. New York: Alfred A. Knopf.

Rogers, A. Robert. 1984. *The library in society*. Littleton, CO: Libraries Unlimited.

Schwartz, Peter and James Ogilvy. 1979. *The emergent paradigm: Changing patterns of thought and belief*. Report issued by the Values and Lifestyles Program, April 1979.

Shannon, Claude E. and Warren Weaver. 1963. *The mathematical theory of communication*. Urbana-Champaign: University of Illinois Press.

Shera, Jesse H. 1976. *Introduction to library science; basic elements of library service*. Littleton, CO: Libraries Unlimited.

Society for Competitive Intelligence Professionals. SCIP Code of Ethics for CI Professionals. http://www.scip.org/ci/ethics.asp (accessed May 30, 2007).

Toffler, Alvin. 1980. *The third wave*. New York: Morrow

U.S. Department of Labor, Bureau of Labor Statistics. *Occupational outlook handbook 2006–2007*. http://www.bls.gov/oco/ (accessed May 30, 2007).

Webster's Collegiate. http://www.merriam-webster.com/dictionary/disseminate (accessed May 30, 2007).

Wiegand, Wayne A. 1996. *Irrepressible reformer: A biography of Melvil Dewey*. Chicago: American Library Association.

Wilson, Patrick. 1977. *Public knowledge and private ignorance*. Westport, CT: Greenwood Press.

Index

About the Authors

ROGER C. GREER has been a creative thinker in the library profession for more than fifty years with experience in two academic libraries (Purdue University and the State University of New York at Potsdam) before earning his Ph.D. at Rutgers University. He is Dean Emeritus of the School of Library and Information Management, University of Southern California, former dean at Syracuse University and Professor Emeritus at Emporia State University. He has been a professor on the faculties of University of Denver. His writings have consisted of a few professional articles, the ideas of which are included in this book. However, his true gift is his ability to articulate his vision for the library and information science field—preferably over a meal at a greasy spoon.

ROBERT "BOB" J. GROVER is former Associate Vice President for Academic Affairs at Emporia State University, where he has also held the position of Dean and Professor of the School of Library and Information Management. He also was Director of the School of Library and Information Science at University of South Florida and Assistant Dean at University of Southern California. His professional experience was in the school library media field. A native Hoosier, he earned his M.L.S. and Ph.D. from Indiana University. He has authored numerous professional articles and several book chapters.

SUSAN G. FOWLER remains active in the information consulting business she founded immediately after earning her M.L.S. from Emporia State University in 1993. Her expertise includes managing special libraries, research and analysis, and the design and implementation of information infrastructures. Her clients include organizations in the fields of law, healthcare, and philanthropy. Ms. Fowler is a member of the library and information science honor society Beta Phi Mu, American Library Association (ALA), Association of American Law Libraries (AALL), and the Kansas Library Association (KLA). She serves her local and state community through membership on a variety of committees. Her biography is listed in the 2006 Marquis *Who's Who in America*.

The three authors have nearly 100 years of combined professional library and information science experience.